BISHOP REGINALD PECOCK

CAMBRIDGE
UNIVERSITY PRESS
LONDON: BENTLEY HOUSE
NEW YORK   TORONTO   BOMBAY
CALCUTTA   MADRAS: MACMILLAN

BISHOP REGINALD PECOCK

*A Study in Ecclesiastical History
and Thought*

BY

V. H. H. GREEN, M.A.

*Formerly Scholar of Trinity Hall, and Lightfoot Scholar of the
University of Cambridge. Fellow of St Augustine's College,
Canterbury. Assistant Master at Sherborne School*

THIRLWALL PRIZE, 1941

CAMBRIDGE
AT THE UNIVERSITY PRESS
1945

PRINTED IN GREAT BRITAIN

CONTENTS

PREFACE

'Who on earth', my friends say to me, 'was Bishop Pecock?' This small and obviously imperfect essay is intended as an answer to that question. Its career has been somewhat chequered. Teaching and lecturing work at a theological college, at a training college and at a school have prevented anything like continuous research into the problems of fifteenth-century history. Apart from this, when the finishing touches were being put to the essay the Luftwaffe treated it with that incivility and disdain, which was so characteristic of the housemaid's attitude to a very much greater work, Carlyle's *French Revolution*. In other words, the manuscript was burned, burned as Abailard's precious writings on Ezekiel had been burned centuries before. The rough copy of the essay which survived provided the foundations for this book. I had hoped to explore further, to have found more documentary evidence for the details of Pecock's career and thought, but the difficulties of our time and my own feeling that there was further and probably more important work to be done in other fields of historical research convinced me that I should not be justified in withholding this short study any longer. This explanation is intended in no sense as an apology. It is merely meant to explain the imperfections and defects of the essay itself.

It is a pleasant task to thank those who have in greater or lesser degree helped this essay on its way. I must particularly acknowledge my indebtedness to the adjudicators of the Thirlwall Prize, 1941, the Chairman of the Degree Committee of the Faculty of Divinity, and to the Trustees of St Deiniol's Library, Hawarden, for the award of a Gladstone Studentship in 1937. Many friends have at one time or another shown an interest in my work, Professor C. W. Previté-Orton who first suggested that Pecock was worthy of study, Professor A. Hamilton Thompson with whom I used to talk most fruitfully at Leeds, Mr C. W.

Crawley of Trinity Hall and the Rev. Dr G. C. Richards, some-time senior Fellow of Pecock's old college, Oriel. My friend and colleague, Dr F. J. Badcock, Librarian of St Augustine's College, Canterbury, has always placed the full facilities of the library at my complete disposal, nor can I forget the help which I have received during past years from Dr Williams's Library of Gordon Square, London. A former pupil, Mr David Munns, has kindly helped me with the Index. I have mentioned some further obligations in the footnotes, but I am grateful to the Rev. G. F. Nuttall, B.D., for so kindly lending me his thesis on 'Faith and Reason in the Works of Bishop Pecock'. I have also to thank the editor of the *Church Quarterly Review* for permission to use my article on 'Bishop Pecock and the English Bible'. The tragic death of Mr J. G. Sikes deprived the world of a real scholar and the author of a personal friend and adviser. Two other scholars of note, Mr B. L. Manning and Dr E. V. Hitchcock, who ex-pressed their interest, and the former of whom gave me invaluable advice, have died since I commenced this study. Finally, it would be the height of discourtesy to omit my thanks to the Cambridge University Press for the helpful suggestions of its proof readers and the patience of its printers. I need hardly add that I am alone responsible for any errors and imperfections.

This essay is intended primarily for students of theology, of history, of English literature and of the medieval and pre-Reforma-tion period in general. I have therefore nearly always retained the wording of the original manuscripts, modified and punctuated by their various editors. I have, however, taken the liberty of substituting the letters 'th' for the O.E. form 'þ'. Wherever possible I have let Bishop Pecock speak for himself so that students of English literature may gather some impression of his style while they are reading about the man and his works.

Dominus tecum!

VIVIAN H. HOWARD GREEN

HOLNICOTE, 1944

CHAPTER I

THE STUDY OF PECOCK

ALTHOUGH REGINALD PECOCK'S importance in fifteenth-century history is undoubted, too little has so far been written about him to enable his real significance to be assessed. The attention which historians of the present century have paid to him is both slight and misleading. In 1932 a writer could still assert that only one, instead of, as in fact, five, out of the bishop's works had been published.[1] The political historians of the period, apart from the ordinary text-book writer, concentrate their attention on the trial, and on the trial alone.[2] This trial scene figures in nearly every history of fifteenth-century England, but it is mentioned as a sudden deviation from the main theme, a rock standing in the middle of the road. It has so far seemed impossible, even in the masterly introduction which Churchill Babington wrote for the 'Rolls' edition of Pecock's *Repressor*, to absorb Pecock into the main stream of fifteenth-century history. Besides the lack of material there is also a diversity of interpretation which inspires yet another writer to give what he, probably foolishly, regards as an integrated study of this learned and rather tragic bishop in relation to his works and to the age in which he was living.

The various attempts to interpret Pecock in themselves provide a valuable essay in historiography, for the oblivion which seemed to cover the bishop like a cloud almost as soon as, if not before, his own age was ended, prevailed with two or three notable exceptions until our own times. Thus the *Bibliographica Britannica* of 1766, which claims to relate something about the 'lives of the most

[1] H. P. Palmer, *The Bad Abbot of Evesham and other Medieval Studies* (Oxford, 1932), 119.
[2] E.g. Sir J. H. Ramsay in his *Lancaster and York* (II, 202 ff.), and Sir C. Oman in his History of England, 1377–1485 (*Political History of England*, ed. W. Hunt and R. L. Poole, IV, 377). Yet both these attempts, gallant as they are, do not really tackle the question of Pecock's real significance.

eminent persons who have flourished in Great Britain and Ireland from the earliest times down to the present day', makes no mention of him.[1] This ignorance was partly due to the misleading estimate of the martyrologist, John Foxe, who, following Bale,[2] classed Pecock with the Protestant martyrs who had suffered for their faith.[3] It is ironical that Pecock should have been treated as a precursor of the Reformation and even more ironical that both Father Parsons,[4] the industrious Jesuit, and the *Index Librorum Prohibitorum et Expurgandorum* of Madrid dated 1667, among others, should have condemned him as a Lutheran professor.

Indeed, the study of Pecock was in reality wholly subordinate to the theological viewpoint of his interpreters, and is in consequence really more revealing of the authors than of their subject. Thus that zealous scholar, Henry Wharton,[5] interested, as befitted Archbishop Sancroft's chaplain, in defending the *Ecclesia Anglicana* against the Romanists and the Dissenters, welcomed the opportunity of editing Pecock's *Book of Faith*, so that it might prove that

[1] It should be noted that in the article on 'Henry Wharton', the latter's edition of the *Book of Faith* is mentioned in a footnote.

[2] *Index Britanniae Scriptorum* (ed. R. L. Poole and M. Bateson (Oxford, 1902), 337 ff.). Bale in his turn was mainly dependent on Gascoigne (*Loci e Libro Veritatum*, ed. J. Thorold Rogers (1881), *passim*).

[3] *Acts and Monuments* (ed. 1684), I, 805. Edward Hall was even wider off the mark, for he thought that Pecock was condemned for lecturing against papal annates and Peter's pence (*Chronicle* (1809), 237).

[4] The copy used was an Italian translation, *Esame del Calendario Protestante detto Foxiano, cioè Volpiano*, 'vedendo lo stesso paragonato col Calendario Cattolico Romano è coi Santi ivi contenuti'. Trans. F. G. Morelli (ed. 1753), II, 255-7.

[5] Wharton, who was one of the greatest scholars of his day, never studied for less than 12 hours a day when in residence at Gonville and Caius College, Cambridge. He assisted both William Cave and Archbishop Tenison in their controversial work, besides producing a great deal of valuable material himself. Bishop Stubbs sums up his scholarship: 'this wonderful man died in 1695 at the age of thirty, having done for the elucidation of English Church History (itself but one of the branches of study in which he was the most eminent scholar of his time) more than anyone before or since' (*Registrum Sacrum Anglicanum* (ed. 1897), iv). *Vide* 'Autobiography' in G. D'Oyly's *Life of William Sancroft* (London, 1821), II, 103 ff.; D. C. Douglas, *English Scholars* (1939), 175-97.

'scripture to be the rule of faith'[1] was an axiom of pre-Reformation Anglican theology. Similarly, Dr Daniel Waterland, Master of Magdalene College, Cambridge, a learned and perspicacious divine, who was as averse to Latitudinarian ideas as he was suspicious of any emphasis on the sentimental or mystical strands in Christianity, stands full square the eighteenth-century churchman when he treats of Pecock in his correspondence with the latter's future biographer, John Lewis. His criticisms and his advice are precise, pithy and valuable, even for the modern scholar, but it is his admiration of Pecock's common-sense rationalism which stands out in this correspondence. He submits very humbly that Mr Wharton makes Pecock more of a Protestant than he really was, and his attitude is best summed up in a letter that he wrote to his friend, John Loveday:

He was a very honest man, and one of the ablest divines of that age. His misfortune was that he undertook to defend a very corrupt Church against the Wiclevites, upon a scriptural and rational foot. It was impossible for him to do it, but by softening and disguising several principles and practices then prevailing. His design was very like to what the Bishop of Meaux [*i.e.* Bossuet] attempted in the last century; but Pecock was not altogether so artful, nor so well-guarded. He made some concessions which were very just, but which so corrupt a state of the Church would not bear. His enemies (some through envy, some through superstitious zeal) took the advantage and aggravated everything to the utmost. And thus a good and great man fell a sacrifice.[2]

This just and favourable estimate, which possesses far greater historical validity than Dean Hook's trenchant judgement of a

---

[1] Preface to the *Book of Faith* (1688), ix: 'it was the commonly received opinion of the Church that scripture is the rule of faith', an opinion not reversed by the 'sentence [i.e. against Pecock] of two or three partial bishops' (*id.* xiii).

[2] Waterland, *Works*, ed. Van Mildert (Oxford, 1823), x, 428. Bishop Van Mildert's life of Waterland should also be consulted with a view to a full understanding of Waterland's position in eighteenth-century church history. His chief writings were directed against Arianisers like Daniel Whitby and Samuel Clarke.

century later,[1] did not soften Lewis's Protestant bias. Lewis, who was the rector of a country parish in Kent,[2] was an earnest, somewhat laborious writer with a faculty for research but unfortunately lacking both Waterland's more balanced scholarship and his serene English prose style. His life of Pecock, which was a sequel to his study of John Wyclif, remains the sole full-length biography of the worthy bishop yet published and is therefore invaluable, but it was written with a view to justifying the 'great and invaluable blessing of the Reformation' and to disproving the 'antiquity of Rome's hold on England'.[3] Lewis believed that both Wyclif and Pecock were bulwarks of 'Protestantism' against the aggressive poison of Rome. His portrait of Pecock is therefore inevitably unbalanced and his book as a whole suffers from his desire to denounce image-worship,[4] 'that absurd and nonsensical doctrine of transubstantiation'[5] and other irrelevancies.[6] After care has been taken, however, to guard against this bias, Lewis's book remains the standard authority on Pecock.

One stage in the interpretation of Pecock has been concluded with Lewis and the information so gathered points to two important facts. In the first place, the writers who have been dealing with Pecock have approached him from a purely propagandist though not necessarily unhistorical angle, with the intention of supporting some factor in their own philosophy of life. Therefore

[1] W. F. Hook, *Lives of the Archbishops of Canterbury* (London, 1867), vol. v. It might be added that Waterland's judgement was more balanced than that of the non-juror, Jeremy Collier (*Ecclesiastical History* (ed. Barham, 1840), III, 390 ff.). His treatment of Pecock is misleading, especially in relation to episcopacy and its effects in England.

[2] 1675–1747, vicar of Minster from 1708 and master of Eastbridge Hospital, Canterbury, from 1717. Henry Wharton had been vicar of Minster in 1688.

[3] *Life of Reynold Pecock* (Oxford, ed. 1820–), vii.

[4] *Id.* 54–60.   [5] *Id.* 163.

[6] E.g. 'one would have thought that so violent a shock, added to the general opposition [in relation to Anselm] which this doctrine of papal supremacy met from all the Western princes, had been enough to shame so groundless and impious an imposture out of the world. But ambition knows no bounds, especially when backed by interest, and flushed and encouraged by the superstitious madness of the people' (*id.* 92).

it is not so much Pecock who passes through yellow manuscript and leather-bound volume as Master John Foxe, Henry Wharton, Archdeacon Waterland and the learned 'minister of Margate'. In the second place, Pecock has been viewed throughout, although with varying emphasis, as a precursor of the Protestant Reformation, a Lutheran before Luther, an eighteenth-century rationalist standing amidst fifteenth-century darkness, a living apologia of the *Ecclesia Anglicana*.[1]

In the nineteenth and twentieth centuries Pecock was no longer regarded, with one or two exceptions, as a piece of scaffolding for the redundant arguments of erudite but controversial churchmen. There was, nevertheless, still little unanimity as to his real significance. Dean Hook, for instance, in his *Lives of the Archbishops of Canterbury*, reacts to Pecock very differently from Lewis and Wharton. Pecock appears in the noble dean's work as an 'asserter of Ultramontane principles and an upholder of the extreme pretensions of the Bishop of Rome',[2] 'an ultra-papist' who even 'if he had escaped persecution in his own age, would not have escaped it entirely in our own'.[3] Churchill Babington, one of the most versatile scholars of the last century,[4] took a very much more balanced view in the introduction to his edition of Pecock's *Repressor*, for he characterises Pecock there as 'the enlightened advocate of toleration in times peculiarly intolerant; he was the acute propounder of a rational piety against unreasoning and most unreasonable opponents'.[5] This viewpoint is reflected and extended in Professor J. L. Morison's later estimate of

[1] Even later, Dr Thomas Short regarded Pecock as a 'promotor of the Reformation...though not a martyr, was a confessor in its cause' (*A Sketch of the History of the Church of England to* 1688 (London, 1840), 70).

[2] *Lives of the Archbishops of Canterbury* (London, 1867), v, 178.

[3] *Id.* v, 293–4.

[4] Babington (1821–89) was an extremely competent natural historian and expert classic who was appointed to the Disney Professorial Chair of Archaeology at Cambridge in 1865. He also edited vols. 1–2 of Higden's *Polychronicon* (*D.N.B.* (Suppl. 1909), XXII, 92–3).

[5] Introduction to *The Repressor of Over Much Blaming of the Clergy* (Rolls, 1860), lix. In another place Dr Babington commented that his type of mind was 'Anglican rather than Roman' (*id.* xxvi).

Pecock as a 'Renaissance man in a land still content with its ancient ways and thoughts'.[1] A writer a few years later hit on the happier formula 'a product of his own day and a child of a later generation'.[2] With a more intensive study of the method of the bishop's thought there has been an inclination to leave the 'Renaissance' and to return to the 'medieval' man. Both Dr E. Hitchcock and Dr Greet, who have together been responsible for the excellent editions of Pecock's work for the Early English Text Society, find that he can no longer be regarded as the sponsor of nineteenth-century liberalism born before his time but rather as a man with 'essentially the Aristotelian, scholastic type of mind'.[3] Dr Greet, indeed, goes so far as to say that 'it was his habit in argument to take extreme positions, but always with recognition of their hypothetical character',[4] thus suggesting, unjustifiably, that Pecock never sincerely held the opinions he circulated but merely relished them as an exercise in logic. Another recent writer, Canon Maynard Smith, calls Pecock a 'thoroughgoing rationalist'.[5] Such, then, have been the opinions which different students of Pecock have held, and it needs little power of observation to detect the extreme diversity of views which characterises both earlier and more modern writers. Thus even though it has been possible for recent scholars to reach a more truly historical and critical view of Pecock's significance in the fifteenth century, there is not as yet any final opinion on the matter nor has an integrated study of Pecock appeared.

There is yet another reason why an essay on Pecock might be written. His own career and works are fascinating in themselves, for the spectacle of a bishop on trial may still interest the twentieth century, whilst his books, once the initial effort has been made,

[1] Introduction to the *Book of Faith* (Glasgow, 1909), 23.
[2] Bishop (then the Rev.) E. M. Blackie in *E.H.R.* (July 1911), 448. Cf. Ten Brink in his *History of English Literature* (trans. W. Clarke Robinson (New York, 1893), II, 335). He calls Pecock the 'enfant terrible of orthodoxy'.
[3] Introduction to the *Donet* (E.E.T.S. 1921), xxi.
[4] Introduction to *The Reule of Chrysten Religioun* (E.E.T.S.), xvi.
[5] *Pre-Reformation England* (London, 1938), 283.

are far less exhausting than Dr Greet would have us believe.[1] But it is doubtful whether any man is worthy of historical study for himself alone. Pecock *qua* Pecock is of only minor importance and interest, but Pecock *qua* fifteenth-century history takes on an altogether different appearance. No longer an isolated phenomenon, he fits into the vast, dramatic background of fifteenth-century history, and in so doing helps us to understand that fascinating but difficult age. There are then two aspects of Pecock to be considered in this study, the Pecock who lived, wrote and thought from *c.* 1390 to *c.* 1460–1, and on the wider canvas the Pecock who reflects the feelings, moods and aspirations of the time in which he was living, who points the way to the age that has passed and to the age that was yet to come.

Finally, it must be admitted that this study, in so far as it is concerned with original research, is a re-examination and integration of evidence rather than a fount of new, undiscovered material. The reasons for this are twofold. In the first place, it has not been possible to discover any really new material nor to have found any of Pecock's long-lost treatises, diligently as it had been hoped that this would have been the case. In the second place, the writer believes in all modesty that the re-examination and the integration of research partially completed, together with the interpretation to which that research must give rise, are frequently as valuable as the opening up of some newly discovered treasure trove. There is perhaps an unfortunate tendency in our own days to exalt new treasure trove rather more than its importance would justify. It is hoped, then, that the short estimate of the diversity of views which have been put forward about Pecock in past years together with the lack of 'any integrated study' of the bishop will amply justify this brief essay on a comparatively little charted sea of fifteenth-century history.

[1] Introduction to the *Reule*, xviii.

CHAPTER II

PECOCK'S EARLY YEARS

REGINALD PECOCK was born in Wales somewhere between 1390 and 1395,[1] although both the exact date and place are unknown. All the evidence agrees on his Welsh parentage: he was, Gascoigne tells us, 'Wallicus origine',[2] whilst the bull of provision issued by Pope Eugenius IV at the time of his elevation to the see of St Asaph speaks of him as 'presbyter dioecesis Menevensis'. One tradition asserts that he was born at Laugharne in Carmarthenshire, but there is no evidence to suggest whether this was so or not.[3] Nor do we know anything about his parentage despite Lewis's hazard that he was probably of 'an honest family, though it was not much known or celebrated'.[4] The name 'Pecok' or 'Pacok' does not give any clue to his surroundings nor to the identity of his family.[5] Indeed, any attempt to visualise his early years is not only by its very nature hypothetical but also comparatively unprofitable. The Wales in which he was brought up

[1] Babington says c. 1395 (Introduction, x) and Lewis c. 1390. The probable date lies somewhere between the two.

[2] Loci e Libro Veritatum, 26, 99, etc. Cf. A Brief Latin Chronicle, ed. J. Gairdner (Camden Soc.), 167: 'nacione Wallicus'; Incert. Chron. in Leland's Collectanea (ed. 1715, II, 409). Babington notes that Bale calls him 'Anglus' in the 1548 edition of the De Brit. Script. but follows Leland in his later edition.

[3] Browne Willis asserts this in his Survey of St Asaph (ed. E. Edwards, London, 1801, 80), but I cannot find the reference in my copy of Fuller's Worthies of Wales (ed. P. Austin Nuttall, 1840, III, 492), apparently Willis's source of information.

[4] The fact of his fellowship establishes that his family would not have been a very rich one. One of his friends, Lyhart (Fellow of Exeter, later Provost of Oriel and Bishop of Norwich), was a miller's son from Lanteglos in Cornwall.

[5] The name Pecock is not infrequent in medieval literature, e.g. Thomas P. of Coggeshall (Cal. Fine Rolls, XVIII, 126), Robert P. (grocer of London) (Cal. Pat. Rolls, Henry VI, VI, 316). Cf. Cal. Pat. Rolls, Henry VI, V, 370; Edward IV, III, 490; Edward III, XVI, 365 (John P., parson of Alderton in Northampton); Cal. Close Rolls, Henry VI, III, 98, 112, 462; Thorne's Chronicle of St Augustine's, Canterbury, ed. A. H. Davis, 412; Reg. Bekynton, I, 134.

was a wild and war-scarred country, yet again to suffer from the rebellion of Glyndwr which took place during Pecock's early childhood. St David's Cathedral, supposing St David's to have been the diocese of his birth, only just escaped the dire fate which overtook the churches of Bangor and St Asaph, for Glyndŵr penetrated as far as south Pembrokeshire in 1401. In short, says Adam of Usk, *velut alter Assur, furoris Dei virga, inauditam tyrannidem ferro et flamma miserrime vibravit.*[1]

Pecock's early education, which probably took place at some school attached to his local church, can have been very little different from that of his contemporaries, nor can his time at Oxford, whither he went in the first decade of the fifteenth century, have been very notable from the educational point of view. It is difficult to find any originality in his contemporary professors, and, in any case, as yet no one has been found to whom any of Pecock's original ideas can be specifically traced. He would have read such works as Ralph Strode's *Logica* and the well-thumbed Biblical commentaries before attaining to his degree. He incepted under a Cistercian monk, probably during the last year of his residence in Oxford, for the degree of Bachelor of Divinity. For this he would have pursued the normal scholastic task.[2] Later he proceeded to the Doctorate of Divinity but, adds

---

[1] *Chronicon Adae de Usk*, ed. Sir E. M. Thompson (London, 1904), 78.

[2] Dr Hastings Rashdall details the course and gives other information relative to studies at Oxford in vol. III of his *Universities of Europe in the Middle Ages* (ed. F. M. Powicke and A. B. Emden, Oxford, 1936), 158–60:

'THEOLOGY—For B.D. (*Admissio ad lecturam libri Sententiarum*):
  For M.A. candidates two years more, i.e. seven years in all.
  For others, two years more, i.e. eight years in all.
  Certain opponencies, number not specified. (N.B. probably one—*Reg. Annalium Coll. Merton.* ed. H. E. Salter, O.H.S., xxvi–xxvii.)

For Licence (*i.e. for the Doctorate*):
  Two years' further study.
  To have lectured on one book of the Bible and on the Sentences.
  An examinatory sermon at St Mary's.
  Eight responsions to non-graduate opponents.
  To dispute (as opponent) with every regent D.D.
  Vespers.
  In the fifteenth century an additional sermon was added by statute.'

Gascoigne, 'fuit doctor in Oxonia per graciam absurdam'. He continues:

Nunquam enim respondit alicui doctori pro forma sua, ut esset doctor, nec aliquem actum in scolis fecit in Oxonia, postquam incepit in theologia....Per omnes annos a die incepcionis suae in Oxonia usque ad diem praesentis scripturae nullum actum fecit scholasticum, nec legendo, nec praedicando, nec disputando, nec determinando.[1]

Even so the interest of Pecock's early years centres on Oxford, for it was to be of a paramount, perhaps even the predominant influence in his life and work. He attended the university at a critical time, since events there and especially in his own college of Oriel must have had a pronounced influence on the future development of his thought and must to a certain extent explain his later antipathy to Lollardy. In November, 1407, Archbishop Arundel had summoned a meeting of the Southern Convocation at Oxford to try to prevent the continued reading and propagation of Wyclif's views and of his writings.[2] As a result of this, a commission consisting of members of the universities of Oxford and Cambridge and the heads of the 'Colleges, Halls and Entries' was appointed to make a monthly inquisition, the object of which was to find out whether the constitutions so passed were observed in the societies under their governance. In addition to this, lecturers were forbidden to make any book which had been written in Wyclif's time the subject of their classes unless it had been licensed by the university or its delegates and by the archbishop. The university not only disliked this unwelcome exercise of primatial power but it regarded the archbishop's interference as illegal and discourteous.[3] Further, the primate's determination

---

[1] *Loci e Libro Veritatum*, 26.

[2] Wilkins, *Concilia*, III, 314–19; H. B. Workman, *John Wyclif*, II, 417–19 (Appendix v); Rashdall, *Universities in the Middle Ages* (ed. Powicke and Emden), III, 130 n.

[3] On Oriel College, *vide* D. W. Rannie, *History of Oriel College* (London, 1900); G. C. Richards and C. L. Shadwell, *The Provosts and Fellows of Oriel College* (Oxford, 1922).

to hold a Visitation of the University[1] particularly exacerbated the 'Independent' party whose Lollardy was in fact but a shield for their dislike of archiepiscopal interference.

Oriel College was the headquarters of the 'Independent' party. Indeed, John Birch and William Simon, two fellows of the college, were the ringleaders in the opposition to Arundel. When the archbishop arrived at St Mary's Church, then as now in the patronage of Oriel, the scene of his visitation, these two dons, who were the proctors, barred the doors against him and later in defiance of his orders celebrated High Mass in the church. The turbulent state of the college was well revealed in the ensuing investigation which was carried out by the archbishop's orders. The provost, John Possell, admitted that he had on occasions risen from his bed to admit the ringleaders into the college past midnight, and that on one night in particular one of the fellows, Thomas Wilton, had gone to the provost's room, called him a liar and had offered to fight him.[2] On the eve of St Peter's Day, Provost Possell accordingly exhorted the college, and Robert Dykes, another of the fellows, and Wilton in particular, to lead a godly and pious life and to refrain from all illegal and injudicious disturbances. The three offenders, however, far from being sobered by this advice, attacked the house of Courtenay, the chancellor of the university, who had inspired Possell to make

[1] *Snappe's Formulary* (ed. H. E. Salter, O.H.S., 1924), 156–75.
[2] The archbishop had left Oxford before Birch celebrated Mass, the town and the university having been placed under an interdict (Rashdall, *id.* III, 132 n.). Birch and Simon were charged: 'fuerunt consentientes...castellacioni ecclesie beate virginis Oxonie contra suum pastorem Archiepiscopum visitantem, et stante interdicto eadem nocte scilicet diei Veneris contra mandatum domini Cantuariensis Iohannes Birche invitis clericis ecclesie excepti claves, valuas aperuit et campanam modo solito pulsari fecit, immo & post crastinum altam missam inibi celebravit.' Simon was also charged 'rediens domum de prelio fatebatur aperte se illis invasoribus affuisse et ipsos sibi bonos socios pernouisse & quando intravit portam collegii non induxit famulum suum secum, sed remisit eum armatum ad pugnam & ad exercitum contra suum Cancellarium insurgentem' (*Snappe's Formulary*, 197). Simon, Dykes and Wilton were all northerners and may have been engaged in traditional conflict against the southerners.

this exhortation, killed a law student, and furthermore refused to appear before Arundel's inquisitorial court to answer the charge of heresy of which they were now accused. John Birch, Simon's colleague at Oriel and as proctor, was further accused of attempting to undermine the archbishop's constitutions by putting forward a motion in *Magna Congregatio*, which would have deprived the twelve persons elected to examine Wyclif's writings of their power to do so. In addition to this he had attempted to attack Richard Courtenay for dissolving the *Magna Congregatio* by dubious and illegal means in the *Parva Congregatio*. In particular, he had endeavoured to persuade the more orthodox members of Oriel to follow him, and to resist the college's repudiation of the bull of Pope Boniface IX which had granted the university exemption from episcopal jurisdiction.[1]

Even the dean of Oriel, John Rote, who had been often suspected of Lollardy, was in reality more interested in Arundel's discomfiture than in the propagation of Wyclif's ideas. 'Let the archbishop', he said at a fellows' meeting on one occasion, 'have a care what he tries to do; once before he tried to visit the university and was banished the kingdom for his pains....I have heard the archbishop say: "Do you think that bishop overseas [*i.e.* the Pope] can give my benefices in England to whomsoever he will? No, by St Thomas."' In this way Rote hoped to stimulate hostility to Arundel within the college. Rote's future career is not without interest although it comes as an anti-climax after his earlier antagonisms. When Provost Possell died in 1414,[2] Rote was elected provost and the Bishop of London duly confirmed the

[1] This bull, issued in 1395, exempted the university from the jurisdiction of all archbishops (inclusive of *legati nati*), bishops and ordinands. The radical character of the measure had aroused opposition. The bull was revoked by John XXIII in November, 1411 (*Cal. Pap. Reg.* VI, 302–4).

[2] Wood says that Corffe succeeded Possell (in 1410?) and that Leyntwardyn succeeded Corffe after a 'great difference had been between Mr John Martill and Mr John Rote...concerning the Provostship'. It is clear that he has muddled up the chronology (*Historia et Antiquitates Universitatis Oxoniensis*, Wood, 1674, II, 105).

election on November 17th, 1414. This election, however, did not pass off successfully, for John Martyll, one of the fellows of Oriel, questioned its validity on the ground of insufficient notice and an appeal was accordingly made to Rome. In the upshot, Rote renounced his claim, and William Corffe, the university's representative at the Council of Constance, was accordingly elected.

In the midst of these upheavals and disturbances Pecock must have been elected to a fellowship at Oriel College. It is sometimes inferred that he succeeded Garsdale as a fellow of the college in 1417, but this is doubtful, as he was probably already a fellow when, with Martyll, Brygon, John Carpenter and Kayll, he disputed the validity of Garsdale's election to the provostship.[1] It seems most likely that Pecock was elected to a fellowship in 1414–15, for the note of expenses 'pro preposito et pekok xi*d*.' would refer to the junior fellow as the *Collector reddituum*. Pecock would probably have taken part in another disputed election, between Nicholas Herry and another fellow in 1424, before he finally left Oxford.

Now it is clear from this brief survey of the fortunes of Oriel College during Pecock's residence there that he had not only been launched into controversy and dispute but he had also come into contact with Lollard opinions and views, although these views were often no more than a screen to shield the struggle between the university and the archbishop. It is hardly true then to aver, as some have done, that Pecock first came into contact with Lollard opinions in London, since a good groundwork for his extensive knowledge of Wyclif's teaching had already been laid during his residence at Oriel.

---

[1] Babington said that he was elected to a fellowship in place of Garsdale, who had been made provost, but in a later note he says that Garsdale was never provost of the college but treasurer of the college from 1409 to 1413. He was fellow and treasurer, in 1411 he appears as 'student of divinity', and was elected to, but subsequently deprived of, the provostship in favour of Leyntwardyn. On Feb. 14th, 1414, he was given leave of absence from his vicarage of Rudstone in Yorkshire (*Cal. Pap. Reg.* VI, 439). I am much indebted to my friend, the Rev. Dr G. C. Richards, sometime Senior Fellow of Oriel College, for help in clarifying the chronology here.

It is a little uncertain to what extent his relations with the Oriel dons—by the statutes all but three of the fellows were bound to be theologians—determined or influenced the course of his opinions. One of his great friends, Walter Lyhart, later Bishop of Norwich, may have succeeded Pecock in his fellowship in 1425, and it is possible that Pecock first came into contact with him when he was teaching in the schools belonging to Exeter College in School Street, for Lyhart was a fellow of Exeter until 1425.

A far more interesting contact is to be found in the presence of Thomas Gascoigne at Oriel during these years, for Gascoigne's dislike of Pecock may well have originated at this time. Gascoigne, who never became a fellow because he was the scion of a wealthy Yorkshire family and therefore ineligible for office, was probably educated at Oriel and certainly spent the greater part of his life there. From 1449 to 1458 the college allowed him to have 'his chamber in the College rent free', a significant indication of his long and fruitful connection with the society. Although he was offered livings on many occasions—he accepted only two offices, the incumbency of St Peter's-in-Cornhill and a prebendal stall at Wells[1]—he spent nearly the whole of his life in the service of the university of which he was many times Chancellor, Vice-Chancellor and Cancellarius Natus or Senior D.D., acting as Chancellor during vacancies. In reading Gascoigne's comments on Pecock, it is necessary to remember this early connection, for it may well account for the learned doctor's antagonism to a more successful, and even more enlightened, contemporary.[2]

[1] He also held the living of Kirk Deighton for a short while.

[2] Miss W. A. Pronger writes of his opposition to Pecock: 'Admittedly Pecock was Gascoigne's *bête noire*, but Gascoigne's interest in him was much less than has been supposed, while the only argument he quotes in detail from Pecock is his sophistical thesis that bishops were not bound to preach. Gascoigne did not understand Pecock. He treats the sermon of 1445 [sic] as if it were the central feature of Pecock's work, whereas for Pecock the doctrine that bishops *qua* bishops were not bound to preach was but a piece of equivocation as he later confessed.... Thus too much weight should not be given to his indifference to Pecock, for Gascoigne's misinterpretation has both obscured the meaning of Pecock's work and exaggerated the bias of his own.

Finally, in addition to the influence of disputes, Lollards, friends and foes, it must be emphatically affirmed that Pecock can only be properly understood with the scholastic theology of contemporary Oxford in one's mind, for if it is, as it obviously is, impossible to understand Wyclif without first assessing the intellectual content of the Oxford where he was taught and where he lectured, so too it is impossible to account for much of the substance, method and form of Pecock's thought unless one constantly remembers that it is not only an English bishop who is speaking but also, and above all, an Oxford don. His repeated emphasis on syllogistic reasoning and his determination to 'educate' the people in logic is a measure of his debt to Oxford.

What propirtees and condiciouns ben requirid to an argument, that he be ful and formal and good, is tauʒt in logik bi ful faire and sure reulis, and may not be tauʒt of me here in this present book. But wolde God it were leerned of al the comon peple in her modiris langage, for thanne thei schulden therbi be putt fro myche ruydnes and boistosenes which thei han now in resonyng; and thanne thei schulden soone knowe and perceue whanne a skile and an argument bindith and whanne he not byndith, that is to seie, whanne he concludith and proueth his conclusioun and whanne he not so dooth; and thanne thei schulden kepe hem silf the better fro falling into errouris, and thei myʒten the sooner come out of errouris bi heering of argumentis maad to hem, if thei into eny errouris weren falle; and thanne thei schulden not be so blunt and so ruyde and vnformal and boistose in resonyng, and that bothe in her arguying and in her answering, as thei now ben; and thanne schulden thei not be so obstinat aʒens clerkis and aʒens her prelatis, as summe of hem now ben, for defaut of perceuyng whanne an argument procedith into his conclusioun needis and whanne he not so dooth but semeth oonli so do. And miche good wolde come forth if a schort compendiose logik were deuysid for al the comoun peple in her modiris langage; and certis to men of court, leernyng the Kingis law of Ynglond in these daies, thilk now seid schort compendiose logik were ful preciose.

The argument struck Gascoigne simply because it was a contradiction of his own convictions that preaching would be a panacea for all ills' (*E.H.R.* LIV, 30). I think that Miss Pronger has perhaps over-simplified the problem.

Into whos making, if God wol graunte leue and leyser, y purpose sumtyme aftir myn othere bisynessis forto assaie.[1]

Pecock, the academic man, had a tremendous respect for the intellect, a respect which partly inspired his own conceit, his whole philosophy of life and certainly overshadowed the events of his career. For all the time, as busy bishop, truculent courtier and humiliated man, the steady pitter-patter of the 'schort compendiose logik' 'ful preciose' is heard. In fine, then, it is apparent that the university's influence on Pecock, with the material evidence at our disposal as scanty as it is, was undoubtedly great and would probably be found to be even greater were the full sources of his early years open to the historian.

A further important contact must have been established by Pecock about this time, with Humphrey, Duke of Gloucester, whose patronage he now obtained.[2] The interval of six or seven years which follows on the vacation of his fellowship is a complete blank although preferment in the diocese of St David's is a possibility. It cannot be established, however, when Pecock came into contact with Gloucester, but it is not unlikely that both Pecock's learning and his zeal for the faith attracted the duke's attention. For Humphrey took a keen interest in the hunting down of heretics and had himself personally attended the trials of Lollard priests in 1431. He was also a great patron of the university—it is said that he himself had studied at Balliol[3]—and he began his gifts to scholarship in 1435 when he presented books

---

[1] *Repressor*, i, 9.

[2] Professor K. H. Vickers writes of this connection: 'the original authorities for these statements cannot be found, but it is significant that Pecock began the propaganda that ended in his disgrace immediately after the death of the man who is said to have been his patron. It may be that the orthodoxy of Humphrey acted as a restraint on the Bishop so long as he lived. However, this cannot be anything but supposition, as there is no real authority on which to base this hypothetical connection' (*Humphrey, Duke of Gloucester* (London, 1907), 389). Leland's statement on which the connection is largely based may, however, be accepted.

[3] Bale says that Gloucester probably 'studied both rhetoric and *res naturales* at Balliol College'.

and money to the university, a token of further gifts in 1439 and in 1444. His patronage was bestowed very generously, both on foreigners and on Englishmen, on Titus Livius of Ferrara, on Bruni, on del Monte and Antonio di Beccaria, whom he employed as his secretary, on John Whetehampstead, the famous abbot of St Albans who was a decided opponent of Pecock, on Bishop Bekynton[1], Capgrave and Lydgate, among many others less famous. It is not surprising then to find Pecock among the famous men whom he took underneath his wing, for Humphrey, *amator virtutis et rei publicae sed præcipue clericorum promotor singularius* as William of Worcester calls him, encouraged learning in general rather than any one branch of study in particular. In this as in other things he resembled the Italian potentates of the Renaissance era. Thus it seems only too probable that it was through Gloucester's patronage that Pecock was promoted rector of St Michael Royal and master of Whittington College, London, in 1431.

[1] He mentions Humphrey, Duke of Gloucester, as one of his three principal benefactors (*Somerset Medieval Wills*, 406). On the rise of English humanism, especially in relation to Humphrey, Duke of Gloucester and his immediate entourage—Whetehampstead in particular—see R. Weiss, *Humanism in England during the 15th century* (1941).

CHAPTER III

PECOCK IN LONDON

THE next thirteen years of Pecock's life are of vital importance, for it was now that he began to write and publish the books which were destined to have so decisive an influence on later events. He was, besides, gaining the requisite knowledge and experience, both for the formation of his opinions and for his career as a bishop and administrator. He had been ordained, it should be mentioned, some eleven years previously, when Bishop Fleming of Lincoln had made him subdeacon on December 21st, 1420, deacon on February 15th and priest on March 8th, 1421, taking his college fellowship as his title.

St Michael Royal, of which Pecock now became rector, had been one of the foundations to benefit under the will of the generous Sir Richard Whittington, the prominent London merchant who was Lord Mayor of London on four occasions. By his will he bequeathed money for the foundation of the college of St Mary and the Holy Ghost, the mastership of which was attached to the rectory of St Michael Royal. The college was to consist of the master, four fellows who were to be clerks who had proceeded to their M.A. degree, two clerks, besides the parish clerk, four choristers and an almshouse to be called God's House Hospital for thirteen poor people. The master was to be chosen a month after the vacancy by the four fellows, who were to communicate their choice forthwith to the wardens of the Mercers' Company, who, in their turn, were to inform the prior and chapter of Christ Church, Canterbury, in whose gift the rectory lay. The stipend of the master was ten marks a year, payable, with the other stipends, once every quarter.

Pecock realised that Whittington's endowment was not as adequate as it might have been, for he complains of inadequately endowed colleges and churches in his *Repressor*:

And perauenture this cause moued deuoute temperal lordis in the oold daies forto so richeli endewe bischopis and othere statis of the chirche; and therfore noman may argue and proue that, as bi strengthe of her riche endewing, that the statis of the chirche ouȝten or schulden be lad into wors plijte than thei schulde be, if thei were porelier endewid; or if thei were not endewid with immouable godis at al. Wold God the bischop writer of this book hadde so sure knowing of his saluacion as he hath experience vpon the trouthe of this now of him affermed sentence.[1]

On the other hand, he may be referring to the notoriously ill-endowed diocese of St Asaph, of which he was then bishop. He makes complaints of a similar nature in *The Reule of Chrysten Religioun* which was of earlier date.[2] In any case Whittington's executors, John Coventry, Jenkin Carpenter and Will Grove, in whose hands the erection of the college now lay, had granted a further £53 per annum, until the college should be sufficiently endowed, in February, 1424. When it was dissolved in the reign of Edward VI the revenues of the college were put at £20. 1s. 8d.[3]

The master was bound by the statutes to offer prayer on behalf of Whittington, his wife Anne, her father and mother, Richard II, Thomas of Woodstock, Edward III, Walter de Waldehof and Jean his wife, Philip de Taylour and Sabina his wife, the present king (*i.e.* Henry VI) and Henry Chichele, the Archbishop of Canterbury. Chichele had granted a licence for the erection of the college and hospital in November, 1424.

When, therefore, Pecock succeeded Richard Puringland as master in July, 1431, he became the head of a comparatively new

---

[1] *Repressor*, II, 307.

[2] *The Reule of Chrysten Religioun*, 331 ff., where he says that 'alle parisch chirches' should be properly endowed and that no local custom should be allowed to interfere with an endowment. He says in respect of this (in relation to both clergy and laity) that 'it wolde seeme the reule of the kingis lawe of engelond is more resonable and more pure and more avoiding the said inconuenientis and myschefis than is the spiritual lawe of the chirche—god sette here helpe and amendement soone' (*id.* 333).

[3] Newcourt, *Repertorium Ecclesiasticum Parochiale Londonense* (London, 1708–10), I, 490 ff.; Stow, *A Survey of London* (1598), ed. W. T. Thoms (London, 1842), 91.

foundation and was henceforth to live amidst environs very different from those to which he had been previously accustomed at Oxford. In July, 1431, too, the church was formally recognised as a collegiate church by the Pope 'with honours, privileges and insignia after the manner of other collegiate churches, and grants indult for the said master, chaplains, clerks and choristers to use and enjoy the like habits, honours and pre-eminence as other persons of such college churches'.[1] A letter of the same date contains the interesting but hardly edifying information that burials were no longer to take place in the first cemetery near the rectory since 'on account of the smells and infections of the dead buried there, the said master could not at certain times live at the said church', but at a more convenient place on the north side of the church.

There are relatively few references to contemporary affairs in Pecock's surviving works nor do they throw much light on the London of his own day. He uses London Bridge to point a metaphor. He refers similarly to the 'going of peple in pilgrimage to the College of Seint Kateryn bisidis London, as y dare putte this into iugement of whom euer hath seen the pilgrimage doon in the vigil of Seint Kateryn bi persoones of London to the seid College'.[2]

There are, however, other indications that Pecock was not altogether inactive in non-ecclesiastical affairs and that he came into fairly close contact with many prominent London business men, more particularly with members of the Mercers' Company.[3]

---

[1] Cal. Pap. Reg. IX, 340.

[2] Repressor, I, 215. He also mentions the services held in St Paul's in memory of Bishop Gravesend of London.

[3] E.g. 'John Wockynge, citizen and vintner of London to Master Reynold Pecoke, clerk, Andrew Michell and Robert Fytlynge, citizens of London gift of all his goods, chattels, and debts moveable and immovable, quick and dead' (Cal. Close Rolls, Henry VI, III, 370). Cf. 'John Forde of Yver co Bukingham to Master John Somerseth chancellor of the exchequer, Reynold Pecoke, William Lichfelde, Sir Edward Wyche, Richard Hakedy, Thomas Burgoyne "gentilman", William Sommaum, their heirs and assigns "quit claim of all lands, rents, reversions and services called Osterley and all lands etc. in the parishes of Northwode, Istelworth, Braynforde, Hestone and Hese co. Middlesex" belonging to Thomas Osterlee etc.' (March 26th, 1443, Cal. Close Rolls, Henry VI, IV, 147–8).

We find evidence of his business with 'Edward Gisors, citizen and grocer of London, Thomas Knollys, citizen and grocer'.[1] There are references to his dealings with the Mercers' Company in the *Reule*[2] and in the *Folewer to the Donet*. In the *Folewer* the son replies to the father:

I wote wel, fadir, that now late in londoun a book of ȝowre writyng which the kunnyngist and wijsist clerkis in ynglond maken ful mych of and preisen it mych, and in which thei fynden noon yuel, was scornyd and reprouyd of mercers seruauntis, whanne the book came into her handis and was of hem rad.[3]

Pecock's views on usury and trade did not differ from the accepted opinions of his age. Usury was worthy of the most vigorous condemnation:

in vseri the leener, bi manassing that he wole not ellis leene, drivith and compellith the borewer to assent forto paie a summe of his owne good bisidis the summe borewid, and that for the borewyng or the leenyng, which is not resonable cause to so compelle, for it is aȝens lawe of kynde, of resoun and of charite.[4]

This does not of course invalidate the assumption that he may have been in frequent contact with prominent London business men of his time.

The passage which refers to his personal dealings with the Lollards, not only in Oxford but also and probably primarily in London, is perhaps more interesting.

I have spoke oft tyme, and bi long leiser, with the wittiest and kunnyngist men of thilk seid soort, contrarie to the chirche, and

---

[1] *Cal. Close Rolls*, Henry VI, iv, 300–1 (April 27th, 1445).

[2] *Reule*, 94: 'herder and derker evidencis in plees of lond, in plees of dette and of trespace, in rekenyngis to be maad of receivers and rente gaderers in the account of an audit, ȝhe in bargeyns making of greet marchaundisis and in rekenyngis making therupon, as a man schal soone wite if he take homlynes [i.e. intimacy] with mercers of london.'

[3] *Folewer*, 176–7.

[4] *Donet*, 68. The argument is expanded in the *Folewer*, 144–6. He says there that the law against unjust usury is not a 'positijf statute of the al hool chirch or of the pope' but 'lawe of kynde and of resoun'. He himself has written a book 'of vsure' (*id.* 146).

which han be holde as dukis amonge hem, and which han loved me
for that y wolde pacientli heere her evydencis, and her motyves,
without exprobracioun. And verrili noon of hem couthe make
eny motyve for her parti so stronge as y my silf couthe have made
therto.[1]

This close relationship which existed between Pecock and his
opponents, together with the academic cast of his mind, resulted
in his writing and publishing a number of books.

So few out of the already written and projected works actually
survive that it is extremely difficult to know how much he actually
wrote whilst he was in London. Yet it may be accepted as an
established fact that he was engaged in working out the sketches
of future publications. In addition, two of his surviving works,
The Reule of Chrysten Religioun and the *Donet*, and possibly the
Poore Mennis Myrrour, an abridged version of the *Donet*, date from
this period although they cannot be pinned down to any one year.
Numerous references to his other books suggest that certain
works had already been published, but it is difficult to know
whether this was so or not owing to the method which he employed when he was engaged in writing his books. He describes
his method in his introduction to the *Reule*:

 fferthermore, thou3 in this present prolog and thou3 after in this
present book I allegge othere bokis whiche were bigunnen longe
after the bigynnyng of this present first book, 3itt no man hath
therupon to wondre, fforwhi y kepte this reule that the former
bokis hadden not her fullist and parfitist filling and eending eer
than the latter bigunne bokis were al moost eendid. And after
that . . . y maad my cours fro book to book that ech of hem my3te
helpe the other to be maad.[2]

If it is then impossible to determine the exact date of publication,
the fact that the *Reule* and the *Donet* had probably been finished or
at least were nearly finished by 1443–4 indicates that Pecock's
mind had reached its full maturity and that his ideas had been

---

[1] *The Book of Faith*, 202.
[2] *The Reule of Chrysten Religioun*, 22.

systematised during his tenure of the mastership of Whittington College.

While, then, he was in London he began to think out and to put into writing a *Summa Theologica*, an all-inclusive survey of the Christian religion written in particular relation to the needs of the century in which he was living. This *Summa*, as it stood, has not survived nor was Pecock able to complete his projected plans, for tragedy swept not only those plans but the very fruit of his labours into the flames. There is no evidence to suggest that Pecock was merely indulging in a kind of mental exercise in order to reach hypothetical conclusions which he did not sincerely hold, as Dr Greet suggests. Sincerity and honesty were among the most notable characteristics which we can glean from a consideration of his works, and which in fact justify us in speaking of his trial as a personal tragedy. Whilst, then, he was working in London, he was formulating an all-inclusive system, a mode of informing his hearers of the orthodox faith which he was vindicating, and of refuting and converting heretics.

Another factor of interest, and, when we consider the detailed relationship of event and personality which help to mould the historical process, of some importance, is based on the fact that one of his friends, Vincent Clement, was rector of the neighbouring church of St Martin Vintry, which then stood at the south corner of Royal or Queen Street and of Upper Thames Street, from November 1439 to 1444. This 'venerabilis et egregius vir', as he is styled in Archbishop Kemp's register, was one of those characters of no very great importance in themselves whose activities are, however, suggestive of significant trends in history and who occupy a key position in the history of their time. Like his friend, Clement was a protégé of Humphrey, Duke of Gloucester, being entitled indeed the duke's orator.[1] He was also like Pecock in that he incurred the wrath of Gascoigne

---

[1] *Cal. Pap. Reg.* VIII, 225. *Correspondence of Thomas Bekynton*, ed. G. Williams (Rolls Series), I, 223: 'orator pridem in Romana curia carissimi avunculi Humfridi etc.'; *Paston Letters*, I, 24.

over the manner of taking his doctor's degree at Oxford.[1] A great deal of Clement's time was spent in passing to and fro between England and the papal court, for he apparently acted as papal ambassador as well as the chief collector of the *Camera Apostolica* in England. Thus in 1441, having just returned from Rome, he was sent by Henry VI to Archbishop Theodoric of Cologne,[2] whilst in May of the next year he represented Thomas Bekynton at Rome and carried his gifts and good wishes to Pope Eugenius IV.[3] In 1443 we find Bekynton telling Biondo of Forli that he owes his elevation to the see of Bath and Wells very largely to the efforts which Clement had made on his behalf at Rome.[4] Later in the year, from August to December, he was urging forward business of the king's relating to indulgences at the papal court, without, however, achieving a successful result. He wrote that his continued lack of success—he was still working for the same objective in the early months of 1444—had exposed him to ill-natured comment in England.[5] In addition to work of this kind abroad, he was engaged on multitudinous papal duties in England, with granting faculties and dispensations, with questions relating to marriage and to usury,[6] with collections of a tenth for a crusade and other financial operations.[7]

Clement's championship of papal claims gained him suitable rewards as well as papal approval.[8] *Sacrae Theologiae Doctor*[9] as he

---

[1] 'Doctori insolenti, qui Oxoniae in theologia incepit in ordine diaconatus existens, gradu suo optento minis et promissis, et diversis litteris regiis et brevibus regiis missis contra eos qui in magna congregacione regencium et non regencium in Oxonia graciam suam petitam ex sua consciencia nega-verunt' (*Loci e Libro Veritatum*, 28). For the letter of the king vide *Correspondence of Thomas Bekynton*, I, 223–5.

[2] *Correspondence of Thomas Bekynton*, I, 131.

[3] *Id.* I, 240, 241, 242. Judicious gifts were also made to the Papal Treasurer, the Papal Secretary (i.e. Biondo of Forli) and the Papal Chamberlain.

[4] *Id.* I, 172.   [5] *Id.* I, 175–6, 179.

[6] *Cal. Pap. Reg.* X, 206–7, 222–3, 227–8, 417, etc.

[7] *Id.* XI, 192–3 etc.   [8] *Id.* VIII, 223–5.

[9] So Lewis (14, 214) based on Gascoigne (*op. cit.*). Henry VI's letter to the University of Oxford (dated Feb. 22nd, 1443) speaks of his great merit: 'habemus itaque doctissimum virum hunc, uti justum est tum propter

was, Clement held posts of a very widely assorted nature,[1] distant
from each other by many miles, some of them successively and
others consecutively, the vicarage of Adisham, Kent, the vicarage
of Wetheringsett in Suffolk, the vicarage of Olney in Bucking-
hamshire, the prebendal stalls of Welton Ryval[2] and Stow Longa[3]
in Lincoln Cathedral, the prebendal stall of Putston Major at
Hereford[4] and of Tervin at Lichfield,[5] the chancellorship and the
treasurership[6] of Lichfield Cathedral, the archdeaconries of Wilt-
shire,[7] Huntingdon,[8] Winchester[9] and Tortosa (in Spain),[10] a
prebendal stall, canonry and the provostship at Valencia Cathedral
and the vicarage of Albal in the same diocese,[11] a canonry at
Salisbury Cathedral, and the rectory of St Peter, Montfort-sur-
Risle[12] in the diocese of Rouen, as well as specific papal offices. It
must be confessed that Clement was put to considerable trouble

scientiam et virtutes suas, tum quod ab uberibus almae vestrae nutritus
educatusque sit, admodum gratum et peculiariter nobis carum.' He therefore
desires that he shall be rewarded by the grant of a D.D. Papal documents still
continue to speak of him as S.T.M. Clement seems to have remained a
subdeacon.

[1] E.g. 1447: 'Motu proprio reservation, for collation to him, of a regular
benefice in commendam for life, of any order, with or without cure and of a
secular benefice, in the realm of England, and one in each of the cities and
dioceses of Bordeaux, Rouen and Valencia, of any value, of any patronage etc.,
with mandate executory to the bishop of Huesca, abbot of the monastery of
St Bernard without the walls of Valencia, the dean of Bordeaux and the archdeacon of Salisbury' (*Cal. Pap. Reg.* x, 37). In 1453 it seems that Clement had
a chance of promotion to a bishopric, for a document of that year enacts that
'in the event of his being promoted to episcopal dignity without the said
realm, and his being consecrated, all the benefices with and without cure, even
incompatible, which he shall hold in the said realm at the time of such promotion, of anysoever value, shall not thereby become void, and that he may
continue, even after such promotion and consecration, and obtaining the
administration of a see, to hold such benefices in commendam therewith' (*Cal.
Pap. Reg.* x, 253).

[2] 1452–8.   [3] 1458–74.   [4] 1453–74 (*Reg. Boulers*, 23).
[5] 1455–8.   [6] 1458–74.   [7] 1458–64.
[8] 1459–74.   [9] 1459?–74.
[10] In 1448 a pension of 150 gold florins from the archdeaconry was assigned
to Clement in 'consideration of the exchange which he proposes to make of
the said archdeaconry' (*Cal. Pap. Reg.* x, 37).
[11] *Cal. Pap. Reg.* x, 252–3.
[12] *Id.* IX, 392. Cf. *Correspondence of Thomas Bekynton*, I, 178.

by difficulties arising out of the tenure of his various benefices. In particular, trouble was constantly occurring over the post which the papal collector held at Valencia. In 1459 a quarrel broke out between the chapter and their absent provost, who was represented, without his knowledge however, by his brother Francis. This ended in a victory for Clement over his enemy, Canon John Pellegrini.[1] A further conflict took place next year, a year that was noticeable for a papal reprimand delivered to Vincent through Nicholas V's special envoy, Francis, Bishop of Terni.[2] Clement's financial operations, of interest as they must be to all students of the medieval papacy, need not detain us.[3] Yet it is perfectly clear that Clement's headquarters were in England, 'dwelling in England' reads a papal letter of 1453,[4] whilst Gascoigne points to his contact with Pecock in 1447.[5]

Perhaps Clement's friendship with Pecock was only important in that it helps us to see the environment in which Pecock was working with greater clarity.[6] Yet his acquaintance with this singularly influential man, friend of king and pope, may have influenced his ideas as well as aided his promotion to high office. There is no reason to think that Clement, who apparently died in 1474, took any action in the trial scene.

Such must have been the situation when Pecock was appointed to the bishopric of St Asaph.

[1] *Cal. Pap. Reg.* XI, 545–6. The question at issue related to the possession of a house formerly inhabited by Canon Peter Romei. Francis Clement had taken on himself the right to give up Vincent's rights in this particular house.

[2] *Id.* XI, 680: 'the pope having long heard that Vincent Clement has behaved unjustly and unworthily in his office of Papal Collector in England.'

[3] *Id.* XI, 26, 376, 383, 495, etc.

[4] *Id.* X, 590.   [5] *Loci e Libro Veritatum*, 28.

[6] A further friend was John or Jenkin Carpenter, Town Clerk of London from 1417 to 1438. Pecock is mentioned in his will (dated March 8th, 1441). He was given a benefaction of 'twenty shillings' and, with William Lichfield, was to see that any of Carpenter's 'good or rare books' were placed in the Library at the Guildhall for the 'profit of students there, and those discoursing to the common people'.

CHAPTER IV

PECOCK AS BISHOP OF ST ASAPH

THE somewhat obscure relationship which had been established between Gloucester, or at least the court, and Pecock must have continued whilst he remained in London, for in 1444 he received the see of St Asaph in succession to John Lowe, who had been translated to Rochester. Pecock wedded his fortunes to those of the already declining house of Lancaster by this action. It is now necessary to give a brief indication of the political and economic trends of the period in so far as they affected the career of the newly promoted prelate in order that the situation may be the more clearly visualised.

There is no period in English history quite so confusing as the Lancastrian nor more difficult of true analysis. This is because the period, like Pecock the man, was a parti-coloured age, characterised by a dying feudalism, an erotic chivalry, a burst of creative intellectual, artistic and commercial activity, flowering with an avidity of life at once curiously negative and yet generative. The actual factors at work in England before, during and after the year 1444, were in themselves only characteristic of this general transitional phase, the course of which was to a very large extent determined by economic activity.

To understand fully the economic activity of the century is in some sense to gain the key to the comprehension of its complicated history. In England this economic activity was intimately associated with the wool trade, represented to this day by the fine perpendicular churches of East Anglia and the splendid remains of former baronial mansions,[1] but chiefly related in the fifteenth century to the rising power and claims of the mercantile class. The latter, whose views are reflected particularly well in the *Libelle of*

---

[1] E.g. Tattershall, Wingfield, Bolton in Wensleydale, mansions which were, it is interesting to note, residences of comparatively minor nobles.

English Polycye,[1] whose author may have been a member of the episcopate, were beginning to regard foreign policy as a means to a commercial end, to visualise the English campaigns in France as a useful method of achieving domination in the Channel, and in particular in the Straits of Dover, because the trade of so many countries 'must needs pass by our English coast...betwixt Dover and Calais', and of giving greater freedom to English trading activity. The *Libelle* reiterates then that the policy of the government should aim at making the English 'masters of the narrow sea...that is the wall of England'.

> For if this sea be kept in time of war
> Who can here pass without danger and woe?

Many representatives of the knightly class were themselves closely associated with mercantile activity. The fortunes of the De la Pole family had been laid by a Hull merchant, William de la Pole, in the fourteenth century, whilst Archbishop Chichele's father was a 'broker or draper' who had bought some land at Higham Ferrers and married the daughter of a gentleman, Anne Pyncheon. Sir John Fastolf himself, we may remember, turning a blind eye to the ecclesiastical condemnation of usury, advanced sums to London merchants 'ad merchandizandum' at 5 % per annum.

The old feudal ideas, however, which were perhaps most actively expressed in the objective ideals of King Henry V in his French war, were still retained and indeed ran their course consecutively with the more novel aims of upper and middle class society. As a result the new economic activity, the infiltration of the merchants into the baronial class and the ideals of the old chivalric and militaristic individualism coincided in the spearhead of what has not been inaccurately termed the 'bastard feudalism'.

The first twenty years of Henry VI's reign were further characterised by the rivalry between Gloucester, who as a cultured

[1] *Libelle of English Polycye* (1436), ed. Sir G. Warner (O.U.P. 1926).

scholar and a feudal knight with little conception of diplomacy was a typical representative of his age, and Cardinal Beaufort, an ambitious prelate whose financial operations are a tribute to his shrewdness rather than to his piety.

Three things stand out amidst these conflicting events. In the first place, the increasing distrust of the Lancastrian monarch and his advisers, which was due to their passive naval and foreign policy, stimulated both the belligerent feelings of the middle class, who were intent on suppressing alien trading establishments, and of the feudal class, who were always eager for adventure.[1] Secondly, the increasing financial difficulties[2] confronting the government, together with the passivity of the king, spurred on the government's desire for peace. Thirdly, there was the rivalry of Gloucester and Suffolk, the newly risen favourite of Henry VI.

The elevation of Reginald Pecock to the see of St Asaph was clearly touched by all these trends, for he was now closely allied to the Lancastrians, to their policy of peace and to the maintenance of the *status quo* in governmental and social matters. Why or when he transferred his allegiance from Gloucester to Suffolk we do not know, but that he did so is undoubted. The few months preceding his appointment were troubled, for an expedition sent to France under Somerset had failed, and finally on February 11th, Suffolk, Moleyns, another adherent of Pecock, and Sir Robert Roos were empowered to conclude peace with 'our uncle in France'. As a result Henry VI was betrothed by proxy to Margaret of Anjou, an event which boded ill for the history of England. All this meant, then, that in the ensuing troubles—the conflicting nature of the interests at stake certainly implied civil war sooner or later—

[1] The feudal wars and riots of the time bear witness to this, e.g. 1441, warfare between Sir William Bonville and the Earl of Devon; 1442, riots in Wales; 1443, in York between the citizens and the Abbot of St Mary's, between the Earl of Northumberland and the Archbishop of York (for this vide *Proceedings*, v, 269–75, 309; *Foedera*, XI, 27).

[2] In 1442 the limited amount of money available for the campaign in France is seen in another loan by Beaufort (*Proceedings*, v, 199).

Pecock would be implicated, if only to a limited extent. This was the situation when he was appointed Bishop of St Asaph.

The bull of provision, confirming Pecock's election, was issued on April 22nd, 1444, and was followed on June 14th by his consecration in the archiepiscopal chapel at Croydon by Archbishop John Stafford.[1] It is unlikely that Pecock spent much of his six years in his diocese, but he was probably more conscientious than Thomas Bourchier, who as Bishop of Ely is popularly supposed to have said mass in his cathedral on one occasion only. Pecock may well indeed have paid some attention to the needs of his somewhat barbaric and neglected see. In any case his work was not without effect in his diocese nor was his tenure of the bishopric without effect on Pecock himself.

For two centuries St Asaph had been one of the cockpits of Great Britain, for its geographical situation, placed as it was close to the garrison fortress of Rhuddlan and on the main line of march for the English armies to north Wales, made it only too frequently the scene of armed conflict and devastation. In the thirteenth century Bishop Howel ap Edynyfed had been forced to live on borrowed money, *destructis episcopalibus caede et incendio mendicare ut de alieno viverent cogebantur*, and to dwell a refugee at Osney Abbey, thus setting an example for other and later Welsh dignitaries. Bishop Robert de Lancaster, for instance, lived at Valle Crucis Abbey during his episcopate. In the fifteenth century St Asaph and St David's had suffered both at the hands of Owen Glyndŵr and of his opponent, Henry IV. The king destroyed the Franciscan monastery of Llandaes, and in retaliation Glyndŵr laid waste the Cistercian abbey of Cwmhir. Then Henry set fire to the abbey of Strata Florida, burned the cathedral and destroyed the bishop's houses at Meliden, Bodidris and St Martin's.

Thus the grim havoc of war bequeathed the bishops of St Asaph a very considerable task, for it needed a century of peace and more before the diocese could be put into shipshape condi-

---

[1] The temporalities had been restored to him on June 8th (*Cal. Pat. Rolls*, Henry VI, IV, 272; I. J. Churchill, *Canterbury Administration*, II, 138).

tion.[1] The bishops of the first half of the fifteenth century seem to have been relatively energetic in the work of reconstruction, but their task was considerably hampered by lack of money. Bishop Robert de Lancaster declared in 1419 that he had largely repaired his cathedral church but that the work could not be continued because the revenues of his see were insufficient. It seems fairly clear that the cathedral had to wait until the end of the century for the work of Bishop Redman before it was finally repaired, whilst it is doubtful, taking into account the fact that two early Tudor bishops, David ap Iorwerth (1500–3) and David ap Owen (1503–13), lived at their respective monasteries of Valle Crucis and Aberconway, if the palace received any attention at all during the century.[2]

Disorder, which was the first characteristic of Pecock's newly acquired see, had as its natural sequel the second important characteristic, poverty. If Whittington College had been insufficiently endowed, the see of St Asaph was even poorer, and in becoming its bishop Pecock had seemingly stepped, to use a vernacular phrase, 'from the frying pan into the fire'. We do not know what measures Pecock took for carrying on the work of reconstruction, but we may infer that he followed in the steps of his predecessors. In June, 1426, an indulgence had been granted to penitents who on the principal feasts of the year and especially on that of St Asaph himself, 'visit and give alms for the repair of the church of St Asaph, which, on account of wars and other calamities, has been burned and despoiled of its books, chalices, vestments and other ornaments and of manors and habitations belonging to the bishop Robert'. During this period the rectories of Meifod, Guilsfield, and Welshpool were held *in commendam*

[1] Even then the see of St Asaph remained a 'Cinderella', a poor diocese usually used as a stepping stone to higher things.

[2] Cf. *Cal. Pat. Rolls*, Henry VI, iv, 348: 'grant...on his petition showing that his cathedral church, bell tower, choir, chalices, vestments and other ornaments there pertaining and palace and other manors there have been burnt in the last Welsh war, that, while he be bishop, he be quit of all tenths, fifteenths, quotas and parcels thereof granted to the king by the clergy of England.'

with the bishopric to increase financial stability. Further, the king remitted the quit-rent owed to him for Gronant-is-y-Môr because of the *exilem statum* of the bishop, first for three years in 1414, then in 1437, in 1449 under Pecock, and in 1452 under his successor.[1] The *Taxatio* of Nicholas IV puts the income of the *temporalia* in 1291 at £33. 5s. (of bishop and chapter) and the *spiritualia* at £287. 10s. It is interesting to observe that in 1535 by the *Valor Ecclesiasticus* of Henry VIII the *temporalia* were worth £25. 10s. and the *spiritualia* £431. 19s. 6d. St Asaph was then and for long centuries to be one of the poorest of the British bishoprics.

In respect of the general diocesan work with which Pecock had perforce to come into contact, our estimate is hindered from the outset by lack of material evidence. According to legend there are grounds for believing that Bishop Goldwell took the registers of the diocese with him when he left the see in 1559 and went to Rome. But of this Browne Willis wrote: 'This is doubtless without the least grounds, for he, being in three years translated thence, left things as he found them at St Asaph, neither was there anything to be met with at Rome about this see, as the Author was told by a gentleman who searched there about our English bishoprics, and in particular was desired to do so about St Asaph.'[2] Whether Willis was right or not the registers are still missing.

We know very little about Pecock's rule of the diocese of St Asaph. He himself gives us some idea of what he believed a bishop's duties to be in the *Reule*. The bishop

is to ouer se that the louȝer curatis fulfille her chargis, and to here the complayntis maad vpon the louȝer curatis and for to helpe amende hem, to gadir togyder the louȝer clergy forto determyne doutis reisid in thi lawe of kynde and of feith, and to devise what counseile may be ȝouun to pryncis and potestatis, and what good

---

[1] 'Pardonavimus eidem nunc Episcopo predictas viginti…marcas per annum nobis, pro predicta placea prati more Bosci Turbarie et Pasture vocata Gronant-is-y-Mor in Com. predict. debit. ac ipsum de redditu sive servitio etc.' (*Cal. Pat. Rolls*, Henry VI, iv, 294—Sept. 15th, 1444).

[2] Browne Willis, *History of St Asaph*, 102.

oportunytees mowe be devisid and kept amonge hem wherby al this forseid officis in alle hise poyntis may be trulier kept and fulfilled.[1]

Could Pecock speak Welsh? If he was to have had any intimacy with the clergy of his diocese it was almost essential that he should have some knowledge of that language. The fact that his own English is so barren of dialectal deviations may indicate this or it may not.[2]

The clergy with whom Pecock would have had to deal may be divided into two sets, the native Welsh and the English who held Welsh benefices with their own livings. Little can be said of the former, but the meagre records at our disposal indicate that they were well in the majority. Here and there we have glimpses of a Byford Lewis, rector of Llandrinio, who is indicted for felony in connection with papal subsidies or some other cleric who has, more by accident than design, by his own misdeeds or desires, attracted the chronicler's attention. Here and again we find evidences of pluralism,[3] of 'a priest of noble birth' who holds the deanery of St Emilion, the rectory of Long Stratton in Norfolk as well as the rectory of Penant Melangell, but generally speaking there was less absenteeism among the Welsh clergy than in the Church in England.

Finally, is there any evidence of Pecock's influence being effective in his diocese? Two points alone are suggestive. First, in 1458 Master Thomas Lempster, Comportionary of Llansannan, was deprived of his benefice for being an adherent of Pecock, his successor being Gilbert Haydock, the king's chaplain, rector of

[1] *Reule*, 327.

[2] Little consideration was made for the Welsh in the matter of the higher clergy. It is true that in the fourteenth century the Black Prince had investigated whether one Alexander Dalby, candidate for the see of Bangor, could preach in Welsh, but it was not part of the government's or the Church's policy to encourage national feeling in what was after all only a lately won district.

[3] The Archdeacon of St Asaph, John Tupney or Tubney (1442–57) apparently only held the rectory of Southfleet in the diocese of Rochester in addition to his own offices.

Newtown and one of the agents sent by the king to Pecock to demand his resignation.[1] Secondly, support for the Lancastrian cause in this region may have been largely due to the few properties held by faithful followers of the royal house in the district, but it may also have been partly due to the exertions of the bishop. When Pecock was promoted to Chichester, he was succeeded by Thomas Knight, Prior of Daventry, a man who was deposed from the bishopric later by another of Pecock's opponents, Bishop Chedworth of Lincoln, for his partisanship of the Lancastrians. Knight's successor, Richard Redman, Abbot of Shap, was a strong Yorkist. We can already see the close connection which existed between politics and religion in the history of the period and which particularly affected Pecock's career. There is thus the minimum of evidence to suggest that Pecock paid some attention to his distant see, but there is more to indicate that he continued to spend most of his time in London.

Whilst he was Bishop of St Asaph, certain other factors come to the fore which are of interest for Pecock's life. In the first place, his theological views were already provoking irritation and dislike, especially in respect of his emphasis on the 'doom of reason'. This is clear from an apologia which he makes in one of the books which was written just before or after his elevation to the bishopric:

Y make protestacioun that it is not myne entent forto holde, defend or fauoure in this book or in eny other bi me writun or to be writun in latyn or in the comoun peplis langage eny errour or heresie, that is to seie, eny conclusioun which is aʒens treuthe and specialy aʒens the feith or lawe of oure lord god. And if eny such it happe me to write or offre or purpose or holde, defende or fauoure, bi eny vnavisidnesse, hastynes or ignoraunce, eer than y may se the treuthe, or bi eny other maner, y schal be redy it to leeve, forsaake, and retrete mekely and deuoutly at the assigne-mentis of myn ordynaries fadris of the chirche after that thei han take sufficient avisyng therupon; ʒhe and it the same y now as for

---

[1] November 7th, 1458. *Cal. Pat. Rolls*, Henry VI, vi, 465. Haydock held many offices in addition to his royal chaplaincy.

thanne, forsake and leeve. In the contrarie maner to this gouer-naunce y was neuer ȝitt hidirto disposid, y thanke my lord god, and y purpose never in contrarie wise to be, howeuer it happe ouer hasty and vndiscreete awaiters and bacbiters in other wise of me feele or diffame.[1]

The theological views which he expounded in his books aroused far less wrath than a sermon which he preached at St Paul's Cross in 1447. This sermon, which was preached on the text *Argue, obsecra, increpa, emenda in omni paciencia et doctrina* (2 Tim. iv. 2) was a reasoned but firm apologia on behalf of non-preaching bishops and of non-residence.[2] Bishops, he submitted, were more im-

[1] *The Reule of Chrysten Religioun*, 29. Cf. *Donet*, 4–5.

[2] The chief points in the sermon were:

'(1) Nullus hominum scit probare quod episcopus in quantum est episcopus et pro quanto est episcopus obligatur ad praedicandum in sua propria persona vulgari populo suae diocesis. Istis terminis et "ad praedicandum" sumptis in suis famosissimis significationibus.

(2) Episcopi non reputarent seipsos esse obligatos ad praedicandum in propriis personis suis vulgari populo suarum diocesium in quantum et pro quanto ipsi sunt episcopi supra alios curatos. Sed episcopi reputarent se esse liberos ab isto onere.

(3) Episcopi in quantum sunt episcopi debent habere abundantiorem Christianae religionis notitiam in materiis quas inferiores curati tenentur populo praedicare aut docere, atque debent habere majorem scientiam ad respondendum ac solvendum difficiles quaestiones quam est requisita haberi ab immediatis inferioribus curatis in quantum ipsi sunt inferiores et immediati curati.

(4) Episcopi habent potestatem ad assumendum et resumendum sibi et ad iterum dimittendum quando eis placet exercitium et opus praedicationis ad populum, quemadmodum habent potestatem ad assumendum et resumendum sibi quodcunque aliud opus curae pertinens immediato curato, quando eis placet; ita quod perinde episcopi non impediantur a meliore opere suarum ordinariarum curarum pro illa vice ab illis debito adimpleri, et quod opus ab illo immediato curato non potest ordinarie impleri.

(5) Episcopi possunt propter diversas causas absentare se a suis diocesibus et fieri non ibidem residentes excusabiliter et meritorie et allocabiliter penes Deum durante toto tempore illarum causarum.

(6) Magis expediens opus potest Christianorum animabus impendi quam est opus praedicationis, isto vocabulo praedicationis capto in sua propriissima et famosissima significatione.

(7) Neque papa neque episcopi Anglicani sunt simoniaci in hoc et per hoc, quod ipsi recipiunt suos episcopatus a papa per provisionem et solvunt papae primos fructus suorum episcopatuum.' (*Abbreviatio Reginaldi Pecok, Repressor*, II, 615–19.)

portant than inferior clergy since both their duties, their sphere of influence and their knowledge were more considerable. Why, then, should so much emphasis be placed on the function of a bishop as a preacher? There was nothing to oblige a bishop to preach, but it may be noted in passing that Pecock himself seems to have carried out this obligation. A bishop, indeed, fulfilled his function better in applying himself to more important work.[1] There is, indeed, every reason, not only why he should not preach but for his leaving the diocese when more important work, work for the good weal of Christendom, calls him so to do. Finally, he urged that neither the Pope nor the English bishops can be properly called simoniacs because they receive their sees by papal provision and subsequently pay firstfruits or annates for them. This sermon, which particularly aroused the wrath of Thomas Gascoigne, seems to have made Pecock unpopular in many circles.[2]

Pecock himself was so well satisfied with his discourse that he felt that he had successfully refuted his opponents, both heretics and Catholics. He told Master Thomas Chapman that no one would now speak evil of bishops or murmur against them, since he had so clearly proved that bishops were not bound to preach nor to do other works of a cure of souls, *sicut clerus et vulgus opinantur, sed tenentur superintendere et quaestionibus aliquorum respondere*. Eventually he had the sermon published and circulated

---

[1] Cf. 'weel y wote, that thou3 the office of preching is ful profitable into the eende of exortacioun, and of remembrauncing, certis it is not so into the eende of best teching' (*Repressor*, I, 88).

[2] Cf. 'certis, such an antetheme he ladde bi space of long tyme, which to summe ful mych plesid. In so mych that summe of the heerers profrid gold oft forto haue had thilk long antetheme writen for deynte had therof. Neuer-theles, for that the precher therof was not wonyd to write his solempne sermons, and for that he was 3ouun to greet bisinessis, he not took the labour forto delyuere it. But what for al this so preciose and so deliciose bifore send in the antetheme, whanne he procedid in the bodi and substaunce and cors of his sermoun vndir this theme: "Amici mei et proximi mei aduersum me appro-pinquauerunt et steterunt", in vndirnemyng and blamyng certeyn prechers, and that for as mych as he wolde that his werk schulde take effect, he dide it scharpli and not without profis therto brou3t, the peple, for what causis bothe god and wijs men knowen wel y-nou3, beere hem anentis the seid precher as wijlde, vnresonable beestis in many kyndis crueli, vnmanli, vncurteisli and vntrewli, with contynuaunce of long tyme' (*Folewer to the Donet*, 104–5).

it among his friends, sending it in particular to Walter Lyhart, whom we have already noticed at Oxford and who was now Bishop of Norwich and a leading Lancastrian, to Adam de Moleyns, another important minister who was Lord Privy Seal and Bishop of Chichester, and to Vincent Clement. Other men, however— Gascoigne naturally says *Omnes*—began to cry, 'Vae, vae, episcopis!'[1]

An analysis of his opponents is instructive, since it seems to indicate that the chief onslaught came from the universities where his works would presumably have had the greatest circulation and where his opinions would have called for most attention. Thus Hugh Damlet, who had been appointed Master of Pembroke Hall, Cambridge, this very same year, offered to prove to the world that Pecock's works contained many heretical opinions. Another of his most persistent enemies was also a don, William Millington, the famous Provost of King's College, Cambridge, who declared in a sermon which he preached at St Paul's Cross that those who patronised Pecock would never prosper if England had her own way.

Besides this Yorkshireman whom Capgrave affirms to have surpassed his predecessors in 'scholastic questions, literary depth and ripeness of character',[2] there were, in addition to the ever-loquacious Gascoigne, opponents of lesser fame. Among them Friar John Bury, who wrote the *Gladius Salomonis* as a reply to Pecock's *Repressor*, stands out. A friend of John Lowe, Bishop of Rochester, another enemy of Pecock's, at whose request the *Gladius* may well have been written,[3] Bury was an Augustinian friar, at one time provincial of Clare in the county of Suffolk and described by one writer as a 'doctor'.[4] This may or may not be

---

[1] *Loci e Libro Veritatum*, 15.

[2] Capgrave, *De Illustribus Henricis*, 133. For Millington *vide* G. Williams, *Cambridge Antiquarian Society Communications*, I, 291 ff.

[3] Bury says of Lowe in the *Gladius*: 'stabilis columna in templo Domini, vir Benjamin, vir geminus ab adolescentia sua, utraque manu ut dextra utens, qui nec sic institit Scripturis, ut humanitatis in se studia aliquando vacasse credantur, etc.' ['Geminus' has same meaning as 'ambidexter'.]

[4] Bale, *Index Britanniae Scriptores*, etc., ed. R. L. Poole and M. Bateman (Oxford, 1902), 186-7.

so, for there is no indication as to which university Bury attended, but he seems, from a survey of his *Gladius* and from the fact that he was supposed to have written a commentary on St Luke's Gospel, to have been a well-educated man. Pecock's successor at Whittington College, Thomas Eborall (1444–64), also carried on a vigorous campaign to discredit his predecessor. It is interesting to note that Eborall had formerly been rector of Kirk Deighton, a living which had been held by Gascoigne for a short time and which was in the gift of Sir Robert Roos, Gascoigne's brother-in-law. Eborall's acquaintance with Gascoigne must then have been fairly considerable.[1] Finally, two London rectors became prominent adherents of the anti-Pecock party, Gilbert Worthington, rector of St Andrew's, Holborn, from 1439 to 1447, and the eloquent preacher, William Lichfield, rector of All Hallows the Great and of St Mary Magdalen, Old Fish Street, until his death in 1448.[2] Lichfield had previously been associated with Pecock in business matters.

As a result of the growing opposition to Pecock, John Stafford, the Archbishop of Canterbury, asked Pecock to give him a justification or at any rate an explanation of the sermon which had caused so much trouble. Although the vindication[3] was hardly successful, it apparently placated Archbishop Stafford, a tactful diplomatist who had himself incurred royal displeasure by his moderation in political affairs.

A few years later[4] Pecock completed his most famous work, the *Repressor*, but its emphasis on the 'doom of reason' as opposed to the scriptures and revelation, made him still less popular in theological circles, and indeed called forth a reply from Friar John Bury in the *Gladius Salomonis*. By 1450 Pecock had already damaged his 'theological' reputation by his heterodox opinions and is already writing as a man who knows that his works will offend many of his readers.

---

[1] *Loci e Libro Veritatum*, 175–6, 215.

[2] Lichfield is said to have composed as many as 3083 sermons but only a few of these have survived.   [3] Babington, *Repressor*, II, 615 ff.

[4] A reference in the *Repressor* to the fact that war with France had now been waged for 34 years makes the date 1449 (*id.* II, 516).

Politically, the declining prestige of the house of Lancaster and its supporters increased his unpopularity. The negotiations with France, which had already led to the marriage of Henry VI with Margaret, were continued with ever-increasing prospect of disaster. At the end of 1445 the king, acting as it seems without the support of Suffolk, agreed to the surrender of Le Mans and all else that he held in Maine to Charles VII 'en faveur et en contemplacion de vous principalment'. This step so angered the middle classes and the army that the province had eventually to be forcibly annexed in 1448. Such activities as these only served to encourage further the belligerency of the English people, who were humiliated by their government's policy of surrender, whilst it encouraged the French king to hope for more gains from the declining power of England. Although the resumption of hostilities was almost certain, the government had sent no new equipment to the army in Normandy, and the renewal of the war was followed by disaster after disaster, the loss of Harfleur, Honfleur, Fresnay and other important towns during the early months of 1450.

The unsuccessful policy which Suffolk favoured in both peace and war must undoubtedly have been furthered and supported by men like Pecock. He certainly gives some indication of his views on these matters in the *Repressor*. It was hardly politic to give an illustration beginning 'if the King of Ynglond dwellid in Gascony, and wolde sende a noble longe letter or epistle into Englond'[1] in the very year when everything was going so badly, and it was even more tactless of him to argue that the religious—even if falling below the standard of the perfectly virtuous life—are doing much more good staying in their own monasteries than by fighting in France 'forto make miche morther of blood, 3he and of soulis, bothe in her owne side and in the Frensch side'.[2] It seems clear that Pecock had by this time definitely allied himself to Suffolk, for these years were also noticeable for an event which added to the increasing dislike and distrust which men felt for Henry VI's chief minister, the downfall and death of Gloucester,

[1] *Repressor*, I, 21.   *Id.* II, 516.

the chief opponent of the prevailing policy of the government. The mysterious circumstances attending his death[1] increased the general disquiet. Agnes Paston voices this in a letter to her son asking for reliable news from France 'tydynggs from beyond see, for here thei arn aferd to telle soche as be reportid'.[2] 'Thus began the trouble of Engelonge for the deth of noble duke. All the comyns of this reame began for to murmure, and were not content', writes the author of the *Polychronicon*. By this time the royal finances, always difficult enough, constituted an insoluble problem and thus added to the anxieties of the government. Since 1433 the royal debt had increased from £168,000 to £373,000, whilst another war threatened to diminish the royal income still further.

Under these circumstances two events occurred, both of them of importance for the understanding of Pecock's career. The first was the murder of the former Lord Privy Seal, Adam de Moleyns, Bishop of Chichester, by a mob of angry seamen at Portsmouth on January 9th, 1450, 'for abriggyng of thair wageȝ'.[3] The second was the downfall and murder of Suffolk himself on May 3rd as a result of the Commons' indictment of his policy the previous February. The satirical Ballad, the *Dirge of Jake Napis*, gives sarcastic testimony to the joy of the country at these ominous events:

---

[1] *Foed.* XI, 178; *Chron. Davies*, 118; W. Gregory, 188; Whetehampstead, I, 179, does not suggest that he was murdered, but this opinion was very current both at home and abroad. Professor Vickers sums up: 'Murder, therefore, is the most probable explanation of the Duke's sudden demise, his relapse into a comatose state might very well be the result of a poison taken with his food... at any rate it is beyond doubt that his destruction was planned if not carried out' (*Humphrey, Duke of Gloucester*, 301–2).

[2] *Letters*, I, 59.

[3] 'And this yeer, the Friday the ix day of Januarye, maister Adam Moleyns, bisshoppe of Chichestre and keper of the kyngis prive seel, whom the kyng sente to Portesmouth forto make paiement of money to certayne soudiers and shipmenne for thair wageȝ; and so it happid that with boisteȝ langage, and also for abriggyng of thair wageȝ, he fil in variaunce with thaym, and thay fil on him and cruelli there kilde him' (*Chron. Davies*, 64). Moleyns had actually resigned the Privy Seal on Dec. 9th (*Foed.* XI, 255).

For the sowles of thes wyse and wurthy,
Adam Moleyns, Suffolke, Sir Robert Ros, thes thre.
And specyally for Jake Napis sowlle that evar was sly,
For his sowle *placebo* and *dirige*.
Executor of this office dirge for to synge,
Shall begynne ye Bisshope of Seynt As.[1]

Thus amidst the thunder of war abroad and of approaching civil conflict, with the murder of yet another bishop, Ayscough of Salisbury,[2] and Jack Cade's rebellion, the two main events of the coming months, Pecock was elevated from St Asaph to Chichester, *omen imminentium cladium.*

[1] Two of the editors of this poem assume that it refers to Pecock's successor, Thomas Knight, presumably basing their identification on the fact that Pecock's appointment to Chichester had already taken place by the time of Suffolk's death. This is true, the *congé d'élire* had been issued on Jan. 30th, but the *temporalia* were not restored to Pecock until June 8th. The identification of the Bishop of St Asaph with Pecock is an obvious conclusion. His successor was little known, even his surname is a conjecture, whilst it takes many months for men to get used to new titles. The author of the *Dirge of Jake Napis* would naturally think of the bishop as Bishop of St Asaph. As a matter of fact both Gairdner's and Wright's editions of this famous ballad are far from satisfactory. Thus the 'Bishop of Hereforthe' is identified by Gairdner with Richard Beauchamp, Bishop of Hereford, whilst Wright has identified him with Reginald Baker (*sic* Boulers), Abbot of St Peter's, Gloucester. Gairdner is obviously correct, for even if Beauchamp had been translated to Salisbury at the time when the *Dirge* was being written, Beauchamp would have been the man in the author's mind. Similarly, Ayscough, the murdered Bishop of Salisbury, is, as Gairdner says, meant rather than his successor Beauchamp in the reference to Salisbury. Strangely enough Wright identifies the Abbot of Gloucester with Reginald Boulers or Butler despite the fact that a few lines previously he had already identified him with the Bishop of Hereford. The main fault of these editions lies in the absence of good notes; many important personages pass by completely unnoticed (*vide* T. Wright, *Political Poems* (Rolls Series), II, 232 ff.; *Stow's Memoranda*, ed. Gairdner (Camden Soc.), 99–103).

[2] Ayscough suffered at Edington as a result of rioting which was perhaps an offshoot of Cade's rebellion. The Chronicler's narrative is graphic: 'aftir that he hadde said masse, and was drawe fro the auter and lad vp to an hille ther...and there thay slow him horribly...and spoillid him vnto the nakid skyn, and rente his blody shirte into pecis.... Thise ii bisshoppis [i.e. Ayscough and Moleyns] were wonder couetous men, and evil beloued among the comune peple' (*Chron. Davies*, 64).

CHAPTER V

PECOCK AS BISHOP OF CHICHESTER

It was on March 23rd, 1450, that Pecock was appointed to the see of Chichester.[1] A week later he went to Leicester where parliament had been sitting and made his profession of obedience and finally on June 8th the temporalities of the see were restored to him. We know next to nothing of events in his diocese during his episcopate, for the register of the see during his rule has not been preserved. It is unlikely that he paid very much attention to business there,[2] and other events of a more momentous character are of greater importance for Pecock's career. The year of his elevation heralded the beginning of the end of English dominion in France; on August 12th, 1450, Cherbourg fell and a contemporary noted that 'we have not now a foote of londe in Normandie'.[3] It was followed on November 1st by the defeat of the English at Blanquefort, 'la male journade',[4] the fall of Bayonne and Bordeaux (which was regained momentarily by Shrewsbury) and the end of English control in Guienne. With the fall of

[1] De Moleyns was murdered on Jan. 9th. Babington is wrong in making it June 9th (*Repressor*, xxxii) (*Cal. Pat. Rolls*, Henry VI, v, 334). The temporalities had actually been committed to Pecock and to Sir Thomas Tyrell, by mainprise of Richard Vernon and Richard Wotton on January 20th, 1450 (*Cal. Fine Rolls*, XVIII, 148).

[2] W. R. W. Stephens, in his *Memorials of the See of Chichester*, follows Lewis and Babington. A few references indicate the nature of routine work in his see, e.g. mandate to admit John Rudyng LL.B. to the prebend of Ewherst and Holyngton (July 18th, 1454, *Cal. Pat. Rolls*, Henry VI, vi, 162); mandate to the dean and chapter to admit Wm. Trasy to the prebend of Bulworthithe (Oct. 31st, 1454, *id.* vi, 195); mandate to the dean and chapter to admit John Woode to prebend of Hoo, Wratlyng and Nenefield to which Pecock had already instituted him (April 26th, 1455, *id.* vi, 216); presentation of Baldwin Hyde for admission to the prebend of Holyngton (Aug. 8th, 1452, *id.* vi, 434); presentation of John Penant to the prebend of Hastyng (April 15th, 1452, *id.* v, 527). Pecock also acted as commissioner for a tax in Sussex in 1450 (*Cal. Fine Rolls*, XVIII, 173).

[3] *Paston Letters*, ed. James Gairdner, I, 139.

[4] *Vide* G. Le Bouvier, *Les Cronicques du feu Roy Charles*, 458–9; Jean Chartier, *Chronique de Charles VII*, 239, 246, etc.

Castillon in 1453 we may say that the end of the so-called Hundred Years War was in sight.

Indeed, 1453, the year in which Constantinople fell before the Turks, marked the end of an epoch in more ways than one. War abroad was paralleled by discontent at home,[1] the rebellion of Jack Cade, the beginning of the faction fight in real earnest which prepared the way for the opening of the Wars of the Roses, the first big battle of which was fought at St Albans in 1455.

The 'Captain of Kent's' rising aimed to overthrow an administration too weak to wage war successfully abroad or to maintain order at home, and many prominent Yorkists were implicated in it. Its demands, which clearly indicate that it was a representative movement, reflecting the aims and desires of the middle and lower classes of society, were of an economic and administrative nature. They included the demand for the abolition of many extortions, the Estreats of the 'Green Wax', unlicensed Purveyance, and the Statute of Labourers which had been re-enacted in 1446. They argued further that unemployment in the weaving industry had been caused by the adverse trade conditions resulting from interrupted communications. They complained of the alienation of crown property, of tyranny and administrative corruption, of the failure of the king to pay his debts and of the general lack of justice. Finally, the rebels fastened on the misdeeds of Suffolk and demanded the recall of the Duke of York, 'late exiled from our...lord's presence'. Cade's rebellion was but the precursor of further troubles, a detailed analysis of which the nature of this essay does not allow. But the rivalry of York and Somerset was only the focal point of disturbance. The periodic illnesses of the king still further weakened an already weak government.[2]

[1] *Vide* e.g. *Paston Letters*, 1, 162, 163; William of Worcester, *Annales Rerum Anglicarum*, 474; *Chronicle of the reigns of Henry IV, V and VI*, ed. J. A. Giles, 42; *A Short English Chronicle*, ed. James Gairdner, 66 ff. One of the best short accounts of Cade's rebellion is to be found in the *Chronicle*, ed. J. S. Davies, 64–8.

[2] 1453. 'ut sensu...caret et memoria...nec valeret pedibus pergere' (*Chron. Giles*, 44). He was again ill in 1456.

In addition to the baronial wars, the renewal of the conflict, for instance, between Sir Thomas Neville and Lord Egremont[1] or between the Earl of Devon and Lord Bonville,[2] which characterised the festering of bastard feudalism, the middle classes of the country, dissatisfied with the failure of the Lancastrian government to safeguard their interests, either pursued a neutral course in the conflict or gave tentative support to the growing power of the Yorkists, support which was later justified by the active economic policy which King Edward IV pursued in their, and his own, favour. Signs of this are already perceptible in parliamentary action, in the statute prohibiting all importation of wrought silk—ribbons, laces and 'corses of Geene' (Genoa) alone excepted,[3] and in the riots of April, 1456, directed against the Italians.[4] At the moment, the privateering and piracy of the French, the unpopular commercial treaties with the Flemings and the Hanseatic League only helped to foster popular feeling against the Lancastrians and in favour of the Duke of York. In August, 1457, for instance, a privateer force under de Brezé, Seneschal of Normandy, 'robbed and spoyled the toune of Sandewyche in Kent abydyng thereynne an hoole day' and on their way home plundered Fowey.[5] These events must be understood if we are to see Pecock's trial in its right setting, for he too was embroiling himself in this anarchy both by his theological and by his political opinions.

There are many indications of the growing opposition to

---

[1] 1453. *Short English Chronicle*, 70. There was open warfare in 1457.

[2] William of Worcester, 475.

[3] *Rot. Parl.* v, 325.

[4] Fabian, 630; *Paston Letters*, 1, 384–7. The trouble started when a Mercer's servant assaulted an Italian. The Lord Mayor imprisoned the servant but the next day the Londoners, the Mercers, released him and sacked several of the houses. John Bocking wrote to John Paston: 'The peas is weel kepte, but the straungiers are soore a dradde, and dar not come on brode.' A week later (May 15th, 1456) he talks of a proclamation made 'or shall be, thorwe London, the pees to be kepte upon grete peynes; and the Lumbards to occupie the merchaundize as thei did til the Counsail or Parlament have otherwise determyned'.

[5] *A Short English Chronicle*, 71; *Chron. Davies*, 74.

Pecock in his works, and 'myne adversaries' who 'bihynde my back allege to the comune peple' who with 'greet rudenesse' attack him because he differs in some places from the teaching of the Fathers are very much to the fore. There are many passages, for instance, in the *Folewer to the Donet*, probably written somewhere about 1455, which reflect the growing criticism with which he had to deal:

> Y make this protestacioun here and now, bifore the fynal vttryng and publischyng of eny of my bookis, englisch or latyn: that y haue be and schal be of noon othir synguler disposicioun in alle my writyngis, englisch or latyn, than ben wonyd to be othire writers of her writyngis.[1]

This plea for toleration appears not infrequently, suggesting again and again that here is a writer who is continually being attacked, and, what is interesting, is bewildered by the storm of criticism which he arouses. Pecock adds that he may be criticised for writing books to instruct laymen but that laymen may very well benefit from what he has written, even if they do not understand the theological implications of all they read. Similarly, he adds, the clergy do not always understand the Latin Bible, but they are doubtless edified by what they read. It is not true, he repeats a few pages later, to say that 'I write and teche therin of my silf and of myn owen heed, as thouȝ y hadde noon autorite for it'.[2]

Another adversary, who had already made his opposition felt, was William Goddard or Godhard, the provincial of the English Franciscans, who apparently 'apechyd hym of hys erysys', possibly in retaliation for the bishop's denunciation of the friars as 'clamatores in pulpitis' or 'pulpit-bawlers'.[3] It seems likely that many of the Lancastrians, possibly the king himself, might have been alienated by his theological views.

---

[1] *Folewer to the Donet*, 5, 6; cf. *id.* 67, 72, 108, 227.   [2] *Id.* 9.

[3] *Greyfriars Chronicle of London*, ed. J. G. Nichols (Camden Soc. 1852, 20). Goddard was buried in the Greyfriars' Church (*Collectanea Typographica et Genealogica*, v, 277). 'Item in epistola sua directa, in titulo "Doctori ordinis fratrum minorum Godard" vocat praedicatores modernos clamatores in pulpitis' (*Loci e Libro Veritatum*, 100).

But it is doubtful whether his theological views would alone have aroused the venom which led to his downfall.[1] It is very difficult to secure evidence of his activities in these years, but he was implicated in the resentment which was increasingly making itself felt against the Lancastrians. The records bear witness to his attendance at the Privy Council from time to time. With the Bishops of Norwich, Salisbury, Bath and de Moleyns he had attended as Bishop of St Asaph on February 1st, 1445, to discuss Suffolk's impending embassy to France.[2] Ten years later, as Bishop of Chichester, on May 14th, 1455, he was among those who signed the letters of credence for instructions to the commissioners who were to be appointed to raise money for the defence of Calais,[3] and a few months later, July 9th, he was nominated one of the triers of the petitions for Gascony and the islands.[4] Later on, November 10th and December 11th, 1455, his name was among others giving the Duke of York power to act

[1] It is clear that his business associations, e.g. with the Mercers' Company, continued. Cf. *Cal. Fine Rolls*, XVIII, 64, 167. 'Whereas the king's servant, Master John Somerseth, chancellor of the Exchequer, built of late a chapel on a piece of ground containing 20 feet in length and 40 feet in breadth, lying at the west end of the bridge of New Braynford, co. Middlesex...the foundation stone of which chapel the king laid with his own hands...the said John intending to found on his piece of ground, held of the king, contiguous to the said chapel, a hospital for nine poor men and a gild in honour of the nine orders of holy angels: the king has granted in frank almoin to Reynold, bishop of St Asaph, Nicholas, bishop of Llandaff, Master John Somerseth, Master Peter Hyrford, Master William Lychfeld...etc., the said piece of ground on the late ancient highway, with the water of Braynt and the soil thereof pertaining to the ancient wooden bridge...and licence for them to found a gild' (*Cal. Pat. Rolls*, Henry VI, v, 29). This is dated Oct. 12th, 1446, when Pecock was Bishop of St Asaph. Evidence of his activity as Bishop of Chichester is to be found in another document (Feb. 5th, 1452): 'Pardon for 40s paid in the hanaper to Thomas Coke, Thomas Tyrell, knight, etc. for acquiring in fee from Reynold, bishop of Chichester, Walter, bishop of Norwich, John Broddesworth, citizen and mercer of London, John Somerseth...a manor or messuage called "Erles"...in Haveryng, co. Essex, and in the meadow called "Brightmaresmade" in Haveryng marsh an acre of meadow' (*Cal. Pat. Rolls*, Henry VI, v, 517).
[2] Nicolas, *Proceedings of the Privy Council* (London, 1837), VI, 32.
[3] *Id.* VI, 240.
[4] *Id.* VI, 262, 275; *Rot. Parl.* V, 279a and App. 453-4.

whilst Henry was ill. But this only shows that he was a not inactive politician. A letter which he wrote to the Lord Mayor of London, Sir Thomas Canning, in 1455, which was so *valde suspiciose perturbacionis fidei et insurrecionis in regno Angliae* that the mayor sent the letter to the king,[1] is, however, an indication of his growing political unpopularity. It must not be thought that Pecock had anything like the prominence in the politics of the day which some of his fellow-prelates, like his friend Lyhart, had. A petition of January 20th, 1451, for instance, which gives a list of some thirty persons accused of 'mysbehaving' and which includes most of the important members of the Lancastrian party does not include Pecock's name. Yet everything indicates that it was a combination of his political and theological views which brought about his ultimate downfall.

A letter which Lord Beaumont wrote to the king[2] gives some idea of the anxiety with which Pecock's views were now regarded. Lord Beaumont began with an eloquent testimony to Henry's reputation as a Christian prince: 'Most cristen prince our allermost dred soverene lord after oppinion of longe before of oon of youre name and lyenage which for excellency of zele and love of God and myghty supportacion of Crysts faith and his Chirch in tyme of nede byfore other princes your noble progenitours ys prophesyed of as wele in the writyng lett with the holy ampull sent from heven and delivered to Seynt Thomas of Cauntbury.' He then notes that it is the king's duty to 'represse the most execrable persones that by sotyll covyns and ymaginatyff wittes sett all these studes to hurt our faith'. It is particularly appropriate that he should write this now because of 'that grete noyze' which 'rennyth that ther shuld be diverse conclusyons labored and

---

[1] *Loci e Libro Veritatum*, 212. Gascoigne has 1456, and the author of the *Short English Chronicle* 1455. Canning's brother was the famous Bristol merchant.

[2] *MSS. Peterborough*, VII, fol. 43. Is this also suggestive? 'Grant for the King's sergeant, Henry Fylongley, keeper of the great wardrobe, of 100£ which Reynold, Bishop of Chichester is held to pay for the escape of Nicholas Brian, late convicted and committed to the bishop's keeping' (Sept. 25th, 1457—*Cal. Pat. Rolls*, Henry VI, VI, 323).

subtilly entended to be emprented in mennes herts by pryvy by also unherd meenes to the most pernicyous and next to pernicyon of our faith'. He then comes to the main point of his letter:

that is sayd that this pecok this Bisshop of Chichester thurgh presumption and curiosite demed by hym in his own wytte but it soner be extincte and undirstond and by your myght and comaundment to be the archiebissop and prelates and doctours examined and yf that be provid so assisted and punished by you of all pepill thought to be he that so shuld be of temporall princes he by whom the chirche shuld in tyme of nede fele hem so releved and born uppe by. And in this do now your wakyr diligence and lat the pepull fele the grete desir ye haff evir had in your hart to the exaltation and continuante of your faith to the worldes end. And now lete passe out into lyght the grete flammes of faith kept and myghty brennyng ever in your brest.

He trusts that

not to take yt to displesur I wryte my pore advice ffirst yf ye have knoulech certayne by wrytynge or other wyse of this matter to send to th archbysshope and the chaunceller and other prelates to take of the best clerkes of bothe universities and with owte delay deuly to examine the ground of the works and that yt be not remissely done ne longe drawen of lenthe the tyme wherebye the puple myght take hurt ffor yf they do ye wyll take yt to grete displesure.[1]

And so the way was prepared for Pecock's fall.[2]

[1] John, first Viscount Beaumont, was one of the chief supporters of the House of Lancaster. After having held the post of Constable, he succeeded Suffolk as Chamberlain in 1450. He was killed at Northampton in 1460.

[2] Pecock had also acted, with John Stokes and Thomas Marsh, as Bishop Bekynton's proctor in 'the coming convocation in London' in 1453 (*Reg. Bekynton*, 1, 199) and again in 1456 (*Id.* 1, 264). He had also been present in London to help in the consecrations of Bishop Booth of Lichfield (at St Paul's, July 9th, 1447) and of Bishop Beauchamp of Hereford (at Lambeth, Feb. 9th, 1449). Dr T. G. Jalland suggests that his papalism led to his fall (*The Church and the Papacy* (1944), 420 n.) but all the evidence suggests that this was an incidental rather than a fundamental reason for his misfortunes.

CHAPTER VI

PECOCK'S TRIAL AND SENTENCE

THE blow actually fell at a council of spiritual and temporal lords, purported to have been held on October 22nd, 1457, when the temporal lords refused to continue with the agenda of the council whilst Pecock remained in their company.[1] The reason for this action is itself uncertain, but it seems only too probable that Pecock had grown more tactless and intransigent in his political opinions. The temporal lords as a whole would hardly have been concerned with purely theological questions, whilst the Yorkists in particular might have thought that they could use Pecock as an instrument through which to strike at the Lancastrian government.

The cry of the temporal peers was taken up by their spiritual colleagues who turned what was either a general or a specific charge into an ecclesiastical examination and requested Archbishop Bourchier to hand them Pecock's books for an examination to be made of his views. In reply to this, Pecock added that he was perfectly willing that the archbishop should have the works that he had written within the last three years, but that he could take no responsibility for the works which he had written previous to that period since they had only been circulated among his private friends and had never received his final corrections.[2]

---

[1] 'Nullus enim dominus temporalis tunc in illo concilio magno regis et regni existens voluit loqui concilium suum nec avisamentum, nec ea quae intellexit pro bono regni ibi exprimere, quousque ille episcopus Pecok esset extra domum illius concilii, magnis doctoribus et pluribus in Theologia ibi in illo concilio regis presentibus' (*Loci e Libro Veritatum*, 210–11).

[2] Some years previously Pecock had made a very similar complaint: '"the donet of cristen religioun" and "the book of cristen religioun" and othire suche of doctrine and of officiyng whiche, bifore the deuyce and setting of this present book, ben runne abrood and copied aȝens my wil and myn entent, as y haue openli prechid at poulis, and that bi vncurtesie and vndiscrecioun of freendis, into whose singuler siȝt y lousid tho writingis to go, and forto not haue go ferthir into tyme thei were bettir examyned of me and approvid of my

4

This reply was not entirely satisfactory, and the archbishop, who appears to have pursued a cautious tacking policy throughout the trial, summoned Pecock to appear before him at Lambeth on November 11th and to bring his books with him. For the moment, he was to withdraw from the Council Chamber. Pecock complied with this request, and apparently left London, probably for his diocese.[1]

The intervening period seems to have been marked by different moves on the part of the chief actors in the coming tragedy. Archbishop Bourchier did not wish to commit himself to either side lest his own position should be undermined in the event of the Yorkist party gaining the upper hand in the councils of the nation. He was personally more of the civil servant than the churchman, and he showed relatively little zeal in his conduct of religious affairs. He was not, however, without ability as a diplomatist,[2] a quality which determined his attitude towards Pecock and which enabled him to crown King Henry VII many years later. Pecock was and, from the attitude taken by Archbishop Stafford some ten years previously, had been a 'thorn' in the archiepiscopal flesh. He was at the same time a bishop, a member of a class in which *esprit de corps* was always strong. The charge of heresy was in itself of so grave a nature that the archbishop had to move slowly. He therefore ordered the accusers to bring their accusations in writing to Lambeth on November 11th, but he warned them not to 'presume in any manner out of court

lordis and fadris of the churche, y wole to be as noon of myn; but in as moche as in me is, y wole thei be rendrid vp aȝen, and bettir formes of the same be to hem deliuered, whanne dewe deliueraunce therof schal be made' (*Donet*, 6–7).

[1] For what follows: *Loci e Libro Veritatum*, 209 ff.; Whetehampstead, *Chron. Monast. St Albani* (Rolls), ed. H. T. Riley (1872), 1, 280 ff.; *Three Fifteenth Century Chronicles* (Brief Latin Chronicle, Camden Soc.), ed. J. Gairdner, 167 ff.; *English Chronicle from 1377 to 1461*, ed. J. S. Davies (Camden Soc.), 75 ff.; Lewis, *Life of Pecock* (1820), 143 ff.

[2] In 1458 he was largely responsible for a temporary reconciliation between the two conflicting parties but he later abandoned the Lancastrian cause. Whetehampstead, describing him with the pen of a flatterer rather than of a critic, calls him 'qui pro tunc cardo erat solidior, fortiorque columna, totius in regno Ecclesiae Anglicanae' (1, 281).

to assert, judge, or preach anything to the prejudice of the afore-said Lord Bishop Reginald whilst this affair of the examination and discussion of his books and conclusions before him or his commissaries was depending and unfinished'.

The king was also informed of the action and probably took some part in the ensuing events, for although he had only recently recovered from one of his bouts of temporary insanity, it may be presumed that his mind was as clear as ever where religious questions were concerned. Harding's statement, so frequently quoted and not without acceptance in his own day, that the king

> could little within his brest conceyve;
> the good from eivill he could uneth perceyue

seems incredible in the face of Henry's known piety and integrity of character. His relations to Pecock could certainly have been determined by his 'religious' rather than by his 'political' views, a fact which probably further clouded an issue already obscure in itself. The theological question, which was basic so far as the king was concerned, probably lost the bishop Henry's sympathy and increased the improbability of an acquittal.[1]

Pecock himself seems to have retired to the country where he occupied himself in erasing and correcting certain phrases in his works which might prove offensive to his judges, for Gascoigne tells us that the books which he brought with him for examination on November 11th were found *in pluribus locis cancellati et rasi in diversis locis, et iterum de novo scripti per eundem episcopum.*

From November 11th until December 3rd when he made his abjuration Pecock's fortunes went from bad to worse. The nine books which he brought with him to Lambeth on November 11th, including the *Repressor* and the *Book of Faith*, were handed by Archbishop Bourchier to twenty-four doctors, some of whom were undoubtedly personal enemies of the bishop. This com-

---

[1] Babington suggests, improbably, that 'this personal feeling may manifest itself in the statutes of King's College, Cambridge, in which Henry directs that no disciple of Wiclif or Pecock shall be suffered to remain there' (xxxiv n.).

mission was to report to the archbishop and his three assessors, with whom the final sentence lay.

The characters of these assessors reveal the disadvantageous position in which Pecock was now placed, for they would all for one reason or another have been biased against him. It has already been noticed that John Lowe, Bishop of Rochester, whom Pecock had succeeded at St Asaph, was one of the most persistent of the bishop's enemies and a patron of his fellow-Augustinian,[1] Friar Bury, with whom he may have been actively associated in the writing of the *Gladius Salomonis*. Although he had been Confessor to Henry VI, he was probably already an avowed Yorkist. Three years later he joined Warwick's army at his diocesan city, and was one of the delegation which the Londoners sent to the Duke of York to find out whether he would accept the crown. The second of the assessors, John Chedworth, Bishop of Lincoln, was far more of a trimmer than Lowe. Despite the fact that his rise to high office was due to the king's attachment to him, he too was now probably veering towards the Yorkist camp. Chedworth had been a Fellow of King's College, Cambridge, under Provost Millington, another opponent of Pecock's, and had actually succeeded him as provost when he was deposed from that office in 1446. His elevation to the see of Lincoln in 1452, in succession to Marmaduke Lumley, was yet another sign of royal patronage. In any case, whether Chedworth was or was not veering towards the Yorkists, his attitude to heterodoxy in general and to the Lollards in particular, suggests that he cannot have viewed the bishop with any great favour. The third of the trio, William Waynflete, Bishop of Winchester, was a more ardent Lancastrian, a personal and trusted friend of Henry VI whose confidence he enjoyed. It is possible that Waynflete represented Henry's views in this matter and was therefore averse to Pecock from a theological rather than from a political standpoint. It is interesting to note that Waynflete had been one of the three prelates (de Moleyns and Stafford

[1] Lowe had been prior of a London house in 1428 and provincial of his order in England.

had been the other two) before whom Pecock had been brought in 1447 in connection with the sermon which he preached at St Paul's Cross.[1] It may be hypothetical to think of Waynflete as the moderate man among the assessors, but he was certainly not present at the final scene of the tragedy, the burning of Pecock's books and the bishop's recantation. Finally, the fact that both Chedworth and Waynflete were collaborators in arranging the new statutes of King's College, Cambridge, is also suggestive. Thus the characters of all three assessors were not such as to give much encouragement to their 'dear brother, Reginald'.

Pecock seems to have recognised this disadvantage, for he requested that he might be judged not by his fellow-bishops but by his peers, his equals in 'intellectual distinction',[2] an unfortunate, tactless remark which was typical of his character and which can only have exacerbated his opponents still further. It may have been at this time that the prominent Yorkist partisan, George Neville, who had been recently appointed Bishop of Exeter, although he was too young to be consecrated to that office,[3] *passionato seu ira commoto*, remarked to Pecock: 'My lord of Chichester through his just judgement God is willing to let you suffer these great reproaches because you have vehemently and shamefully censured and denied the true and holy words of the Blessed Jerome, St Augustine, of that holy doctor, Gregory, and other saints.' Pecock replied that he repented of having written his works without sufficient knowledge of the matters in question. On the other hand, Bishop Neville may have addressed this remark, as Gascoigne indicates,[4] to Pecock when the commissioners reported that they had found many errors and heretical views in the bishop's works, as they had promised they would prove *suis pileis utentes* before the king. Whether this report was unanimous or not is not known, but the report was accepted by

---

[1] *Loci e Libro Veritatum*, 31.   [2] *Loci e Libro Veritatum*, 213.

[3] Bishop Edmund Lacy had died in Sept. 1455, and Neville was appointed in March, 1456, being at that time about twenty-five years of age. He was given the temporalities then (*Foed.* XI, 376) but was not consecrated until Dec. 1458.   [4] *Loci e Libro Veritatum*, 213.

Bourchier and his fellow-bishops and it probably provided a basis for the seven points of Pecock's retractation, as well as for the semi-official condemnation which the archbishop called on Dr Pinchbeck, the rector of St Mary Abchurch, to read at St Paul's Cross the following Sunday. A few days later, on November 21st, in all probability at Lambeth Palace, Pecock was again examined and made a recantation of certain conclusions which he had reached in his writings. This examination prepared the way for the final thrust, what we may call the trial scene of November 28th.

The trial of November 28th was the climax of Pecock's career. It is uncertain whether this took place at Lambeth in the presence of certain secular lords, the two chief participants being Lord Scales and Sir Thomas Stanley, and ecclesiastical notabilities as Gascoigne suggested[1] or, as Whetehampstead believed, before the king in full council at Westminster. Babington thought that he may have been examined in both places about the same time, but it seems more likely that Lambeth would have been the scene of his trial. After various preliminaries Archbishop Bourchier addressed Pecock in these terms:

Dear Brother (*Condilecte Frater*), since all heretics are blinded by the light of their own understandings, and will not own the perverse obstinacy of their own conclusions, we shall not dispute with you in many words (for we see that you abound more in talk than in reasoning) but briefly show you that you have manifestly presumed to contravene the sayings of the more authentic doctors. For as regards the descent of Christ into hell, the Tarentine doctor in an enquiry of his into the three creeds says that it was left out of the Nicene and Athanasian creeds, because no heresy had then arisen against it, nor was any great question made about it. As to the authority of the Catholic Church, the doctor Augustine says, unless the authority of the Catholic Church moved me, I should not believe the Gospel. As to the power of councils, the doctor Gregory says (and his words are placed in the Canon *Distinct XV*), that the four sacred councils of Nicaea, Constantinople, Ephesus and Chalcedon are not less to be

[1] *Id.* 214. On Lord Scales see *D.N.B.* L, 395–6.

honoured and reverenced than the four holy Gospels. For in them (as he asserts) as on a square corner stone the structure of the sacred faith is raised; and in them the rule of good life and manners consists. The other doctors also say with one voice that although the sacred councils may not err in matter of faith, because in every general council, where two or three are gathered together in Christ's name, His Holy Spirit is there in the midst of them, who does not suffer them to err in faith or to depart from the way of truth. As regards the sense and understanding of Scripture, the doctor Jerome says, that whoever understands or expounds it otherwise than the meaning of the Holy Spirit requires, is an undoubted heretic. With whom agrees the Lincoln doctor thus saying: Whoever excogitates any opinion contrary to Scripture, if he be publicly teaching it and obstinately adhere to it, is to be counted for an heretic. Accordingly, Master, seeing that you are convicted not only of holding what is contrary to the sayings of all these doctors, but moreover contradict them; it behoves us, according to the doctrine of Doctor Jerome, to cut you off from the body of the Universal Church as rotten flesh, and to drive you from the fold as a scabbed sheep, that you may not have the power to corrupt or infect the whole flock. Choose, therefore, for yourself one of these things: whether you had rather retract from your errors, and make a public abjuration, and so, for the future agree with the rest of Christ's faithful in your opinions; or whether you will incur the penalty of the canons, and not only suffer the reproach of degradation, but also, moreover, be delivered over to the secular arm, that, because you have attempted to plunder the treasury of the faith by force, you may become, according to the saying of the prophet, the fuel of the fire as well as the food of the burning. Choose one of these two for the alternative is the immediate coercion of heretics.

Although he cannot have been ignorant of the fate which was meted out to heretics Pecock seems to have been somewhat taken aback at these grim alternatives. After standing silent for a few minutes he replied: 'I am in a strait betwixt these two alternatives and hesitate in despair as to what I shall choose. If I defend my opinions and positions, I must be burned to death: if I do not, I shall be a byword and a reproach. Yet it is better to incur the taunts of the people than to forsake the law of faith and to depart after death into hellfire and the place of torment. I choose, therefore, to make an abjuration, and intend for the future so to live that no suspicion shall rise against me all the days of my life.'

Pecock has been frequently blamed for thus giving way, for, it has been argued, his action revealed either cowardice, gross inconsistency or both. Although it is true that Pecock was not of the stuff of which heroes are made, the explanation of his abjuration is comparatively simple, for his recantation was in accordance with the views which he had put forward time and time again. This has been too rarely emphasised. It is true that he believed that his own intellectual standpoint was right: 'if in tho maters which y write and teche, y folewe the doom of resoun and grounde hem there, it is not trewe that y seie, write and teche therin of my silf and of myn owen heed as thouȝ y hadde noon autorite for it.'[1] Indeed, his appeal to Rome clearly indicated his belief in his own innocence.

At the same time his views also most certainly allowed, indeed demanded, his obedience to right and proper authority, the authority of the Catholic Church which he had throughout his life tried to make more palatable to heretics as well as to believers by attempting to base it less on revealed scripture than on man's power of reason. That in the ultimate analysis Pecock's appeal to reason constituted a denial of all ultimate authority save that of the individual is beside the point, because the bishop would never have recognised the validity of this logical inference any more than John Wyclif would have recognised the validity of the communistic inferences of dominion based on grace. In a short discussion on the Eucharist Pecock said that a heretic is a man who will not recede from errors which have been clearly proved to be wrong and to have been as clearly condemned, but he also, with an obvious reference to his own position, affirmed that it is not sinful for a man to proceed reasonably from an actual article of faith to other truths, providing 'that he be redy to forsake his errour as soone as he may dresse hym silf bettir into trouthe'.[2]

[1] *Folewer to the Donet*, 9.   [2] *The Reule of Chrysten Religioun*, 96.

Pecock would, then, have been inconsistent if he had stood out against higher authority in a way which would have brought him perilously near to those Lollards whose individualistic arrogance he had soundly trounced and to his own definition of what constituted heresy. Further, he had averred his willingness to submit to proper authority should it order him to renounce any or all of his views:

y schal be redy it to leeve, forsaake, and retrete mekely and deuoutly at the assignementis of myn ordynaries fadris of the chirche after that thei han take sufficient avisyng therupon.[1]

It must also be remembered that hell fire, the experience of which Pecock affirmed to be the effect of breaking the law of faith, was a very real thing, even to a scholar such as the bishop. It was a physical probability, not an academic possibility, which almost certainly swayed men's actions. In a passage which bears a remarkable resemblance to a similar passage in Wyclif's writings, Pecock speaks of hell fire as

passing greet lothynes and gastnes in seyng horrible thingis, in heeryng of gastful thingis, in smellyng of moost grevose stenchis, taastyng of most squaymose and moost vnsauery taastis, in touching, feelyng and suffring moost peynful thingis to the

---

[1] *The Reule of Chrysten Religioun*, 29. Cf. *Donet*, 4: 'fferthirmore, sithen an errour or heresye is not the ynke writen, neithir the voice spokun, but it is the meenyng or the vndirstondyng of the writer or speker signified bi thilk ynke writen or bi thilk voice spokun...therfore y desire and aske for charite that noon harder or hastier holding or iuging be made anentis me.' He says that reference should be made to the general argument of his work and of his other writings and if the meaning is not then clear 'recours may be had to my persoon forto aske of me, while y am in this lijf'. He adds: 'god send to be reders in my bokis suche men as wolen gladli aspie aftir my meenyng in my wordis, and saue and defende me a3ens alle othire in contrarie maner disposid reders or heerers.' He will, indeed, thank any one who suggests an amendment of his views 'for helthe of cristen peplis soulis' (*id.* 5).

The Rev. F. A. Hannick in an otherwise disappointing dissertation, *Reginald Pecock* (Washington, 1922, 13) suggests that 'Pecock did the obvious thing....Had he acted otherwise his principles regarding authority, set forth in the *Repressor* and the *Book of Faith*, could be naught but inconsistencies'.

touche, lothid and hatid cumpanye, ffere in ymagynacioun and mynde vpon chaunge of peynes to come.[1]

Although Pecock's retractation may have been partly caused by panic, evoked by the hornet's nest which he had aroused, it is at the same time true to say that it was more in tune with all that we know of Pecock's life and character than has sometimes been admitted.

On Saturday, December 3rd, he went to Lambeth and there made his retractation in the presence of the archbishop and the twenty-four doctors who had presumably formed the commission which had previously reported on his works. Next day, December 4th,[2] the public recantation was read at St Paul's Cross, long one of the chief centres of ecclesiastical life in England. Bishop Brunton, emphasising the central position which it occupied, wrote: 'in that place [London] there is a greater devotion and a more intelligent people, and therefore, it is to be presumed, greater fruit. Moreover, because each bishop of England has subjects as parishioners in London, therefore when he gives instruction there, it is as though he were preaching to his own people and to the other churches of England in addition.' Bishop Brunton[3] was not alone in emphasising the importance of St Paul's Cross. The chroniclers witness to the interest which the general public showed in Pecock's recantation, for there were, says Gascoigne with pardonable medieval exaggeration, no less than twenty thousand people gathered round the Cross that Sunday to see the strange spectacle of the public humiliation of an important bishop.

Pecock, who was arrayed in his episcopal robes, was accompanied by the archbishop, his old enemy Lowe of Rochester,

[1] *Reule*, 144. Both Pecock and Wyclif agree that one of the pleasures experienced by the inhabitants of heaven will be the sight of the damned in torment: 'damned men in hell do ever good to saints in heaven for their bliss is more savoury for pains that they see in them' (*De Ecclesia*, ed. J. Loserth, 1886).

[2] The author of the *Chronicles of the Grey Friars of London* (ed. J. G. Nichols (Camden Soc., 1852), 20) makes the date Nov. 27th. This is inaccurate.

[3] MS. Harl. 3760, fol. 60, cited in G. R. Owst, *Preaching in Medieval England*.

Kempe, Bishop of London, the Bishop of Durham and many other clergy. It is noticeable that neither Bishop Chedworth of Lincoln nor the Lancastrian Waynflete of Winchester were present. After certain preliminaries, Pecock knelt down at the archbishop's feet in supplication and read his recantation, the form of which has been preserved:

In the name of the Holy Trinity, Father, Son and Holy Ghost, I Reginald Pecock, Bishop of Chichester, unworthy, of mine own pure, free will, without any man's coercion, or dread, confess and acknowledge that I have before time, presuming of mine own natural wit, and preferring the judgement of natural reason before the New and Old Testaments, and the authority and determination of our mother, Holy Church, have held, felt, written and taught otherwise than the Holy Roman and Universal Church teaches and observes, and besides this against the true Catholic and apostolic faith, I have made, written, taken out and published many varying, perilous and pernicious doctrines, books, works and writings, which contain heresies and errors contrary to the catholic faith and the determination of Holy Church. In particular I have taught these errors:

(1) It is not necessary for salvation to believe that our Lord Jesus Christ descended into hell after death.

(2) It is not necessary to salvation to believe in the Holy Spirit.

(3) It is not necessary for salvation to believe in the Holy Catholic Church.

(4) It is not necessary for salvation to believe in the Communion of Saints.

(5) That the Universal Church can err in matters of faith.

(6) It is not necessary for salvation to believe and hold that those things which a general council of the universal Church determines, approves or legislates in favour of the faith and for the salvation of souls, must be held and approved by the whole of those faithful to Christ, and that that which it reproves or condemns or holds to be contrary to the catholic faith or goodly customs are thereby held and believed to be reproved and condemned.

(7) It is quite lawful for any one to interpret holy scripture in the literal sense, nor is it to be maintained for salvation for any one to cleave to any other sense.[1]

[1] Wilkins, *Concilia*, III, 576. For No. (7) *vide* Whetehampstead, I, 286.

Wherefore, I, a miserable sinner, which have now walked in darkness here for some long time, have, by the mercy and infinite goodness of God, been led back into the right way and light of truth, and considering myself to have sinned grievously and to have taught and infected the people of God in a wicked manner, return and come again to the unity of our mother Holy Church, and all heresies and errors written and contained in my said books, works and writings here-before this time, I solemnly and openly revoke and renounce in the presence of the most reverend father in God; before this time I have judicially abjured these heresies and errors in due and legal form before the most reverend father in God, my lord of Canterbury, submitting myself, being then and also at this time a very contrite and penitent sinner, to the correction of the Church and of my lord of Canterbury. In addition to this exhorting and requiring in the name and virtue of Almighty God into the salvation of your souls and of mine, that no man give faith or credence to my said pernicious doctrines, heresies, and errors; neither my said books, hold or read in any wise; but that they bring all such books, works and writings as suspect of heresy (dealing in all godly haste) unto my said lord of Canterbury or to his commissaries or deputies for the prevention of many inconveniences and great perils to souls which might otherwise ensue of the contrary. And in addition to this declaration of my conversion and repentance, I hereby make full and open assent that these my said books, works and writings, for considerations and causes rehearsed above, be deputed unto the fire and be burnt in public for an example and to the terror of all others.

The charges with which Pecock was faced were of two distinct kinds. In the first place certain of the charges were based on Pecock's own writings. The first charge was, as we shall see, well authenticated,[1] whilst the third, fifth and sixth accusations may be based on the general tenor of Pecock's thought and on his own distinction between the words 'believe' and 'believe in'.[2] The second, third and seventh charges were never countenanced by Pecock for he explicitly affirms his belief in the communion of saints[3] and in the Holy Trinity,[4] although he admitted to the

---

[1] *Vide* p. 174 ff.   [2] *Book of Faith*, 283 ff.
[3] *Donet*, 104: 'I beleeue the comunyng of seintis to be.'
[4] 'God is thre persons', 'thre persoones ben oon God' (*Repressor*, I, 39, 83).

holding of such opinions in the panic of the moment. In fact, the only significant charge was the first, and this was relatively unimportant as compared with the two real elements in Pecock's trial. The first of these is contained in the words of the abjuration, 'presuming of mine own natural wit, and preferring the judgement of natural reason before the New and Old Testaments, and the authority and determination of our mother, Holy Church', and was substantially correct. The second is found in the general circumstances of his trial, the political ideas which made him unpopular with the great lords.

At the conclusion of his speech Pecock stepped forward and picking up a number of his books, three folios and eleven quartos in all, handed them to the executioner who then threw them into a fire which had been kindled for this purpose near by. The crowd, possibly spurred on by the drama of the moment, pressed forward and would, had they been able, have forced the bishop to follow his literary compositions into the flames. As he watched the fruits of a life's work slowly burn away, we are told that Pecock bitterly exclaimed: 'My pride and presumption have brought these troubles and reproaches upon me.' After his abjuration, Bourchier sent him under nominal arrest to Canterbury and then to Maidstone where he awaited the promulgation of the final sentence.

It cannot, however, have been very long before Pecock regretted his recantation and appealed to Rome against the unjust sentence of the archbishop. Gascoigne tells us that he made the following comment at Canterbury after his abjuration:

> Wyt hath wunder that reson kan not tel;
> How a moder is mayd and God is man.[1]

The verse certainly indicates, if it is genuine, that Pecock hardly retained his belief in the mastery of reason. The grounds of Pecock's appeal are uncertain, but that it was favourably received

---

[1] *Loci e Libro Veritatum*, 217. Gascoigne continues:
> 'Leve reson, beleve ye wonder;
> Beleve hath mastry and reson is under.'

at Rome is clear from the rescript which Pope Calixtus III sent in reply. It is indeed possible that Pecock's appeal might have been successful, for he was friendly towards ultramontanes like Vincent Clement and the English hierarchy was not popular at Rome,[1] had it not been for the fact that his appeal coincided with the death of Calixtus. In any case, Calixtus' reply had been very favourable to Pecock. He sent a rescript to Bourchier requesting him to restore Pecock to his bishopric, and John Stokes, the Archdeacon of Ely, was apparently commissioned to do this:

Quem idem nos auctoritate apostolica et simili scientia absolvimus et cum eo dispensamus eumque restituimus reponimus et rehabilitamus, et infamie maculam abolemus per presentes supplendo etiam omnes defectus tam juris quam facti, si qui forsan absolutione dispensatione rehabilitatione et restitutione archidiaconi hujusmodi intervenissent. Et insuper eidem Reginaldo episcopo Cicestren. Efficacis defensionis subsidio assistens facias eum pacifica dicte ecclesie Cicestren. Possessione gaudere, et non permittas ipsum premissorum occasione in judicio vel extra, publice vel occulte, directe vel indirecte, aut quovis alio quesito colore quomodolibet molestare aut ei iniurias vel offensas irrogari.[2]

Whilst Calixtus was endeavouring to restore Pecock to his see, the bishop's opponents were already at work on a very different task. John Milverton, the provincial of the Carmelites, who had long been hostile to Pecock, sent a letter to Rome outlining the reasons for Pecock's condemnation and citing his recantation. It was probably Pecock's attack on the friars as 'clamatores in pulpitis' which aroused the hostility of Milverton and Goddard, who were both prominent members of their orders. The government could not remain inactive because the crumbling power of the Lancastrian house would be still further damaged if Pecock's appeal was allowed at Rome. The Yorkists would have found this equally unacceptable. All forces in Church and State combined against Pecock.

[1] Evidence abounds in plenty to prove this point, e.g. *Official Correspondence of Thomas Bekynton*, ed. G. Williams, 1872, II, 58, 155, 251, etc. The tension is an interesting comment on the growth of national feeling in England and on reactions to the conciliar movement.

[2] *Arch. Vatic. Reg. Vatic.* Calixti III, vol. 462, fol. 326–7; cited in *Cal. Pap. Letters*, XI, 76–8; *vide* also *Reg. Bourchier* (July 27th, 1458).

Accordingly in September, 1458,[1] the king issued a commission to the Bishop of St Asaph and Dr Robert Stillington, a Canon of Wells, ordering them to summon a number of doctors of divinity and law to discuss the legal implications of, and the possible moves to be made as a result of, the papal rescript. This commission, which included at least two of Pecock's avowed enemies, Dr Damlet and Dr Pinchbeck, and probably more, reported that 'his Highness should send an ambassador to the pope who should represent to him the Bishop's pernicious heresies, and the dangers accruing to the Church from them; and should desire that he cassate the bull of restitution, and appoint to the see a pious and learned bishop to be nominated by the king'. Secondly, they advised that 'since by the process and recantation of Pecock they think that he was infected with heresy long before he was translated to the see of Chichester, that translation was *ipso facto* void'.

In reply Henry VI congratulated the commissioners on their work, adding that he would like to be informed of the actual heresies of which the bishop was guilty. Henry also took care to inform the bishop, who had probably been very hopeful of full restitution after Calixtus's reply to his appeal, of the findings of the commissioners through two of his agents, John Derby and Gilbert Haydock. They informed Pecock that the king would grant him an adequate pension if he would resign his see. Failing that the 'uttermost rigour of the law' would be 'inflicted on him'.

Although the details are obscure it seems likely that Pecock still hoped that his sentence might be reversed, but he ultimately complied with the king's wishes. Meanwhile, Pope Calixtus died on August 6th, 1458, and was succeeded by the versatile, scholarly Pius II, who was elected on the 19th. Next April, Pius wrote to the Archbishop of Canterbury, to the Bishops of London and Winchester and to the Bishop of Terni (if in England) asking them to investigate the accusations brought against Pecock, especially in relation to his relapse into heresy, to try to find out

---

[1] Pecock was still performing his episcopal duties in August, 1458 (*Cal. Pat. Rolls*, Henry VI, vi, 434). On Stillington see *D.N.B.* liv, 378–9.

where any books which he might have hidden could be found, and, if he was guilty, to send him to Rome under 'a sure and good guard' or to let the ecclesiastical and civil authorities proceed against him in England.[1] The reference to a 'relapse' is interesting, but the implications are uncertain. It may have been put forward as a reason for the pontifical change of front or it may possibly refer to the appeal of Pecock. There is the minimum of evidence to indicate that Pecock continued to hold the opinions which he had but a little previously so vigorously refuted. In any case the terms of the papal letter do not seem to have allowed room for very much doubt as to Pecock's guilt, and the subsequent appointment of John Arundel, the king's physician and Archdeacon of Richmond, to the see of Chichester was an *ipso facto* confirmation of the bishop's deposition.

So with the House of Lancaster tottering to its fall, with Henry VI himself averse to Pecock's reinstatement and on the brink of another breakdown in health, with the Papal Curia either convinced of his guilt or of the inexpediency of interfering in England at this juncture, he disappears into the obscurity from which the circumstances of his trial and of his opinions had first brought him. The deprived prelate was sent to the Abbey of Thorney, in Cambridgeshire. Forty pounds a year was allotted for his upkeep there and Abbot Lyle of Thorney was instructed to give him:

a secret close chamber (having a chimney) and convenience within the abbey, where he may have sight to some altar to hear mass; and that he pass not the said chamber. To have but one person that is sad and well disposed to make his bed, and to make his fire, as he shall need. That he have no books to look on, but only a breviary, a mass book, a psalter, a legend and a Bible. That he have nothing to write with; no stuff to write upon. That he have competent fuel according to his age, and as his necessity shall require. That he be served daily of meat and drink as a brother of the abbey is served when he is excused from the

---

[1] *Arch. Vatic. Reg. Vatic.* Pii II, vol. 499, fol. 63; *Annales Ecclesiastici*, Baronius, ed. Theiner, xxviii, 190 ff.; *Cal. Pap. Letters*, xi, 529 (April 7th, 1459).

freytour and somewhat better after [the first quarter] as his disposition and reasonable appetite shall desire, conveniently after the good discretion of the said abbot.[1]

Although authorities differ, it is generally assumed, in the absence of evidence to the contrary, that he died at Thorney somewhere about 1460–1. Both Bale and Foxe suggest that he was 'privily made away', but Bale, who was Foxe's main authority, was writing many years after the event and his assumption is no more than a hypothesis. The chronicler Hall says that he died in his 'awne house', but this may well mean that he died in his own chamber, and therefore at Thorney. Dr Waterland cites a MS. chronicle which asserts:

> His bookes brent at Paulis Cross,
> He in Newgate kept
> All hys liffe after, for the heresyes
> He had hept.[2]

Although Newgate was yet another institution to benefit from the generosity of Sir Richard Whittington, the verse cannot be regarded as satisfactory evidence. The probability of Pecock's death at Thorney in or about 1460 remains.

Although the authorities had successfully accomplished their main object, they were still fully determined to crush any influence which Pecock may have had in England. Did he have many followers? His books, we are told, 'cost moche gooddes',[3] and it is therefore unlikely that many read them outside the universities. Master Lempster of Llansannan passes from history.[4] So too does Master John Orle or Horley, the bishop's chaplain whom Gascoigne does not seem to have found too unpleasant a man.[5] Gascoigne mentions one incident of some interest. *Nuper unus quasi xxti annorum scholaris in grammatica Oxoniae* was accused of various heresies one of which charged him *quod comedebat carnes omni feria sexta*.[6] He was brought before Bishop Alnwick of

---

[1] *Wharton MSS.* 577 (Lambeth), No. 80.
[2] Waterland, *Works*, x, 235. Cf. *Chron. Davies*, 77.
[3] *Greyfriars Chronicle*, 20.   [4] *Vide* p. 33 of this essay.
[5] *Loci e Libro Veritatum*, 35, 42.   [6] *Id.* 29.

Lincoln and imprisoned at Wallingford. As Alnwick died in 1449 the case occurred before that year. Then, *abjuratus factus est monachus Abendonae* (Abingdon), he told the abbot that he had learned all his errors from Bishop Pecock *et a nullo alio*. Although the story must be regarded with a certain amount of suspicion, it serves to confirm the fact that it was the universities, and Oxford in particular, which favoured Pecock's ideas.

The ecclesiastical authorities took immediate steps to stifle any following that Pecock may have had. With the minimum of delay Bourchier sent copies of Pecock's recantation to the bishops of the dioceses within his province requesting them to publish it. In the following March he wrote to Bishop Kempe of London urging him to seek out Pecock's followers or any who read his books within his own diocese or in the southern province.[1] There were, he added, many men and women who possessed copies of Pecock's original English works as well as translations of the scriptures into English, both of which *decrevimus comburendos*. The bishop was also to persuade his episcopal brethren to search for Pecock's books and to warn all those who did not surrender such books within a fortnight that they would make themselves liable to the penalty of excommunication. The effects of this letter are unknown but, as Bishop Grey of Ely reported two months later, there seemed neither followers nor books to be found.

Pecock's influence seems to have been confined to the universities, and even there it never reached very marked proportions. The suspicious attitude which the ecclesiastical authorities adopted proves, however, that 'Pecockism' was regarded as a potential danger to Church and State. It was only natural that his influence at the universities should have been greater there than elsewhere, for although his books, as we can see from the abridgements of which the *Poore Mennis Myrrour* is the best surviving example, were intended for a wider audience, they were in fact too

---

[1] *Vide* Ely MSS. (ref. *Reg. Grey*, March 21st, 1457); *Hist. Manus.* 12th Report, Part IX, 385; *Reg. Bekynton*, March 10th, 1457, I, 302–3.

learned, too emphatic on the need for logical thought, to catch the attention, let alone the interest, of any but the intellectual. It was not surprising then that the universities were also circularised by the archbishop. The university authorities had written to the archbishop in November of the trial year protesting their loyalty and declaring their abhorrence of all heretical and heterodox ideas and opinions. They followed up this action, which in itself reveals the timidity of the university as contrasted with its fight for independence fifty years previously, by a solemn procession which was headed by the chancellor, Dr Thomas Chandler, on December 17th, a fortnight after Pecock's recantation, to Quatrevoix or Carfax. At this place every book of Pecock's that could be found in Oxford was piled on to a bonfire and burned.

Nearly twenty years later, King Edward IV wrote to the university urging the then chancellor and heads of houses to search for Wyclif's and Pecock's books, and to punish any of their followers who could be found 'so that by your effectual support and abilities this new found venomous sect might be the rather suppressed and overthrown to the honour of God and the exaltation of the true faith of the Church'. It is clear from this that Pecock's opinions still caused concern, for eight days after this letter had been sent to the university Edward wrote a letter to Pope Sixtus IV specifically mentioning Pecock's heresy and asking for Sixtus's aid in the matter:

Concerning the same matter Pope Sixtus' immediate predecessors issued letters, of which a copy is enclosed. But as other national disturbances supervened, and in consequence of the death of him who gave the letters, they did not receive due execution. Moreover, after the death of the said Reginald, the writings and treatises composed by him multiplied in such wise that not only the laity but churchmen and scholastic graduates scarcely studied anything else, so that the pestiferous virus circulated in many human breasts, and ere long would have spread immensely had not the Almighty revealed the confessions of certain penitents for the easier dispersion of the remaining followers of the sect. We beseech you, therefore, to dispatch other apostolic letters, by whose authority proceedings may be instituted from time to time against all holders of books and treatises edited by the said Reginald, and of any other erroneous books soever.[1]

This interesting document certainly indicates that Pecock had a greater following than the evidence at our disposal suggests. The paucity of manuscript material associated with his writings would be surprising if Pecock's opinions had been as popular as Edward IV implies. This seems to have been the last direct action which was taken against the bishop. The other evidence which we possess in relation to the university of Oxford comes from a royal injunction ordering the university to withhold the degree of doctor of divinity from Master John Haycock who was suspected of holding 'the superstitious, erroneous and damned opinions of Reginald Pecock'.[2]

If then Oxford University was tainted by Pecock's heretical opinions, it is probable that Cambridge University also housed some of his followers and works, although a letter from William Grey, Bishop of Ely, in whose diocese Cambridge was situated, reveals that he could find *nullum tamen in nostris civitate diocesi...qui hujusmodi libros aliquem librum hujusmodi habuit sic sapiebat*, a fact which indicates that the poison cannot have thrust very deep. The statutes of both King's[3] and Queens'

---

[1] *Cal. State Pap.* (Venetian), 1, No. 451, 134 (Feb. 24th, 1475/6).

[2] *Wharton MSS.* No. 577 (Lambeth). Cf. also the charge made against him 'volebat sapere ultra quam oportuit' in an anonymous sermon of 1483 (*Cotton MSS.* Cleopatra E. III).

[3] I am indebted to Mr John Saltmarsh, Fellow of King's College, for information relating to this topic. He writes: 'It is correct that the Statutes of King's College contained a clause enforcing an oath against the heresies of Wycliffe and Pecock. Thorold Rogers infers from this that the Statutes in their present form dated from some time subsequent to Pecock's condemnation. An examination of the two original manuscripts in our Muniment Room has convinced me that this is not the case. The clause against Wycliffe and Pecock is added as a kind of postscript after the "Amen" of the main body of the Statutes. This postscript is further written into each copy by the same hand, which is not the hand of the remainder of either copy. The main body of the Statutes I believe to date from a revision in 1453. You will find my reasons for this in *C.A.S. Communications*, Volume 33, page 86.' The question

Colleges[1] include a clause which orders every member of the College, at the end of the scholar's 'three probationary years', to take an oath against the damnable errors of Wyclif and Pecock. This oath, which was added to the original statutes of 1453 some years later, most probably in 1458–9, was rescinded when the new statutes were compiled as a result of the report of the first Royal Commission on the university. After that all is silent, save for the voice of a solitary historian or controversialist ironically clapping the bishop for his valiant defence of the 'Protestant' religion.

remains, did William Millington, who as we have seen was one of the most prominent of Pecock's antagonists, have anything, even indirectly, to do with the formulation of this clause? Millington died in 1466; the facts of his career are obscure owing to his having been frequently confused with John Millington of Clare Hall, but his relations with King's College had been strained since his deposition from the provostship. It is clear from his correspondence with Bishop Bekynton (*Correspondence*, ed. G. Williams, II, 157–74; G. Williams, *C.A.S. Communications*, I, 291 ff.) that he did not approve of the first statutes, and his subsequent deprivation was partly brought about by his refusal to accept the statutes. It must be remembered that Chedworth, later Bishop of Lincoln and one of the assessors at Pecock's trial, who succeeded Millington as provost, was also an enemy of Pecock. The additional clause against Pecock in the statutes of King's was not therefore directly due to Millington's activities, but it may of course indirectly reflect his influence at King's at an earlier date. As Babington says it is just possible that Henry VI as the founder of King's may have had something to do with the insertion of this clause in the statutes.

[1] The statutes of Queens' College, which was founded by Queen Margaret of Anjou in 1448 and later refounded by Elizabeth Woodville, also indirectly reflect Millington's influence, as he had much to do with the compilation of the statutes of 1448. The original charter of foundation affirms that the college was founded 'for the extirpation of heresies and errors and the increase of the faith' (*Cal. Charter Rolls*, VI, 74). The addition of the oath against Wyclif and Pecock probably occurred at the same time as the addition of the oath to the statutes of King's College. The present statutes date from 1475 'but slightly revised...in 1529' (*The Universities of Europe in the Middle Ages*, Rashdall, ed. Emden and Powicke, III, 321). It is not without interest that the names of Hugh Damlet and Peter Hyrford (a former follower of Wyclif and a pensioner of Pembroke Hall, Cambridge) occur among the commissioners appointed to draw up statutes for the new foundation. They were old foes of Pecock and members of the royal commission which examined his heresies (*Loci e Libro Veritatum*, 189, 208).

CHAPTER VII

PECOCK'S CHARACTER

A BRIEF analysis of Pecock's character completes the picture of his life, and forms in addition an important factor for the unravelling of his significance in history.

Pecock is said to have had a handsome and dignified appearance, although his countenance was somewhat marred by a skin disease of an apparently hereditary character.[1] There is no surviving portrait or memorial.

The most obvious defect in his character was a personal vanity, which was of so naïve a quality as to be almost comical and which obtrudes in all his works. 'I preie thee, Sir,' he cried to his Lollard opponents, 'seie to me where in Holi Scripture is ȝouen the hundrid parti of the teching upon matrimonie which y teche in a book mad upon *Matrimonie*, and in the firste partie of *Cristen religioun*.'[2] He was never tired of exalting and advertising his own works which were, so he clearly believed, the most effective and persuasive means for converting the Lollards from their folly and of teaching the laity the fundamentals of the Christian religion. 'And therfore', he writes, 'it schal be riȝt profitable that this book with hisse purtenauncis schulde be taken of alle thi cristen peple into vse of ful bisy, ech day studiyng, leernyng and comunyng and afterward therupon remembering, and if not in ech day, ȝitt in holy daies, and that as bisili as peple ben in werk daies y-occupied aboute worldis wynnyng.'[3]

He repeats in yet another place that his books must be seriously studied and frequently consulted by laymen if they wish to know 'that larger, hiȝer and profitabler leernyng and kunning of feith'.[4]

---

[1] 'Valde fuit dispositus ad lepram corporis et plures de parentela sua fuerunt corpore leprosi' (*Loci e Libro Veritatum*, 29).
[2] *Repressor*, I, 15.
[3] *The Reule of Chrysten Religioun*, 13.   [4] *Book of Faith*, 118.

The laity may well find it impossible to be convinced of the truth unless they use his books.[1] Thus, speaking of the comparative significance of the Ten Commandments and the Seven Deadly Sins as compared with his own 'Four Tables' he says: 'And therwith al it schal be oute of cours, of ioynt, and oute of limb, oute of ordre, and oute of dewe processe to gider clumprid, that it schal never serue to teche, to leerne and to remembre and to reporte so fair and so esili and so profitabli as schal therto serve the foorme of the iiii seid tablis aftir that thilk foorme be had a while in haunt and vse of remembring.'[2] Perhaps, he adds, the Christian faith has never been put before the laity so 'cleerli and feelyngli and comprehensiveli'.[3] It would be as well that 'prelatis and othere myȝty men of good' who wished to overcome the horrid forces of Lollardy[4] should purchase and peruse these learned books, so much more intelligible than many of the articles of faith.[5]

Pecock's vanity was coupled with a certain amount of tactlessness which might well savour of arrogance to the superficial observer. His allusion to the king and Gascony is typical of this.[6] In fine, it was one of the forces which helped to bring about his fall. Pecock, the handsome, boastful bird, was identified with the vain and tactless bishop. Abbot Whetehampstead wrote of him with scornful and envenomed pen,[7] recording the while the following verse:

---

[1] *Repressor*, I, 128. 'And without the writing of this present first parti and of *The iust apprising*, or with out sum other writing lijk to hem, tho persoones wolen in no wise be so conuicted and ouercome, as assay therto mad bifore this present day thoruȝ this sixti wyntris by his ther yn vneffectual speding makith opeh experimental witnessing.' Cf. *Donet*, 28.

[2] *Donet*, 147.

[3] *Folewer to the Donet*, 176.

[4] *Book of Faith*, 117.   [5] *Reule*, 91.

[6] *Repressor*, I, 22.

[7] 'Sic etiam intoxicator ille impiissimus, qui perfidiae venenum imbiberat, ut ipsum imbibitum effunderet iterum, ac populum simplicem in fide infective informaret, expuit ipsum modo taliterque evomuit, quod,
        "Dum sol dat radium, Mars gerit aut gladium"
ipsum rebibere, seu reglutire, nullatenus ausus erit.'

Sic deplumatus pavo fuit, et spoliatus,
   Sicque sibi siluit, vox quia rauca fuit.
Sic dudum volucris, quae nomen habebat honoris,
   Bubo non pavo dicitur esse modo.
Nomine privari vult atque gradu spoliari,
   Qui violat fidei dogmata, sive Dei.
Ne sic priveris, haec qui legis, aut spolieris,
   Nec basse tendas nec nimis alta petas.
Dum medium tenuit, currum patris bene rexit;
   Alta sed ut petiit, Phaëton, ab arce ruit.

Pecock himself seems to have recognised that his self-conceit made him unpopular. 'Now schal y seie what y haue herde to be seid of me: "this man seith and techith mych thing, but he seith al of him silf and of his owen heed, fforwhi he alleggith not for him alwey hooli scripture or summe doctoures"',[1] but he also said that men were mistaken in thinking that his opinions were only reflections of his personal vanity.

It must indeed be recognised that his naïve self-conceit and his tactless demeanour are almost certainly overbalanced by his sincerity. The ardour with which he wrote his books not only mirrors the vanity but also the sincerity of his character and aims:

And thouȝ these wordis and manye mo whiche y write in this present book and in summe othire bokis, mow be takun as for wordis of veyn glorye or of pryde and of presumpcioun vpon my silf, and as wordis of indignacioun or envye as anentis othire men and her writingis, lord god, thou knowist that y seie hem not, neithir write hem, vndir thilk corrupcioun and y beseche that y neuer so do. And, lorde, thou knowist that for zele to thi trewe seruice, y seie hem with schame and with drede, lest y schal for hem be amys deemed. In lasse thanne what y now seie here for myn excuse be therfro a defence and a coueryng.[2]

This prayer is by no means the only witness to the sincerity of his motives; there are many other phrases in his books which reflect his sincerity and honesty. 'And therfore into plesaunce bi which y wolde plese God and serue to God, and do sumwhat into

---

[1] *Folewer to the Donet*, 8.   [2] *Donet*, 81.

goostli profite of myn euene Cristen, and for drede of God y
write and outre what y now haue outrid.'[1]

He believed that the work he was doing was the work which
God would have him do, the education of the Christian laity to a
more perfect understanding of Christianity and the refutation of
heretical ideas. He was, he admits in one of his books, 'moved by
zeel to dresse men of the laife into so good service of god',
although 'y was not born into the ricches of so cleer witt to
leerne, neither into so faire vttryng of the hiȝest maters whiche y
haue writtun, as y haue fonde gentil men of the layfe to conceive'.[2]
It is clear that Pecock was more guilty of deceiving himself than
others, since he sincerely believed that his writing was irrefutable,
not so much on account of the fact that it represented his own
work as because of the validity of its contents. If any man knows
better or shall find anything 'wherbi he may amende the doctryne
whiche y am aboute to write...y schal not lette him, but y schal
therfore thanke him; for god knowith that for helthe of cristen
peplis soulis, and for noon victorie to be wonne bi me in my side,
neithir for enye glorie or rewarde to be had a this side god, y
sette me into the labour of my bokis makyng'.[3] Thus it was
largely his sincere care for 'cristen peplis soulis' which led him to
write his books.

He was not, it is apparent, a very pious man if we mean by
piety the devotional exercises of a contemplative monk. Pecock's
idea of God is essentially chilly, more comparable to the not un-
mathematical deity whom Sir Isaac Newton worshipped than to
Him of whom St Bernard and St Francis spoke so lovingly. There
is none of the semi-Platonic *amor Dei*, the cream and blossom of
an otherwise sterile medieval mystic. The symbolism, the semi-
erotic poetry and mysticism which Huizinga has pictured in the
Waning of the Middle Ages was altogether alien to Pecock's
character. But though he was neither a mystic nor a monk, he
seems to have carried out his episcopal duties well and he constantly recommended and urged his fellow-Christians to carry out

[1] *Repressor*, 1, 89–90.   [2] *Reule*, 20–1.   [3] *Donet*, 5.

their religious obligations. The prayers with which he commences some of his chapters in the *Reule* are the best testimony to his devotion. Prayer, he said later in the book, is an essential part of the Christian's life. He thought that the 'long formal preiers as men vsen in bookis'[1] were less effective than the 'schort smert fiery deuoute preiers whiche wolen be seid in iii or iiii or in fewe wordis accordaunt to oure entent for the tyme'. 'In the desir is al the pith of preier.'[2] If Pecock's devotion cannot be compared 'with that of the contemporary author of the *Imitatio Christi*', it was worthy of his position as a bishop of the Catholic Church.

He has sometimes been accused of cowardice, and although too much has been made of this charge, we have seen that there are grounds for thinking, as Babington said, that 'he retracted errors which he had never uttered, and he retracted utterances which he knew to be truths. But, indeed, he seems to have been so confused and bewildered, as scarcely to know what he said or what he had not said.'[3] We must not forget the circumstances, the stress of the moment, the conflicting emotions which clouded the clarity of his mental vision and weakened his determination. He did not lack courage to put forward views which he knew would offend many people and yet which he believed necessary for their spiritual well-being. His action at the trial may have been somewhat unheroic, but it is a testimony to his humanity. Pecock was no St Paul.

It may be that his vanity often turned his sincerity into self-conceit, and that his honesty, so it has been asserted, sometimes savoured of hypocrisy. Yet if he was vain, he was also sincere, and if he was honest, he was only a hypocrite in the stress of the moment. However severely he attacked the emphasis which the Lollards laid on preaching or however vigorously he defended non-preaching prelates, he himself seems to have preached frequently and well. His scholarship is no less sincere, no less honest than his character. He rarely distorts his quotations nor does he

[1] *Reule*, 397.　　　　[2] *Id.* 398.
[3] Babington, Introduction to the *Repressor*, l-li.

conceal matter which, as he must have realised from the repeated attacks made upon him, would be offensive to his adversaries. In short, he was a very human character, rather self-assertive, tactless and vain, bitterly depressed by his trial, yet unconscious of his vanity, even proud of his modesty, sincere, religious and honest.

But there is one aspect of his character more fundamental still because it is basic to the understanding of the man. It is a commonplace to talk about the 'political' or 'economic' man, but we rarely have occasion to use the phrase 'academic' man; yet, as we have seen, that is what in effect Pecock was. Unless we understand that it was the method of university scholarship, the quiddities and quantities which Thomas Hobbes so despised, the splendid and trivial aroma of the schoolroom which inspired and stimulated him, we shall have failed to analyse Pecock's real importance. It is the 'syllogism' and all the system which the syllogism symbolised which imperils as well as establishes the validity of his position. He is far more of the academician than the saint, far more in some ways at least the scholar than the man. He is perhaps too much the university professor, far more so than John Wyclif, to bring very much of the breath of reality into his work. Yet Pecock's life, his character, is as finely suggestive of the 'waning' of the Middle Ages as any over-decorated board or ornate, erotic poem. But the centre piece of that life, the spearhead of his character, is his thought, without which indeed he would be of little interest or significance.

CHAPTER VIII

PECOCK AS A SCHOLAR

ALTHOUGH PECOCK's character was essentially academic, the evidence at our disposal suggests that he was certainly more of the logician than the scholar. The use which he makes of the books which he had at his disposal,[1] and of the Bible and the Fathers in particular, proves that he had no particular claim to great scholarship, at any rate by comparison with his more learned contemporaries.

The foundation stone on which his knowledge rested was naturally the Bible, from which he quotes directly no less than 420 times in his surviving works and to which he makes well over 400 references.[2] The majority of these citations were taken from an English version of the Bible, but he also used the Vulgate; direct quotations from the Latin version are very few in number except in the case of *The Reule of Chrysten Religioun*, the earliest of his surviving works. The source of Pecock's English texts will be discussed when Pecock's claim to be a translator of the Bible into English is analysed.[3] He not only makes far fewer allusions and scriptural references than the majority of his contemporaries —the slight *De Ente Praedicamenti* has over 500 quotations from the Bible alone[4]—but he also, as we shall see, asserted that the Bible was subordinate to the 'doom of reason'. Yet he confesses that the reading of the Bible is 'miche delectable and swete, and drawith the reders into deuocioun and a loue to God and fro loue and deinte of the world'.[5]

His use of the patristic writings is again less full and more critical than that of the majority of his contemporaries and prede-

---

[1] It might be mentioned that a catalogue of books, dating from 1375 (*Collectanea*, O.H.S. 1, 59), indicates that there were at least 100 volumes in the library of Oriel College.

[2] An analysis of these texts will be found in Appendix I.

[3] *Vide* pp. 193 ff.

[4] Wyclif, *De Ente Praedicamenti*, ed. R. Beer (1891). [5] *Repressor*, 1, 66.

cessors. Thus Wyclif's *De Compositione Hominis*,[1] a slight work probably based on his lecture notes, includes some 103 citations from the Bible, 70 from Aristotle and 67 from St Augustine. Pecock's contemporary, Gascoigne, far surpassed him in the use of the Fathers, for his works contain over 2200 quotations from St Jerome and 550 from St Augustine.[2] Pecock averred that there is no reason for accepting a statement from St Jerome merely because St Jerome said it, but only because what St Jerome says is true. The seventeenth-century scholar, Wharton, however, acknowledges that his comments on the Fathers were 'far beyond the genius and vulgar learning of that age'.[3] Pecock used the Fathers as authorities for his statements and for confirming the truth of the ideas which he puts forward.

St Augustine was the most influential of all the Fathers in the medieval period, and, as one would expect, references to his works abound in Pecock's surviving books. Even so, however, they are not very numerous. He alludes to a number of St Augustine's books, the medieval classic *De Civitate Dei*,[4] *De Baptismo*,[5] *De Bono Conjugali*,[6] *De Genesi ad Litteram*,[7] *De Trinitate*,[8] *Liber de diversis questionibus octoginta tribus*,[9] and the quaintly named 'book of the soulis quantite'.[10] In some cases he takes his quotations direct from these books, but elsewhere his references are obviously secondhand. When he refers to St Augustine as saying that the third commandment is not necessarily binding on Christian men and women but that due attention should be paid to its meaning, his source is the *Glossa Ordinaria*, once attributed to the ninth-

---

[1] Wyclif, *De Compositione Hominis*, ed. R. Beer (1884).
[2] W. Pronger, *E.H.R.* LIV, 34.
[3] Introduction to the *Book of Faith* (1688).
[4] *Reule* (lib. x, cap. IV), 264; *Folewer to the Donet* (lib. IX, cap. IV), 100, 113; *Repressor* (lib. VIII, cap. XXIII, XXIV), 1, 240.
[5] *Book of Faith*, 115: 'wherto thei [i.e. Lollards] alleggen witnessing of Seynt Austyn in his book of Baptym aȝens Donatistis, that the chirche may erre in determynyng articlis for feith.' [6] *Reule*, 349.
[7] *Id.* 466. [8] *Id.* 466; *Folewer to the Donet*, 67; *Book of Faith*, 122.
[9] Q. LII (Migne, *Patrologia Latina*, XL, 34), *Donet*, 4; *Folewer to the Donet*, 67.
[10] *Folewer to the Donet*, 34.

century scholar, Walafrid Strabo.[1] Pecock said that his interpretation of Holy Scripture was based on the methods which St
Augustine himself adopted; 'and so Austin knoulechid himself
hunte out the dew litteral vndirstonding of Holi Scripture'.[2] In
a similar fashion he urges that the doctor said that 'scripture con-
teyneth mych thyng within him which the writer therof took bi
resoun' in confirmation of his own views.[3] Pecock employed
his writings to contradict St Thomas Aquinas.[4] He quotes
extensively from one of Augustine's sermons in the *Repressor*,[5]
whilst he uses Augustine's book on heresies for his own summary
of the heretical sects who were the precursors of the Lollards.[6]

St Jerome receives a certain amount of attention together with
some chastisement, a fact which drew upon Pecock the wrath of
Gascoigne, who was a fervent admirer of the bitter-almond-
tongued saint.[7] He made occasional use of the prologues which
Jerome wrote to the different books of the Vulgate.[8] He uses him

[1] *Donet*, 156. *Vide* B. Smalley, *Recherches de Théologie ancienne et médiévale*,
IX (1927), 365–400.

[2] *Repressor*, I, 178; cf. *Donet*, 4; *Folewer to the Donet*, 66–7. To what book was
Pecock referring? Babington (I, 178 n.) suggests Augustine's *De Genesi ad
Litteram*, Lib. VIII: 'Aut si et ipse [Adam sc.] figurate intelligendus est, quis
genuit Cain et Abel et Seth? An et ipsi figurate tantum fuerunt, non etiam
homines ex hominibus nati? De proximo ergo attendant istam presum-
tionem quo tendat, et conentur nobiscum cuncta primitus quae gesta nar-
rantur in expressionem proprietatis accipere' (ed. Benedict (Antwerp, 1700),
III, 170). This assumption is borne out by the fact that we have proof of
Pecock's acquaintance with this work. Dr Hitchcock suggests the *Liber de
diversis questionibus octoginta tribus*, LII (Migne, *Pat. Lat.* XL, 34) referred to by
Pecock in the *Donet*. This is very possible; indeed it is more than probable that
Pecock had more than one passage in his mind at the time.

[3] *Folewer to the Donet*, 9.   [4] *Id.* 100.

[5] *Repressor*, II, 328–30. The passage in question, which Pecock has translated into English, is taken from *Sermones*, CCCXI, cap. 9 (*Opera*, V, 873–4, ed.
Benedict, Antwerp (1700)): 'Ipsum laudavit Scriptura...possideris. Non
faciunt...adsit usus rerum bonarum.' Pecock also quotes from the *De
Civitate Dei* (lib. VI, cap. XXIII), where Augustine refers to a book by 'Hermes
Trismegistus' (*Repressor*, I, 240). The book to which Augustine refers is
probably the Neoplatonic *Asclepius* (*id.* 241 n.).

[6] *Liber de Haeresiis*; *Repressor*, II, 497 ff.

[7] *Loci e Libro Veritatum*, 49, 99.

[8] *Repressor*, I, 57, 126; *Reule*, 466; *Book of Faith*, 269. Cf. *Repressor*, II,
437–8: 'Galat. ii.c. toward the myddis, Poul clepid Peter Cephas; and as Ierom

to discredit the inspired authority of the Apocrypha[1] and in his treatment of the Donation of Constantine.[2] Elsewhere he mentions the *Vita Malchi*[3] which he had certainly read and employs the *De Viris Illustribus*.[4] He also quotes from the *Epistolae*.[5]

Few of the other Fathers receive very much attention, not because Pecock had not read them, but because he seems to have been sparing in his citations and skilful in the employment of his authorities. St Ambrose is introduced in two passages in the *Repressor*[6] but merely as means of confirming Pecock's con-

---

witnessith, Cephas is no word of Hebrew, but it is a word of Grew, in which langage it is as myche to seie as *heed*; and it is also a word of Sire tunge, in which it is as miche to seie as *fundament*, or *ground*, or *stable*.' (Cf. Jerome: 'In evangelio et in aliis Pauli epistolis et in hac quoque ipsa (ad Galatas) modo *Cephas*, modo *Petrus* scribitur. Non quo aliud significet Petrus, aliud Cephas: sed quod quam nos Latine et Graece *petram* vocemus, hanc Hebraei et Syri propter linguae inter se viciniam *Cephan* nuncupent' (in *Ep. ad Gal.* lib. 1, cap. 2, *Opera*, VII, 409 (ed. Vallars)).) Optatus of Milevis perpetrated much the same error in the fourth century (Optatus, lib. II, 31, ed. 1702). It is clear that Pecock did not know Greek although he may have been acquainted with the alphabet. Professor J. L. Morison writes: 'At least three mistakes, impossible even to a beginner, reveal the tenuity of his information; for he fancies that Peter's Aramaic name is connected with κεφαλή, he explains orthodoxy etymologically as "right glory", and...he speaks of the "ioustis and othere turnementis and maistries" celebrated at "the hil Olympe"' (Introduction to the *Book of Faith*, 46).

[1] *Repressor*, 1, 251.   [2] *Id.* II, 355.

[3] 'Sithen the chirche wexid in dignitees, he decrecid in vertues' (*id.* II, 322). 'Postquam ad Christianos principes venerit, potentia quidem et divitiis major sed virtutibus minor facta sit' (Vit. Malchi, *Opera*, II, 41, ed. Vallars). Pecock naturally contradicts this statement.

[4] *Repressor*, II, 354.

[5] Ad Paulinum (*Reule*, 384), *Epistola*, LVIII, 7; Ad Demetriadem (*id.* 382, 384), Migne, *Pat. Lat. Epistola*, CXXX, 11; Ad Eustochium (*id.* 422), *id.* XXII, 35). One citation is in English and the other in Latin.

[6] *De Obitu Theodosii Oratio*, cap. 40 (*Opera*, II, 1209, ed. Benedict) (*Repressor*, II, 355); *De Mysteriis*, c. 8 (*Op.* II, 336); *De Sacramentis*, lib. IV, cap. 2 (*Op.* II, 366). In regard to the two latter works, Babington says 'each of these works is doubtful or spurious' (*Repressor*, 1, 170 n.). The authenticity of *De Mysteriis* was challenged at the time of the Reformation and by Professor Loofs, but the 'many parallels and points of contact between *De Mysteriis* and the undisputed writings of Ambrose afford convincing evidence that the former treatise is a work of his composition' (F. Homes Dudden, *St Ambrose*, II, 698). The *De Sacramentis* embodies much of the *De Mysteriis*, including the passage to which Pecock refers, but it had peculiarities which make it unlikely to be a genuine work of St Ambrose (Homes Dudden, II, 706).

clusions. St Hilary receives honourable mention,[1] but no other Father except Pope Gregory the Great is used by Pecock in his surviving works. St Gregory is cited in support of a statement by St Paul in which the latter 'preise himsilf or his owne kunnyng and hise owne werkis, and forto blame an othire mannys kunnyng and hise werkis'.[2] Elsewhere, Pecock roused a hornet's nest by contradicting a famous statement of Gregory's on the virtues of faith.[3]

This was not, however, the full extent of his indebtedness to pre-medieval authors. His discussion on the Donation of Constantine discloses his acquaintance with historical writings; Socrates, Sozomen, Theodoret, Eusebius and Cassiodorus are referred to here.[4] In other passages Pecock frequently refers to the *Tripartite History* of Cassiodorus[5] and the *Ecclesiastical History* of Eusebius,[6] a work which he uses with some facility and historical skill. The early *Decretals* are also introduced as a proof of the accuracy of Pecock's historical assumptions at this point.[7] The seventh-century encyclopaedist, Isidore of Seville, a fount of medieval *data et facta*, is used with St Augustine for his information on the pre-Lollard heresies.[8] Incidentally, Pecock also mentions the books of Epiphanius of Salamis and Filaster of Brescia on the same subject for those who wish for a fuller knowledge of this topic.[9] With the exception of the books

[1] A direct citation from the *De Trinitate* (lib. iv, 835, ed. Benedict; lib. ii, 803). Cf. *Donet*, 4.

[2] *Donet*, 82–3. The *Regula Pastoralis* (cap. i, ii) is a source in the *Reule*, 467, 472. The *super Ezechielem* in the *Book of Faith*, 265.

[3] *Book of Faith*, 149.

[4] 'The ful famose and credible storie clepid *The iii. departid storie*, moost credible next to the storie of Eusebie clepid *The chirchis storie*, and was mad and compilid for thilk entent that it schulde be contynued in progresse and in processe to *The chirchis storie*' (*Repressor*, ii, 355). The three aforementioned historians, of course, make up the *Historia Tripartita*.

[5] E.g. *Repressor*, ii, 352 ff., 361, 365, 376; *Book of Faith*, 283, 298.

[6] E.g. *Repressor*, ii, 352 ff.; *Donet*, 133; *Book of Faith*, 298. He also refers to the author's *Vita Constantini*.

[7] All in the *Repressor* and generally in relation to the historical questions related to the Donation of Constantine.

[8] *Repressor*, ii, 501.   [9] *Id.* ii, 501.

attributed to the Pseudo-Dionysius, this list completes Pecock's debt to writers of the patristic age. There are many references to this writer, whose works were so long popular in the medieval academic world, in his books,[1] but none of them are of sufficient importance to justify special mention. It may be concluded from this brief analysis that Pecock's obligations to the Fathers were slight and that his use of their works, which were to be found in any large library such as that possessed by Oriel College, was less extensive than that of his contemporaries and adversaries.

It is but a short step once again from the Fathers themselves to the medieval theologians whose works were so interlarded with patristic references. Pecock made full use of Gratian's *Summa*,[2] the probable source of many of his patristic references. He recommends the reading of the ever-popular work of the twelfth-century monk, Clement of Llanthony's *Concordia quatuor Evangelistarum*, and he actually uses it to illustrate his arguments in two places in the *Reule*.[3] Another work which he recommends is William of Nottingham's *Conflation of the Gospels*.[4] He had evidently studied the *Grecismus*, a book written by another medieval hammer of the heretics, Eberhard of Bethune.[5] He refers, too, to a book of a rather different nature, the well-known *Liber Diaetarum* of Isaak ben Salomon Israeli.[6] Other medieval scholars with whose works he showed himself to be acquainted and whom he mentions by name include the converted Jew, Petrus Alphonsus,

[1] E.g. *Repressor*, I, 61, 170, 225; II, 418, 425, 446, 459, 460; *Reule*, 313, 462; *Book of Faith*, 185, 188, 189, 193, 257. The chief books mentioned are: *De divinis nominibus*, *De coelesti hierarchia*, *De ecclesiastica hierarchia*.

[2] *Repressor*, II, 354, 359, 364–5, 407, 408; *Book of Faith*, 299, 300, 301.

[3] *Reule*, 211, 493.

[4] *Id.* 211. William of Nottingham (who died in *c*. 1251) was a Franciscan-provincial in England from 1240 to 1251—and a student of the Bible whose commentary on the gospels was much appreciated in the middle ages. He followed the method adopted by Clement of Llanthony.

[5] *Reule*, 251.

[6] *Folewer to the Donet*, 109; J. Guttmann, *Die philosophischen Lehren des Isaak ben Salomon Israeli*, Münster, 1911.

the Oxford philosopher, Robert Holcot,[1] Johannes Januensis[2] and Nicholas of Salerno.[3] Of Petrus Alphonsus he writes:

Petir Alfons of Hispayn, a ful wise and kunnyng Iewe in al the laws of Iewis. Forwhi, aftir that he was excellentli leerned in the lawe of Iewis, his wisdom drove him to this that he wolde examyne at the fulle the sect of Sarracenye, also the secte of Cristen men thoruȝ alle her evydencis, whiche myȝten be gete, and so he dide. And bicause that aftir he had examyned alle thre sectis he founde Cristen secte passe alle the othere and bicame a Cristen man, and maad a book of disputacioun betwixe Cristen lawe and Iewis lawe, in which booke he knowlechith of him silf what y now have rehercid of him.[4]

He also used the medieval historians to confirm statements which he made in relation to the Donation of Constantine; Martinus Oppaviensis (Polonus),[5] Petrus Comestor,[6] 'the Master of Stories', and Gerald of Wales[7] are mentioned in the *Repressor*, although Pecock's attribution of a book called *Cosmographia Hiberniae* to Gerald in itself constitutes a minor problem. He mentions Bede by name.[8] Such sources as these are clearly of a subordinate nature, but his indebtedness to medieval theologians is in a very different category, even though it is impossible to ascertain the exact extent.

Nothing reveals the eclectic nature of Pecock's scholarship so much as an analysis of his references to medieval theologians, few

[1] *Book of Faith*, 208. Holcot, an Oxford Nominalist who died in 1349; for his numerous works *vide D.N.B.* IX, 1008–9.

[2] *Summa quae vocatur Catholicon*; *Repressor*, I, 33; *Book of Faith*, 286.

[3] *Antidotarium* (printed in *Opera Joannis Mesuae* (1479), i.e. Yuhanna ibn Masawaih; *Book of Faith*, 286).

[4] *Book of Faith*, 136 (*Dialogi in quibus impiae Judaeorum opiniones confutuntur*, Cologne, 1536).

[5] *Chronicon pontificum et imperatorum* (to 1277); *Repressor*, II, 364; *Book of Faith*, 255.

[6] *Historia Scholastica* (Migne, *Patrologiae Cursus Completus*, CXCVIII; *Repressor*, II, 529–30; *Donet*, 157; *Book of Faith*, 262, 270).

[7] *Repressor*, II, 350–6. The passage does not occur in the *Topographia Hibernica*, but in *Libri de Invectionibus*, VI, cap. XXVII (*Opera*, R.S. I, 192).

[8] *Book of Faith*, 285.

as these are; at the same time the very eclecticism of his own theology makes it exceedingly difficult to establish his indebtedness with any degree of accuracy. He pays very little attention to the Augustinian theologians of the early Middle Ages. There are a few references, for instance, to St Bernard, and his writings are used to support a reference to Aristotle.[1] He quotes at length in one place from the *Flores Bernardi*.[2] He says further that he treats of the 'othire writingis' of St Bernard and Hugh of St Victor in his 'book of worschiping',[3] but this does not survive. The arguments which the Lollards based on the prophetic writings, the well-known *Scivias*, of Bernard's contemporary, St Hildegarde of Bingen, are dismissed by Pecock as unworthy of consideration by reason of their obvious falsity:

To the iiii bifore maad argument, proceding vpon the reuelacioun and prophecie ȝouun to Seinte Hildegard, it is to be seid thus: Whether it be trewe or no what sche seide and wroot of the persoones holding the iiii ordris of beggeris and of her ordre, this y dare seie, that among the reuelaciouns and prophecies, whiche ben ascriued to hir, is conteyned vntrouthe contrarie to the trewe feith; and for to it proue y durst leie in plegge my lijf, how euer it be that her prophecies and reuelacions weren approued.[4]

The only other pre-Thomist thinker of importance to whose writings Pecock refers is Henry of Ghent, but the reference is hardly courteous:

And if thilk doctour Henric, which is clepid 'The Solempne Doctor' hadde blessid him silf fro this now seid perel, he and hise

---

[1] *Folewer to the Donet*, 56: 'and this same maner forto take "wisdom" seynt bernard alowide, whanne he wole that a kunnyng whanne it is had so that it sauerith, thanne to be sauerer in it it is "wijsdom".'

[2] *Repressor*, II, 409. The *Flores Bernardi* are a collection of extracts from genuine and spurious works of St Bernard, first made by William of Tournai. The references are to St Bernard, *Epist. St Bernard*, 2 (*Op.* I, 120, ed. Par. 1839) and Gaufrid, *Declam. ex Bernard* (inter S. Bernard. *Op.* II, 612)—cited *Repressor*, II, 409 n., 410 n.

[3] *Reule*, 384.

[4] *Repressor*, II, 495. For the argument which the Lollards used *vide id.* II, 483.

felowers hadden not falle into this dotage.... Certis y mai wel seie
that this opinioun is a dotage.[1]

Pecock's most important debt was to the Thomist and Scotist
thinkers of his own age. Neither of the two schools proved entirely acceptable to Pecock, for the worthy bishop was hard to
please and facile in criticism. Duns Scotus's opinions on the
Creed[2] displeased him whilst St Thomas Aquinas was accused of
inconsistency. 'And so y kanne not wite but that bothe he is
contrari to him silf, and also without sufficient skile he forberith
in the first place alleggid forto clepe affeccions "passions".
And therfore, sone, let vs passe ouer this contrauersie.'[3]

Behind the façade of Aquinas and Scotus there stands the potent
figure of Aristotle, who for Pecock as for nearly every other
fifteenth-century scholar was the 'philosophir', whose judgements
are as valid and as divinely inspired as those of the doctors of the
Church themselves. 'Also hethen philosophiris bi her studie in
naturall witt', he writes, 'founden and grauntiden all hem to be
doon; and that these philosophiris so founden and grauntide bi
her naturall witt, it is to be holde. For whi thei hem silf knewe of
noon reuelacioun mad to hem bi God ther upon; and if eny such
reuelacioun hadde be maad to hem, their schulden bifore othere
men haue knowe it so to be made to hem.'[4] Pecock's knowledge
of Aristotle was of course taken from Latin translations of his
works. When, for instance, he wished to prove that riches are not

[1] *Repressor*, ii, 411. The reference 'forto seie and holde stifly, that prelatis
of the chirche in the clergie ben not very lordis of the vnmouable goodis
whiche ben ʒouun or bitake to hem, but thei ben fruyte vsers of tho godis
hauyng therwith power to dispense in almes al that is ouer it that is to be take
into her nede' (*vide* Henr. Gandav. *Aurea Quodlibeta* (n. vii), 441 (ed. Venice,
1613)).

[2] *Book of Faith*, 304.

[3] *Folewer to the Donet*, 101. Cf. *Donet*, 107; Aquinas, *Summa Theologica*, Pt. i
(2nd Part), Q. xxxv. Pecock (*Folewer*, 100) gives exact references: 'iᵃ 2ᵉ,
quaestio 22ᵃ, articulo 3°... iᵃ 2ᵉ, quaestio 59ᵃ, articulo 5ᵗᵒ.'

[4] *Repressor*, i, 14. The 'inspiration' of pagan philosophers was acknow-
ledged by many a medieval thinker but it was an 'inspiration' through
revelation, not through 'naturall witt'. Cf. Abailard, Migne, *P.L.* clxxviii,
cap. 1126, 1144, 1155. I owe this reference to Mr Nuttall.

evil in themselves but only evil when wrongly used he cites Aristotle's *Ethica Nicomachea* as his chief authority.[1] He also referred to this work when he was distinguishing between active and passive worshipping, whilst in other places he referred to Aristotle's *Peri Hermeneias* and *De Praedicamentis*.

But Aristotle's influence was more than that of an authority, because despite the vagueness of Pecock's knowledge he seems to have been in some cases at least the inspiration of the thought itself, particularly in Pecock's discursus on psychology where he not infrequently refers to actual chapters and verses. Pecock's definition of fantasy 'forto forge and compowne, or to sette to gedir in seemyng, thingis whiche ben not to gedir, and whiche maken not oon thing in kynde' is identical with that of Aristotle, whilst he is like the philosopher in that he associates the imagination with memory.[2] He follows Aristotle in saying that taste and touch are not only necessary for all men but are the two things indispensable to all creatures.[3] Finally, he uses Aristotle to support his definition of reason; Aristotle, like Pecock, urged that whereas the bodily senses are so closely related that they cannot survive death, reason forms a divinely inspired and immortal faculty because it is not dependent on the body nor indeed on any natural cause.[4]

In some cases Pecock failed to grasp Aristotle's meaning, and in others he openly criticises him. Thus Pecock retains all the 'common sensibles' mentioned by Aristotle with the exception of time which he omits.[5] In another place Pecock not only fails to

---

[1] *Repressor*, ii, 308; *Nicomachean Ethics* trs. Welldon, Bk. iv, cap. i, 99. Vide *A Catalogue of editions of Aristotle's Nicomachean Ethics printed in the 15th century*, H. C. Chandler (Oxford, 1868). Professor J. L. Morison says: 'Aristotle, in spite of the occasional mention of definite titles, he seems to have known very vaguely indeed, being by no means as learned as his greater predecessors, and suggesting by his vagueness that his quotations were obtained not even from a medieval handbook, but from references in other men's writings' (*Book of Faith*, 46–7).

[2] Cf. *Donet*, 10; *Folewer to the Donet*, 26; *De Anima*, ii, 6.

[3] *Folewer to the Donet*, 21–2.   [4] *Id.* 9.

[5] *Id.* 10. 'Mouing, reste, greetnes, noumbre and figure.' Cf. *De Anima*, ii, 6.

grasp Aristotle's distinction between a 'non-voluntary' and an 'involuntary' act, but he has misunderstood another passage in Aristotle's book which asserts that certain actions are more voluntary than involuntary; Pecock, however, affirms that they are more involuntary than voluntary.[1] Similarly, he does not scruple to criticise and even contradict the 'philosophir':

What was Aristotil othir than a louer of trouth, and therfore a laborer bisi forto fynde the knowyng of treuth, both for him silf and for othire?...And thouȝ many wolen folewe Aristotil for reuerence of Aristotil more than for reuerence of trouth to be defendid and publischid, as ful oft such inparfitnes is wonyd to be vsid in scole of philosofie and in scole of dyuynyte, the more reuth is; ȝit it likith not to me forto so reuerence and folewe Aristotil aȝens treuth, ffor wel y wote it was neuyr Aristotilis wil that eny man schulde so do.[2]

He brings out Aristotle's assertion that wisdom was a 'kunnyngal virtue' as an objection to his own theory of 'kunnyngal virtues', and then dismisses it as a mistaken notion resulting from Aristotle's method of approach to his subject.[3] Even though Aristotle's philosophy is so criticised he remains a potent authority whose teaching may be clearly if somewhat vaguely glimpsed through the obscurities of Pecock's dialectic.[4] At the same time he once again emphasises that 'the philosophir seith, and resoun, which is more than the philosophir, seith that wherebi a man knowith the partie that is riȝt, he may knowe the partie which therto is vnriȝt and that bi vertu and strengthe of the knowing wherbi he knowith that this partie is riȝt, sithen it is so

[1] *Folewer to the Donet*, 148, 151; *Ethica Nicomachea*, Bk. III, cap. I.

[2] *Folewer to the Donet*, 151-2.

[3] *Id.* p. 54; *Ethica Nicomachea*, Bk. VI, cap. 7. Pecock replies that although there is an apparent distinction between his view and that of Aristotle, the difference is purely superficial and that wisdom is implied in his own 'kunnyngal virtues' and therefore 'it folewith not that Aristotil and y in the thing in it silf and in the veri philosofie discorden' (*Folewer to the Donet*, 61).

[4] E.g. *Folewer to the Donet*, 54; *Ethica*, Bk. VI, cap. 7. *Folewer to the Donet*, 75; *Ethica*, Bks. II and III. *Folewer to the Donet*, 77; *Ethica*, Bk. I, cap. I. *Folewer to the Donet*, 93; *Ethica*, Bk. II, cap. 5. *Folewer to the Donet*, 99; *Ethica*, Bk. VI, cap. 9.

that no thing is vnriȝt aȝens riȝt but for that it is contrarie to the riȝt and distroieth the riȝt'.[1] Reason is the crown of the philosopher and it dwarfs everything that does not harmonise with it into complete insignificance.

The close contact between Aristotelian and scholastic thought is symbolised by the fact that in one place Pecock refers to St Thomas Aquinas's commentary on the *Ethica*.[2] Pecock's debt to the scholastic thinkers was obviously great, and he must have been well acquainted with their works even though there are comparatively few references to them in his surviving books. He appears as an eclectic writer. Dr Greet is correct when he says that his theology is 'an extraordinary combination of opposing schools'. Although his method is theologically akin to that of Aquinas, he paid, for instance, very little attention to the practical significance of grace which St Thomas had emphasised,[3] and he is equally remiss when he is speaking on the Holy Ghost. The self-inspiration of the mind which Duns Scotus affirms—Dr Greet also rightly comments that the early chapters of the *Reule* contain arguments not dissimilar in character to Duns Scotus's vestigial arguments for the existence of God[4]—finds its place in Pecock's thought but he discards his emphasis on the authority of the Church.[5] Where Scotus has subordinated the 'doom of reason' as being of probable significance only whereas the decrees of the Church are of absolute significance, Pecock makes the 'doom of reason' into an absolute. Pecock also copied Duns Scotus in affirming that the merit which the Christian can derive from Christ's death on the Cross is limited,[6] and that good works have

---

[1] *Reule*, 25. *Ethica Nicomachea*, Bk. v, cap. 1.

[2] *Reule*, 252: 'Thomas of Alquyn...vpon "Aristotil etikis", jᵉ book, xvj chapiter', i.e. St Thomas Aquinas, *In Aristotelis X Libros Ethicorum ad Nicomachum Commentaria*, lib. 1, lectio 18. *Opera Omnia*, xxv (S. E. Fretté, Paris, 1871–80).

[3] Cf. *Summa Theologica*, ii, q. cix, art. 1–10; q. ix, art. 1–9.

[4] Duns Scotus, *Opus Oxoniense*, i, d. 3, q. 5 (ed. Lyons, 1639).

[5] *Id.* ii, d. 42; *Reportata Parisiensia*, iii, d. 3; d. 23.

[6] *Reule*, 7, 214–19. Cf. Duns Scotus, *Opus Oxoniense*, iii, d. 9; St Thomas Aquinas, *Summa Theologica*, iii, q. xlix, art. 1, 4, 5.

an intrinsic value.[1] Pecock's debt to these two thinkers, and to others of lesser distinction, was undoubted.

Yet the actual references to them in his works are few and far between. One critical reference to St Thomas's *Summa* has already been mentioned.[2] The only reference to Duns Scotus, outside the *Book of Faith*, occurs in the *Reule*, where his *Super Quartum Sentenciarum* is mentioned.[3]

When the evidence at our disposal has been added up, it indicates that although Reginald Pecock was not a great scholar and was indeed far less well acquainted with patristic writings than many of his contemporaries, he was sufficiently well versed in patristic and scholastic learning for the task which he had undertaken. He was certainly not a Renaissance scholar; there is no glimmer of such learning as was to enlighten both Oxford and Cambridge in the later years of the fifteenth century. He had no knowledge of Greek and no appreciation of the classics outside Aristotle, whose writings he knew at second-hand or in Latin translations. His emphasis on the syllogism was purely medieval, but he had a vigorous, well-trained mind which made him view some subjects with greater realism than his more learned contemporaries and to group the knowledge at his command in a more original and distinctive way.

---

[1] *Reule*, 157, 159–60, 473.   [2] *Vide* p. 78, n. 4.
[3] '"The greet clerk doctor subtilis", super 4^m sentenciarum distinccio (xliij), quaescio (j)' (*Reule*, 26, 27).

CHAPTER IX

THE LOLLARDS

BISHOP REGINALD PECOCK had two aims, to persuade the Lollards of the folly of their ways and to 'educate' the laity and clergy of his own Church. Both these aims were complementary to each other, and the means which he used to bring them to a successful fulfilment were identical. Furthermore, the thought which characterised the means led to the rise of an increasingly vigorous opposition and formed the basis on which the charges brought against him at his trial were founded. It is important, then, to examine the essentials of his attack on the Lollards and to estimate the significance of any other ideas which provoked a critical hostility during his lifetime.

The Repressor of Over Much Blaming of the Clergy is the book in which he replies to his Lollard opponents. In fact, this book is not only important for his replies, but also for the light which it throws on Lollard thought during the middle years of the fifteenth century. The evidence indicates that it was written about the year 1449, but it was not published until some five or six years later.[1] It is uncertain whether the Repressor formed a reply to Wyclif's own works or to works written by his followers. Pecock himself gives very few clues, for the Lollard ideas are embodied in the text of the book itself. Babington pointed out that he seems to have very definitely answered certain arguments, especially in relation to the worship of images,[2] against doing a less good work when a better work may be done, against the religious orders,[3] the hierarchy and endowments,[4] which appear in two Lollard

---

[1] Repressor, II, 516, 517. Pecock speaks of the war having been carried on between England and France for 34 years. The war may be said to have commenced with the siege of Harfleur, August 17th, 1415. But the book was not immediately published (Book of Faith, 119).

[2] The Apology of the Lollards (ed. J. H. Todd), 83, 85, 100.

[3] Remonstrance against Romish Corruptions in the Church, ed. J. H. Forshall (London, 1851), 88.   [4] Id. 55 ff., 184.

tracts, published under the titles *Apology for the Lollards* and *Remonstrance against Romish Corruptions in the Church* (1395). He refers to the works of 'oon clerk (but verili to seie oon heretik)',[1] meaning John Wyclif, but there is insufficient evidence to indicate whether he had actually read Wyclif's Latin or English books. Inasmuch as he never mentions any of their titles it is improbable that he had read the Latin books. It is clear that he had used the Wycliffite version of the Scriptures.[2] It seems improbable that Pecock was actually answering the arguments put forward by any particular work whether of John Wyclif or of his later followers. He was endeavouring to reply to the arguments which the Lollards of his own day were using and with which his own experience at Oxford and London would have made him familiar.

The *Repressor* is then the focus point around which a discussion of Pecock's thought must first centre, but it was not the only book which Pecock wrote to controvert the Lollards. *The Reule of Chrysten Religioun*, *The Donet*, *The Book of Faith*, *The Folewer to the Donet*, *The Afore-Crier*, *The Book of the Church*, *The Book of Divine Office*, *The Book of Eucharist*, *The Book of Sacraments*, *The Book of Worshipping* and many another[3] are all mentioned in connection with the *Summa Theologica*, which he was so carefully and so earnestly compiling against his adversaries. Many of these books have not survived and some may never have been written. Others were an abridgement of fuller, less comprehensible versions. Of the existing books, the *Poore Mennis Myrrour* is an abridgement of the *Donet*, whilst none of the existing books are as complete as they should be. Yet they all formed an integral part of the reply which Pecock gave to Lollardy.

It is impossible to grasp the significance of Pecock's reply without first understanding something of Lollardy itself, the founder

---

[1] *Repressor*, II, 413: 'Ferthermore it is to wite, that oon clerk, (but verili to seie oon heretik) tempereth the firste opinioun rehercid bifore...and seith in this maner, that if the clergie mys vse habituali or customabili his vnmouable endewing, the clergie may leefulli and ou3te be dispoilid of thilk endewing bi the temporal lordis and ellis not.'

[2] *Vide* p. 193 ff.   [3] *Vide* Appendix II.

of the movement, its characteristic ideas and the history of its evolution as a historical and theological revolt. Yet it is not easy to estimate the real significance of Lollardy, for students have so long associated John Wyclif with that much-hackneyed phrase the 'Morning Star of the Reformation'.[1] In reality Lollardy is a parti-coloured movement, intersected with differing ideas and marked by varying phases of intensity of effort and action.

Its founder, John Wyclif, was quite as much a scholar as Pecock, an Oxford don spending most of his life in the academic society of Balliol, Canterbury Hall[2] and Queen's College. His intervention in political affairs was infinitely more disastrous (if not for him, at least for England) than Pecock's own appearance on that somewhat inglorious field of human activity.

In the first place the most important and the most interesting feature of Wyclif's activity—and here again popular opinion has been partly deceived by the emphasis which it has placed on his English as opposed to his Latin works—is in reality his intellectual development, enshrined within his many writings. Educated in a scholastic environment more or less wholly dominated by Thomist and Aristotelian influence but lately agitated by the provocative thought of Duns Scotus and William of Occam, Wyclif first comes into prominence as a philosopher passionately interested in the problems at issue between the competing realist and nominalist schools of thought. As a result of his education he emerged a hyper-realist with a faith in the infallibility of logic to which Pecock himself, had he been then alive, could not have objected.

His early works are interesting to the modern historian for two reasons, the relative significance of his mental and philosophical exercises, and for the way in which they give some indication of

[1] The late Professor J. P. Whitney rightly said: 'We can no longer regard Wyclif as a "Reformer before the Reformation"....Had all he suggested been carried out we should have had chaos not reformation, a world in which his beloved Bible and his Christ would have had little power' ('A Note on the Work of the Wyclif Society' in *Essays Presented to R. L. Poole*, 112).

[2] H. S. Cronin, in *T.R.H.S.* VIII, 55–75.

the channels along which his thought was later to be canalised. As a realist his arguments in *De Logica*[1] and *De Ente*[2] centre round the dispute between the validity of the universal as opposed to the singular. He believed that realist philosophy was an inseparable part of divine truth, without which it was impossible to appreciate the more fundamental postulates of the Christian faith, belief in eternal punishment, the resurrection of the dead, the proper interpretation of the Incarnation as well as such trivial matters as the obedience which one should pay to the dean of one's faculty. Every *figura* pointed to a necessary reality, since the universal must be the intrinsic and formal cause of any and every particular *ens*. The universal had almost as much fascination for Wyclif the scholar as the 'doom of reason' had for Pecock. 'Impossibile est hominem caritate diligere, nisi in re ponat sentenciam de universalibus.'[3] He believed that universals existed *ex parte rei*,[4] for 'ydea ergo est essentialiter natura divina et formaliter ratio, secundum quam Deus intelligit creaturas'.[5] They formed, then, the archetypes, the exemplars, the created realities of God,[6] which men also possess in so far as they have been formed in the image of God.

When he carried his realist philosophy forward into the interpretation of Christian doctrine he found himself in increasingly deep water. The Paschal Lamb, for instance, as a figure of Christ must be Christ, although it is less perfectly so than the Host.[7]

[1] Wyclif, *De Logica*, ed. M. H. Dziewicki, vols. i–iii (1893–99). In the introduction he says: 'I have been induced by friends of God's word to compose a treatise in explanation of the logic of Holy Scripture....I propose, with the object of sharpening the faculties of believing minds, to examine processes of proof for propositions which are drawn from Scripture' (cited in *John Wyclif*, Lechler).

[2] Wyclif, *De Ente Librorum Duorum* (Excerpta), ed. M. H. Dziewicki (1909). In view of the work of Dr Harrison Thomson, it need hardly be added that many of the early works of Wyclif have been inaccurately ascribed to him.

[3] Wyclif, *De Ente*, Bk. i, t. 4.

[4] Wyclif, *Trialogus* (ed. Lechler, 1869), i, 85.

[5] *Id.* 66. Cf. 'ydea est, veritas absolute necessaria' (*id.* 61).

[6] *Id.* 63: 'Si [Deus] illud intelligit, illud habet rationem objectivam, secundum quam terminat intellectivitatem divinam.'

[7] Wyclif, *De Apostasia*, ed. M. H. Dziewicki (1889), 98.

Similarly, in his *De Benedicta Incarnatione*, he shows that Christ took on not the 'individual man' but the 'communis natura' of mankind, the divine exemplar, which made him 'verissime et univoce' man's friend and brother.[1] In one of his later works, *De Apostasia*, he says that Christ assumed the 'communis natura' at the Last Judgement. This later development does not, however, affect this illustration of his realist thought, which is in itself certainly in opposition to the teaching of Abailard, Peter Lombard and Aquinas himself.

This extreme philosophic realism formed the intellectual compulsion which drew him on the one hand towards a denial of transubstantiation, and on the other hand led him to formulate the necessitarian views which in some ways anticipated the even more deterministic creed of John Calvin. His earliest works already question the current doctrine by implication, for they deny the possibility of annihilation, 'per idem videtur nihil posse annihilari',[2] but it was some time before he reached his final viewpoint. In the *De Benedicta Incarnatione* he still speaks of the 'miraculosa transubstantiatio', and although he realises that the views of some of the saints are not in agreement with the orthodox doctrine,[3] he falls back upon the Christian's faith. The further and final viewpoint, which is developed in the two tractates *De Eucharistia*[4] and *De Apostasia*,[5] is difficult to interpret.

[1] Wyclif, *De Benedicta Incarnatione*, ed. Harris (1886), 71, 144–5, etc.

[2] Wyclif, *De Logica*, II, 192; *De Ente*, Bk. II, cap. XII–XIV. In another place, however, he agrees with Archbishop Richard of Armagh when the latter declares that 'God can annihilate if He chooses' but the quotation is qualified. Wyclif elsewhere predicates a *corpus mathematicum*.

[3] *De Benedicta Incarnatione*, 190.

[4] Wyclif, *De Eucharistia Tractatus Maior: Tractatus de Eucharistia et Poenitentia sive de Confessione*, ed. J. Loserth (1892). Cf. *Trialogus*, 248: 'Inter omnes haereses, quae unquam in ecclesia pullularunt, nunquam considero aliquam plus callide per hypocritas introductam et multiplicius populum defraudantem; nam spoliat populum, facit ipsum committere idolatriam, negat fidem Scripturae, et per consequens ex infidelitate multipliciter ad iracundiam provocat veritatem.' In 1381 Wyclif confessed: 'I was long in error as regards this heresy of accidents without a subject.' His final view is not very clear and hardly capable of a true scientific analysis. Dr Darwell Stone has some useful references, e.g. 'by virtue of the sacramental words, both the body and blood

There was a similar development in his views on man's freedom of will. The *De Ente* and the *De Logica*[1] find him uncertain, but the later *De Ecclesia* postulates 'omnia futura de necessitate eveniunt'. Bearing his views on the omniscience and omni-governance of God in mind, we can easily see that it needed but a short step forward to call the church the 'universitas predesti-natorum'. It is true that this philosophic conclusion, influenced as it was by the writings of Augustine and Thomas Bradwardine,[2] was confirmed by his personal experience of the Great Schism and by the recent accusations of heresy which the Church had brought against him.[3] It must have been with a certain personal bitterness, perhaps justified by the circumstances, that he sought to prove that the hierarchy and the Church were not identical but rather

of Christ is really and actually in every part of it'. 'The bread is really and actually the very same body of Christ. Nevertheless I do not dare to say that this bread is the body of Christ essentially or substantially or corporally or identically (*identice*)' (Shirley, *Fasc. Ziz.* 115–16). Cf. *Trialogus*, p. 258, *De Eucharistia*, cap. 4, 111–12. Dr Stone concludes: 'He was endeavouring in a scholastic fashion to assert the real presence of the body and blood of Christ in the consecrated Sacraments, while distinguishing the way in which He is present on the altar from the way in which He is present in Heaven, and main-taining the real character of the bread and wine after consecration, and attempting to avoid what seemed to him the insuperable logical contradictions of the current explanations' (Darwell Stone, *History of the Doctrine of the Holy Eucharist* (1909), I, 368). Pecock's reaction to Wyclif on this point is not fully available. Fox quite unjustifiably believed that he was a follower of Wyclif in denying transubstantiation (*Acts and Monuments* (1684), p. 85). Pecock's *Book of Sacraments* is lost, but all the evidence indicates that Pecock would never have questioned the current belief: *Reule*, 95–6 (but cf. pp. 312–17, where he said that the act of celebration is not supernatural in itself), *Donet*, 35. In the *Repressor* he writes: 'in special thei abhorren aboue alle othere... the sacrament of the auter, the preciose bodi and blood of Crist... in so miche that thei not oonli scornen it, but thei haaten it, myscallen it bi foule names, and wolen not come her thankis into the bodili chirche, whilis thilke sacrament is halewid, tretid and vsid in the masse' (*op. cit.* II, 563).

[5] *De Apostasia*, ed. Dziewicki, caps. III–V.

---

[1] *De Logica*, ed. Dziewicki, II, 192.

[2] *De Causa Dei*, ed. Savile (1618). An English study of Bradwardine would be a useful contribution to medieval history.

[3] *De Ecclesia* was written c. 1377–8. Wyclif's condemnation was affirmed in papal bulls issued by Gregory XI on May 22nd, 1377 (Walsingham, *Historia Anglicana*, ed. H. T. Riley, I, 345–53).

inimical to each other.[1] Although he accepted the normal medieval division of the Church into three parts, one militant here on earth, one triumphant in Paradise and one asleep in Purgatory, he was of the opinion that the Church can only consist of those who have been predestined to salvation by election.[2] Thus no man can know whether he be of the Church or of the Devil nor whether God has imprinted the priestly character in his soul or not. He took great joy in telling his readers that a fat abbot who governs a monastery may well be a devil incarnate in God's sight.[3] He interpreted the reception of Trajan into Heaven, a popular medieval story, in a very novel way, for Trajan was not saved through the prayers of Pope Gregory I, but by predestination.[4]

Wyclif contrasted the 'foreknown' who form another body with the Devil or Antichrist at their head with the elect who have been redeemed by Christ. This idea had been simmering in his mind for a long time, since even in the early De Ente[5] he wrote that 'God eternally intended to damn each of the foreknown for the beauty of the world'. Although the text is mutilated and the meaning seems to be 'in prevision of the sins that each of them commits and which he will not repent',[6] the sentence has a

[1] Wyclif, Select English Works, ed. Arnold, III, 447: 'Whanne men speken of holy Chirche, thei understonden anoon prelatis and prestis, monkis and chanouns, and freris, and alle men that han crownes [that have the tonsure] thouȝ thei lyven nevere so cursedly aȝenst Goddis lawe, and clepen not ne holden seculeris men of holy Chirche, thouȝ thei lyven nevere so trewely after Goddis lawe, and enden in perfect charite. But netheles alle that schullen be savyd in blisse of hevene ben membris of holy Chirche, and ne moo.'

[2] De Ecclesia, 8, 11, 125; 74, 111; De Blasphemia (ed. M. H. Dziewicki, 1893), 86; Trialogus, p. 152; Sel. Eng. Works, III, 102, 339, etc. Cf. a remark which he made in one of his sermons: 'Secundum catholicos, ecclesia est predestinatorum universitas, et sic est triplex ecclesia scilicet, ecclesia triumphantium in coelo, ecclesia militantium hic in mundo, et ecclesia dormientium in purgatorio.'   [3] De Ecclesia, 57–8, 92.

[4] Id. 530–3.   [5] De Ente, ed. M. H. Dziewicki, cap. XXII.

[6] This is Dziewicki's comment. Later in the chapter Wyclif adds, 'Deus omnia peccata necessabit ad esse'. Dziewicki rightly says that there is a clear distinction between Wyclif's view of free will and Calvin's 'irresistible grace', but Dziewicki is inclined to modify the theological implications of Wyclif's predestinarianism. Cf. Lechler, Wyclif, 290: 'His meaning rather is this; that when predestination to punishment is viewed passively, it is seen to be the

decidedly deterministic sound. When he was asked the question, should a damned soul which by prevision saw its own fate accept its own damnation, he replied that such an acceptance would reveal a state of mind incompatible with that belonging to a damned soul. If it was then objected that a lost soul had no obligations towards God, it might then be urged that it was considerably freer than other souls. This, Wyclif said, was untrue, since the lost soul is mistaken in its freedom, being in fact a slave of sin and therefore far from free. The 'foreknown' or the *praesciti* do not have a place in the church and do not gain the same satisfaction from their participation in the Sacraments of the Church as the ordinary 'elect' would.

Now it should be noticed that these two very important revolutionary aspects of Wyclif's thought, with all their rather indefinite implications in the sphere of feudal contract and dominion and social and political life, were thus part of an intellectual superstructure erected on the foundations of philosophical realism. It may of course be argued that it was only the cast of his mind and the environment of his life which led him away from the logic of reason[1] to the merit of faith. Indeed, the influence of the nascent nationalism which the fourteenth-century Englishman embodied in popular poetry, as well as the social movements which we associate with the Peasants' Revolt, must also have helped to mould Wyclif's thought. But the pre-eminence is intellectual rather than environmental—with one qualification.

result of the concurrent working of several causes—(1) God Himself; (2) the *esse intelligibile* of the creature; (3) the future entrance of sin or crime.' He cites the *Trialogus*: 'Intelligendo autem passive predestinationem vel praeparationem ad poenam, videtur, quod illae sunt a Deo, ab esse intelligibili creaturae, et a futuritione criminis concausatae' (*id.* 122).

[1] Thus in the *De Benedicta Incarnatione* Wyclif wrote: 'in hoc tamen excedit secta Christiana quascunque alias, quod maxime archana sue fidei copiose probari possunt, miracula explanari in naturali lumine evidenciis et exemplaribus philosophicis, necnon omnes impugnatorum argucie evidenter tolli eciam ex naturalibus et propriis eorum principiis' (p. 159). This passage is an interesting one but does not agree with what Wyclif himself says elsewhere, even in the same book. The *De Benedicta* is, as Mr B. L. Manning has said, extremely important from the theological point of view.

Wyclif was not only an Oxford don but a don with a social conscience and a veneration for scriptural truth that was very early apparent in his writings. He was also, it must be added, a Christian priest with a fervent sense of his responsibilities. Even in the *De Logica* he referred the bishops of his own day to the apostolic ways of the primitive church—'sicut vixerunt Apostoli in ecclesia primitiva, sic etiam tenentur episcopi vivere circa finem mundi'—and in the proemium he declared that his work was based more on the 'logic of scripture' than the 'logic of reason'.[1] He championed this opinion with even greater vigour after he realised that his own intellectual viewpoint was in full and complete agreement with what he understood of the teaching of the Bible. Further, he not only found an outlet for his theoretical views by putting forward a practical political programme which happened to coincide with the selfish political ambitions of John of Gaunt and his feudal following, as well as with the growing distrust which the increasingly powerful mercantile class had of aliens living in England, but he also popularised those views through his own English writings and sermons and through the preaching of his followers.

Thus Wyclif's views percolated in three or even four quite different layers of society, in academic Oxford, in feudal baronies, in mercantile London and Bristol, and in a fourth *stratum*, partly rural and partly urban, perhaps best characterised by the anachronistic term, 'lower middle class'. In the first place, the intellectual movement, which had its headquarters at Oxford and which we associate with men like Repingdon, Aston, Ashwardby (of Oriel), Greenhurst and many others, almost completely disappeared except where, as we have seen from the story of Pecock's early days, it coalesced with the anti-episcopal independent party in Oxford University.[2] It was unable to withstand the repressive

[1] *De Logica*, I, 69.
[2] Repingdon's career ended in a cardinalate. A forceful, not unattractive character, there is no reason to believe that his acceptance of Lollardy and his recantation were not sincere. Greenhurst of New College and Lechlade of Merton are merely shadowy characters. It is true that some of the Lollards,

policy, adopted in the first instance by Bishop Courtenay and continued by Arundel, a policy which, it should be noted, had received implicit governmental sanction in *De Haeretico Comburendo*.[1]

The 'baronial' party was the next to vanish. Here again religious opinions were merged in feudal feeling, especially in the selfish and greedy personality of John of Gaunt. After Gaunt had ceased to patronise the movement, possibly because he was fearful of the revolutionary implications of Wyclif's theory of *dominium*, other barons, Sir Thomas Latimer, Sir John Montague, Sir John Pecche, Sir Reginald de Hulton, Sir Lewis Clifford, Sir John Cheyne and last, but not least, Sir John Oldcastle, patronised the Lollard cause. How far religious and political elements were merged in this section of Lollard society is open to question. Latimer certainly invited Lollards to his house at Braybrooke, and owned copies of Wyclif's works which he loaned to Czech scholars. Oldcastle himself was a sincere Lollard,[2] but there are very few cases in which Lollard thought was not influenced by political and economic motives. For Wyclif himself, as for later reformers, the reformation of the Church and national independence were closely bound together. The Gaunt trend only

e.g. William James, who was still suspected of Lollardy as late as 1420, remained more faithful than Repingdon or Aston had been but the repeated attempts of the Archbishop to enforce his will on the University met with final success (*vide* Hastings Rashdall, *Universities in the Middle Ages*, ed. Powicke and Emden, III, 135). The most forceful Lollard produced by Oxford was Peter Payne, the Principal of St Edmund Hall, who continued his career on the Continent after his excommunication in 1416.

[1] Gee and Hardy, *Documents illustrative of English Church History* (1896), 133–7 (2 Henry IV, cap. 15).

[2] *Fasciculi Zizaniorum*, ed. W. W. Shirley (1858), 433 ff.; 'Sir John Oldcastle' in the *English Historical Review* (xx, 1905, 434–55 and 638–57) by Prof. W. T. Waugh seems to prove that Oldcastle was sincere in his religious opinions. His chaplain had been cited for preaching Lollardy as early as 1410. He had contact with the Bohemians, with Hus himself (through Richard Wyche) and with Wok of Waldstein. Waugh accounts for the rebellion thus: 'The Lollards were goaded into action by the impossibility of putting their theories into practice as long as king and prelates remained prosperous' (*id.* 650).

disappeared in Lollardy after the failure of Oldcastle's rebellion and his subsequent execution.

Although it is at times difficult to perceive in what ways baronial and mercantile Lollardy were different, there is nevertheless a distinction. Whilst the barons wished to confiscate Church property in order to increase both their power and their wealth, the merchant classes, amongst whom there must have been a few Lollards,[1] regarded the Church from a political and national point of view, which was itself based on economic feeling. Their suspicions of alien traders, and of alien monks in particular, their desire to foster English trade and to defeat the French all inclined to make them harbour anti-clerical views. The majority were, however, both anti-clerical and anti-Lollard, for Lollardy itself, by the implications of its theory of *dominium*, fostered certain views which the merchants would instantly distrust.

Thus the only important section of the Lollard movement which really endured until Pecock's day, and even that was wearing thin by 1450, was that most imbued with popular and social teaching. It originated with the teaching of Wyclif's Poor Preachers, and its most typical adherent, the eccentric William Swynderby, is deserving of an article to himself. He was an individualist whose rough eloquence attracted a large following around Leicester where he emphasised the social implications of Lollard teaching. On the other hand, it must be remembered that fairly conclusive evidence has disproved the thesis that Wyclif's ideas were at all responsible for the Peasants' Revolt.[2] It was

[1] This is apparent from the petition which was sent to Parliament in 1395 (Gee and Hardy, *Documents*, 126 ff.) and from Lollard influence in the Parliament of 1410, largely responsible for the radical scheme of disendowment put forward in that year. An analysis of Lollard personalities is also suggestive. Thus a brief glance shows that the knight Sir Roger Acton, who was associated with Oldcastle, was actually of low birth, the son of a weaver who had gained distinction in the Welsh wars (*Chronicon Adae de Usk*, ed. E. M. Thompson (1904), 121), whilst many of Oldcastle's followers must have been London tradesmen, e.g. Parchmynes, the fuller William Dene whom Henry V pardoned, etc.

[2] [2]Cf. Ernst Troeltsch, *The Social Teaching of the Christian Churches* (1931), I, 358: 'The primary motive was not a reaction among the lower orders, but

indeed only after Wyclif's death in 1384 that the social teaching
of the Wycliffite movement comes really to the fore. Wyclif's
writings may sometimes be distinguished from those of later
Lollards by the emphasis which later writers place on the social
implications of Wyclif's teaching. Thus the 31st conclusion of the
series of Latin propositions known as the *XXXVII Conclusiones*
declares that 'secular lords ought to be adorned or clothed with
righteousness to God and men both rich and poor, and to treat
reasonably and charitably their tenants and subjects and servants
or bondmen'. 'Simple priests than hanno benefices bi doom of
chirche now, owen to be apaied with symple liflode and clothinge,
in preynge deuoutli for hemsilf and peple and in usinge medeful
werkis', says yet another contemporary document.[1] The simple
priest, who appealed to the lower classes, the weavers and their
comrades, against the riches and endowments of the Church,
urging them to restore simple, pure ways of living within the
Church and a fairer economic standard of life within the world,
formed the mainstay of the Lollard movement in the later years.
The Lollard teaching emphasised the fact that 'poor men have
naked sides and dead walls have a great plenty of waste gold'.[2]

The chief centres of the Lollard movement in the early years of
the fifteenth century were towns associated with industry where
there was likely to be a number of poor or middle-class people
receptive of Lollard preaching.[3] One of the most striking facts

national sentiment and the desire for political independence.' The discussion
in R. L. Poole, *Medieval Thought and Learning* (1920), 246 ff., gives the best
interpretation of Wyclif's theory of *dominium*. *Vide* also Troeltsch, *id.* 358 ff.
and notes, 437–9.

[1] *The Remonstrance against Romish Corruptions in the Church* (so entitled by the
editor, the Rev. J. Forshall, 1851), 97.

[2] Wyclif, *English Works*, ed. Matthew (1880), 91.

[3] Thus Foxe has a long list of suspected Lollards at Norwich (*Acts and
Monuments*, III, 589–90). He also refers to suspects at Tenterden, Cranbrook,
Rolvenden, Benenden, and Woodchurch in the prosperous Weald of Kent. In
1387 we find the Bishop of Worcester complaining of Lollard activities in his
diocese, probably referring to the activity of the Poor Preachers in Bristol and
in Gloucester. The Lollards were also numerous in London and in parts of
Norfolk and Suffolk.

about the later Lollard movement is the absence of important or original literature which is in itself an indication that the movement had lost its original intellectual stimulus. With the possible exception of John Purvey, Wyclif's works formed the mainspring of the intellectual side of the Lollard movement, even in Bohemia where Hus and his followers never produced a literature in any way comparable to that of Wyclif. In many cases, indeed, they merely copied his works.[1]

All this proves that the later movement was a social, pious or religious agitation whose vitality was emotional and economic rather than intellectual and academic. Even a partial and incomplete analysis of the personalities of the later Lollard movement is suggestive of this. There was a sprinkling of Oxford Lollards, old offenders like Richard Wyche,[2] William James,[3] and Ralph Mungyn who was accused among other things of denying the right of private property, and finally the exiled firebrand, Peter Payne of St Edmund Hall. The less distinguished Lollards gathered round this small group of men. Thus an examination of the contacts made by Mungyn reveal that he had not only sold Wyclif's *Trialogus* and other books to a Hampshire priest, John Botte by name, but that he was also associated with one Nicholas Hooper, a servant of Oldcastle, and with Thomas Garenter, the chaplain of a prominent London merchant named Shadworth.

---

[1] It is fairly certain that J. Loserth (in *Wiclif and Huss*, trans. M. J. Evans, 1884; *Huss und Wiclif*, 2nd ed. Munich and Berlin, 1925) exaggerated the extent of Hus's debt to Wyclif, but the indebtedness remains very great as a comparison of Hus's *De Ecclesia* (trans. D. S. Schaff, N.Y. 1915) with Wyclif's work on the same subject shows. 'Hus', says Professor R. R. Betts, 'was no mechanical echo of Wyclif. He owed as much and more to his own native forerunners, to Milic, Matthias of Janov, Adalbertus Ranconis and a hundred others' (*History*, XXIV, n.s. No. 94, 106). Cf. R. R. Betts, 'English and Czech Influences on Hus' in *T.R.H.S.* 4th ser. XXI, 1939, and F. Zilka, 'The Czech Reformation in its Relation to the World Reformation' in the *Slavonic Review*, VIII.

[2] For Wyche vide *Fasciculi Zizaniorum*, 370 ff., 501 ff.; Wilkins, *Concilia*, III, 394–5; Gairdner, *Lollardy and Reformation in England* (1908), I, 172 ff.

[3] He recanted in 1420.

The scanty evidence further suggests that the main propagandists of Lollard teaching were parish priests and important
members of their flocks. Norfolk, as Foxe indicates, was one of
the main centres of Lollard propaganda, but the main interest of
this analysis is the way in which it reveals the social classes from
which the lay Lollards came. Thus a certain John Claydon, termed
a carrier of London, owned Wycliffite literature which was read
out to him, for he was unable to read, by his friends, John Fullar
and Richard Turning, a master baker. We may observe Richard
Hounden, woolpacker,[1] John Florence, turner, of Shelton in the
diocese of Norwich, John Beverley of Southcreek, a labourer,
John Skilley of Flixton, a miller, among other Lollards whose
misty personalities now and again appear on the stage of history,
whilst the names of Lollards whom Bishop Courtenay interro-
gated at Leicester in 1389 indicate their various callings, Smith,
Scryvener, Tailor and Goldsmith. Finally, Professor Trevelyan
tells how a London apprentice of the name of Colleyn deserted his
master in order to preach Lollardy, and with another poor priest
was lodged with John Fox, the mayor of Northampton.[2] These
details may be trivial but they help to reveal the change in the
composition of the Lollard movement between the years which
saw its inauguration by Wyclif at Oxford and the publication of
Pecock's *Repressor*.

The stern action of the government and of the Church,
symbolised in the first instance in the burning of William Sawtre,[3]
together with the fervent, skilful attacks made on the Lollard
position by Netter and Pecock, were so generally successful that

---

[1] Fabyan, *The New Chronicle of England and France*, ed. H. Ellis (1811), 602;
Gregory, 171. Hounden was burned, Jan. 20th, 1430.

[2] G. M. Trevelyan, *England in the Age of Wyclif* (1899), 320. Another Lollard leader was a weaver who was also a bailiff of the town of Abingdon.

[3] *Fasc. Ziz.* 408–11. Convocation instituted proceedings against Sawtre
whilst the bill *De Haeretico* was before Parliament and before it became law.
The royal writ was issued for his execution on Feb. 26th, 1401 (Hardy,
Documents, 138). Letters Patent against the Lollards were issued at the request
of Courtenay in 1384 (*id.* 110). The Lollards, says Pecock, hold the 'now late
brenned men in Ynglond to be martiris' (*Book of Faith*, 192).

Lollardy was of very slight importance by the year 1450.[1] Yet it not only challenged the medieval view of society and the Christian doctrine of salvation, as interpreted by the medieval Church, but it almost inevitably fitted in with the general change in the conception of life which was expressed in Pecock's own thought as well as in Wyclif's dependence on scriptural truth. In that sense both Wyclif and Pecock are heralds of the Renaissance.

With these facts in mind it will be easier to understand how far a reply to Lollardy in the middle years of the fifteenth century was necessary, and how far that reply was successful. Of the various attempts to justify the ways of the hierarchy to the ordinary man, the man on the 'mead bench' as well as to the Oxford don, no single tract was entirely successful. Perhaps Hoccleve's poem on *Sir John Oldcastle*, the story of 'a manly knyght and shoon ful cleer in famous worthynesse' who became the companion of 'cursid caitifs, heires of dirknesse' and was thus perverted to 'ffeendly doctryne' was the most telling of the replies which were written by orthodox writers to Lollard preachers. His main argument was:

> Lete holy chirche medle of the doctryne
> Of Crystes lawes and of his byleeue,
> And lete alle othir folke therto enclyne,
> And of our feith noon argumentis maaue.
> For if we might our feith by reson preeue,
> We sholde no meryt of our feith haue.
> But now a dayes a Bailiff or Reeue
> Or man of craft wole in it dote or rave.[2]

---

[1] It is uncertain to what extent Lollardy was a real danger between 1425 and 1450. Archbishop Chichele told Convocation on Nov. 16th, 1428, that the chief reason for summoning them lay in the necessity for counteracting heretical teaching which was increasing in the province of Canterbury. Pecock himself gives a not dissimilar impression (e.g. *Repressor*, I, 86–7). A movement like the agitation led by Jack Sharpe of Wigmoreland in 1431 (vide *Historia Anglicana*, Walsingham, II, 282–3; *St Alban's Chronicle*, I, 63, etc.) which had a vigorous social impulse shows the latent discontent in the country. The authorities averred that they feared that the 'fals feelshipp' would destroy the Church.

[2] T. Wright, *Political Poems* (R.S. 1861), II, contains many other poems written against the Lollards. Perhaps the most interesting of these literary

This contrast between faith and reason is doubly interesting in view of Pecock's own position. Although Hoccleve chiefly emphasises ecclesiastical authority, his verses, full of a vigorous national sentiment—Oldcastle as a chivalric knight should be fighting with the king in France—were probably far more effective than the pompous theological tomes of Netter and Pecock:

> Remembre you heuene is a miry place
> And helle is ful of sharp adversitee.[1]

Other repudiations of the Lollard arguments were made in Wyclif's own time by the Carmelite John Cunningham in the three *Determinationes*,[2] by the Franciscan John Tissington[3] and the Benedictine Wells,[4] but they are not important enough to detain either historian or theologian. Despite a certain skilful use of dialectic, as employed for instance in Cunningham's attack on the literal interpretation of scripture,[5] the replies, some of which were interlarded with personal abuse, were as wholly dependent on the interpretation of texts taken from scripture as Wyclif's own writings.[6] They were, in addition, completely bound by scholastic arguments. Thus three replies alone stand out as worthy of attention, that made by an author usually identified with Roger Dymok, that made by Thomas Netter of Walden, and that made by Reginald Pecock.

pamphlets was the reply given by Friar John of Walsingham, writing under the name of Daw Topias, to the Lollard 'Jack Upland' (ii, 16–114). Hoccleve's poem is to be found in *Minor Poems*, ed. F. J. Furnivall (E.E.T.S.), 1892, 8 ff.

[1] Hoccleve, *op. cit.* p. 23.

[2] *Fasciculi Zizaniorum*, ed. Shirley, 3–103; H. B. Workman, *John Wyclif* (O.U.P. 1926), i, 120 ff.

[3] *Fasc. Ziz.* 133 ff.   [4] *Id.* 239–41.

[5] 'Daemonium habes', said the Jews to Jesus (John x, 20) and 'Non sum propheta nec filius prophetae', said Amos to Amaziah (Amos vii, 14). Would Wyclif have accepted the literal truth of these statements, Cunningham asks? and so on (*Fasc. Ziz.* 20–1).

[6] Another eminent opponent of Wyclif was the Thomist philosopher, Ralph Strode, whose text-book on logic, *Logica*, Pecock had very probably read. It was an exhaustive study of syllogistic reasoning, and was still studied at Padua as late as 1488. He wrote 'logical works which were printed in 1488 and 1507 with commentaries by Italian logicians' (Rashdall, *op. cit.* i, 247). Strode was a fellow of Merton College.

Dymok's work was probably first compiled as a series of lectures based on the Lollard *porrectio* to Parliament of 1395.[1] The book itself, to which the title *Liber Contra XII Errores et Hereses Lollardorum*[2] has been given, does not contain any very original matter or arguments, but it is a clear and lucid statement of the Catholic objections to the Lollard arguments which had been embodied in the petition of 1395. It was dedicated to the king whose duty it was, so Dymok pointed out, to defend the Church against her enemies.[3] He begins with a defence of the temporalities of the Church against those who wished to have them confiscated[4] and proceeds with his arguments, which are mainly of a scriptural nature, on behalf of celibacy,[5] the priesthood,[6] the sacrifice of the mass,[7] the sacraments of confirmation and extreme unction,[8] the undertaking of secular office by the clergy,[9] endowments and religious orders,[10] pilgrimages and image worship,[11] confession,[12] the 'righteous war'[13] and the performance of vows of chastity by

---

[1] *Fasc. Ziz.* 360. Mr Cronin rightly comments (in his Introduction to *Dymok*): 'when times were bad or had been better, and when taxation threatened to be heavier or to fall on unaccustomed shoulders the Lollards proper got a better hearing' (xliii). This was the situation in 1395.

[2] Ed. H. S. Cronin (Wyclif Society). Dymok (*c.* 1351–1418) was a Dominican doctor, probably prior of the Black Friars at Boston (*Dymok*, Introduction, xi–xv).

[3] *Dymok*, 1 ff.: 'Istam autem solitudinem vestre conuersacionis perverse atque doctrine pestifere demonstratis in publicacione libelli famosi et eiusdem expansione apud Westmonasterium in ostio Aule Regalis, in pleno parliamento, in conspectu omnium prelatorum, procerum, nobilium et huius regni populi universi. Qui libellus manifestam continet blasphemiam divine majestatis et gloriose matris eius et scandalum ecclesie sacrosancte et tocius generis humani dedecus et iniuriam manifestam, prout ex sequentibus, Deo adiuvante, liquebit' (*id.* 15).

[4] *Id.* 30–51.   [5] *Id.* 71–89.   [6] *Id.* 51–71.
[7] *Id.* 89–112.   [8] *Id.* 114–40.   [9] *Id.* 145–55.
[10] *Id.* 160–79.   [11] *Id.* 180–206.   [12] *Id.* 207–36.

[13] *Id.* 228–58. It is uncertain how far the Lollards would have been pacifists in the modern sense of the word. It is very doubtful whether Wyclif would have been a pacifist, but he did say, and even this was unusual and courageous, considering that he was at that time patronised by Gaunt's party and that England had been at war with France, that the king had no right to conquer foreign territory, merely for the sake of dominating that territory. Pecock was to have dealt with the question of war in that part of the *Repressor* which has not survived (*id.* II, 565).

women.[1] Although the book is straightforward and clear, it lacks the systematic argumentation of Pecock as well as the philosophical or theological assumptions on which he bases his general argument.

This is also true, though perhaps less so, of Netter's *Doctrinale*. Netter was a prominent English ecclesiastic, an Oxford scholar 'most learned in the Holy Scriptures' and well versed in Aristotelian philosophy, provincial prior of the Carmelites and confessor to Henry V by whom he was entrusted with many diplomatic missions. As a pupil of one of Wyclif's opponents, Woodford, he was a fervent champion of the Church, actively associating himself with the trials of Oldcastle, Taylor and William White and entering into controversy with Peter Payne and another Oxford scholar, John Luck. His *Doctrinale Antiquitatum Fidei Ecclesie Catholicae contra Wiclevistas et Hussitas*,[2] which was dedicated to Pope Martin V, was a well-argued attack on the Lollard position. He commences by refuting the Lollard dependence on the scriptures. Scripture is not the sole rule of faith, and for that very reason the Pope and the Church are not worthy of condemnation when they put forward statements which are not actually confirmed by Biblical texts. The so-called Lollard simplicity and their contempt for learning is really no more than heretical ignorance and sinful self-centred pride. He then proceeds to a vindication of the hierarchy and the religious orders along the well-established lines of medieval apologia. He later supplemented this book with some work on the sacraments. Netter's argument, contained within the bounds of his erudite books, has greater unity than that of Dymok, but even so Pecock's *Repressor* remains not only more interesting for its theological-historical thought, but also because it formed the most satisfactory answer to Lollard arguments.[3] Thus

---

[1] *Dymok*, 272-90.

[2] Ed. Père Blanciotti, Venice, 1757. A new edition is badly needed. Netter lived *c.* 1376-1430.

[3] In his *England in the Age of Wycliffe*, G. M. Trevelyan writes of Pecock: 'As his book is addressed to the layman, Pecock refrains from brandishing

we may conclude that Pecock's work was important because it was the most satisfactory reply to Lollard arguments, because it was written in the English language and because it was grounded on a partly original philosophy.

Church authorities, as all previous defenders of orthodoxy had done, and adopts the tone, not of a pope speaking "ex cathedrà", but of a man taking his readers into his confidence.' He adds 'the effective part of his argument is purely negative' (345). In his preface to the English translation of the work on *John Wycliffe and his English Precursors* (1884) Professor Gotthard Lechler writes: 'In the summer of 1840, I studied in the University Library of Cambridge the MS. of *Repressor*—the interesting polemical treatise of the rationalising Bishop Pecock....By that perusal I was conducted into the history of the Lollards; and from them I saw myself thrown back upon Wycliffe himself.'

CHAPTER X

PECOCK'S REPLY TO THE LOLLARDS (1)

(a) INTRODUCTION

PECOCK'S *Repressor* was then at once an attack and a defence, a polemic against Lollardy and an apologia on behalf of the Church and in particular of those aspects of the Church which Wyclif and his followers had so bitterly attacked. He wished to show the Lollards the errors of their ways, and why the Church was right, and, what was more, not only to proclaim like their other adversaries that the Church was right but to persuade them that this was so. This is clear from the first chapter of the *Repressor* where Pecock introduces his argument:

And for as miche as after it what is write, Rom. xᵉ.c., manie han *zeel of good wille, but not aftir kunnyng,* and han ther with take upon hem forto vndirnyme and blame openli and scherpli bothe in speche and in writing the clergie of Goddis hool chirche in erthe and forto bere an hond upon the seid clergie that he is gilti in summe gouernauncis as in defautis, whiche gouernauncis tho blamers kunnen not schewe, teche, and proue to be defautis and synnes; and han therbi maad ful miche indignacioun, disturblaunce, cisme, and othere yuelis, forto rise and be contynued in manie persoones bi long tyme of manye ʒeeris.[1]

Pecock therefore proposes to refute his opponents 'bi writing of this present book in the comoun peplis langage pleinli and openli and schortli, and to be clepid *The repressing of over miche wijting the clergie...* that God for his godenes and charite ceese the sooner in the comoun peple such vnwijs and ouerhasti vndirnyming and blamyng maad upon the clergie'.[2] It is the 'vntrewe and

---

[1] *Repressor*, I, 2-3. Cf. *Book of Faith*, 138, where he argues that if Christian clerks do not prepare some intellectual defence of their faith 'the postis and the pilers of oure feith' will be 'so unleernyd and nakid' that 'myche multitude' will follow the Lollards.

[2] *Repressor*, I, 3-4. Later he mentions the 'Wiclifistis' as the last sect in a list of heretics and adds that their views may be ascertained from the 'vii principal gouernauncis touchid and rehercid bi the proces of this present

ouerhasti vndirnyming and blamyng' upon which he fastens and which he seeks to rebuff throughout his work.

He does not differ from Dymok or Netter in his aims except, and this is important, in so far as the method which he adopts to controvert his opponents is persuasive rather than dogmatic. He aims to 'wynne the lay children of the chirche into obedience', so that, 'bi processe of tyme, aftir that this and other bokis schulen be publischid',[1] the wanderers might be brought back into the fold from which they had so long strayed. But he will accomplish this aim by the weapons of reason rather than by force, and he commenced his writing with a clearly formulated viewpoint of which the essential factor was the 'doom of reason', and the necessity for subordinating everything, including the scriptures and faith, to it.

(b) THE LOLLARDS AND THE SCRIPTURES

The authority of scripture was the rock on which later Lollard teaching was founded. The scriptures formed an all-inclusive, divinely inspired book of belief and conduct. Wyclif may well have reached this conclusion through his own intellectual development,[2] but he laid increasing stress on the scriptures in his later works. They are the 'lex Dei et fides ecclesie'.[3] 'Scriptura sacra est praecipua auctoritas cuilibet cristiano et regula fidei et locius perfeccionis humane',[4] a viewpoint that is emphasised time and time again in Wyclif's De Veritate Sacrae Scripturae.

book...and in wors and horribler maner, as it is open in the book of Wiclijf and of othere being of his sect' (II, 501). In another place he mentions 'Bible men' 'to whom and aзens whom this book is principaly maad' (id. I, 85).

[1] Book of Faith, 113. Cf. 'otherwise than bi fier and swerd or hangement; thouз y wole not seie but that the bothe now seid meenys ben good', but it is, at least, better to try persuasion first (id. 139). Cf. St Bernard, In Cant. Cant. LXVI, 12.

[2] 'The value of an English Bible was not the foundation stone in John Wyclif's theory for the reform of the church and state, but the practical measure to which his theories led him, at the end of his life' (M. Deanesly, The Lollard Bible, 1920, 225).

[3] The Bible, he says, is first and highest in religion, is necessary to salvation and is inspired by Christ Himself. 'Ignorare scripturas est ignorare Christum, cum Christus sit scriptura, quam debemus cognoscere' (De Veritate Sacrae Scripturae).   [4] De Veritate Sacrae Scripturae (ed. Buddensieg, 1905), I.

If anything, his followers made more of the authority of scripture than Wyclif himself. Thus the pamphlet *The Holi Prophete David seith*,[1] urged that scripture must be the rule of life for every-body. 'He that redith scriptures of God and wole fynde God, and his good lyuynge is maad as the leght of lampe bifore hise iyen of his herte, and openeth the waie of treuthe.' The Bible alone, then, without the aid of human traditions or laws, scholars or trained interpreters, is an all-sufficient rule for all problems of Church and State. 'They wenen', says Pecock, 'that noo bischop or archideken or doctour or eny other such persoon of the clergie cometh into the trewe and dew vndirstonding of Holi Scripture; and therfore thei trowen that ech bischop and ech such other clerk bileeueth amys and techith amys... [and] thei trowen to the doctrine which thei fynden among hem silf bi studiyng in the Bible oonli.'[2]

The Lollards would not, therefore, accept any ordinance which was not in complete agreement with the teaching of the Bible or was at least confirmed by scripture, for scripture was above all other books.[3] A man could not use his *dominium* rightly unless he understood the scriptures. In Wyclif's *Dialogus sive Speculum Ecclesie Militantis*[4] 'Veritas' continually applies the test of scripture which his opponent 'Mendacium' as carefully evades. All non-biblical literature must therefore rest on the authority of the Bible because in scripture *est omnis veritas*. This is the standard which must be applied to all activities, to papal decrees, laws of the realm, church services, endowments of priests and colleges, and religious orders. Where its application seemed inapt, there the object of the application must be discarded.

---

[1] Printed in M. Deanesly, *The Lollard Bible*, Appendix IV, 445–56.

[2] *Repressor*, I, 102. In the pamphlet *The Holi Prophete David seith*, Purvey, the probable author, advises his readers to 'enquere mekeli of every lerned man...the trewe vndirstondyng of hooli writ, and be thei not obstinat in ther owne wit but gyue credence to wiser men that han the sperit of wisdom and of grace'. This advice was not very general.

[3] Wyclif says: 'Neither the testimony of Augustine nor Jerome nor any other saint should be accepted except in so far as it was based upon scripture.' Pecock would have substituted the word 'reason'. The citation is taken from H. B. Workman, *Wyclif*, II, 150.   [4] Ed. A. W. Pollard (1886).

The Lollards further argued that the interpretation of scripture could be safely left to every true and humble Christian. They 'taken that who euer is a persoon of saluacion schal soone vndir-stonde the trewe meenyng of Holi Scripture...and ferthirmore alle hem which ben bifore clepid knowen men thei holden forto be children of saluacioun or ny3e to saluacioun, and alle othere men and wommen thei holden as erring scheep in perel of perisching'.[1] Wyclif himself had said that 'he that keepeth meek-ness and charity hath the true understanding and perfection of all Holy Writ', for 'Christ did not write His laws on tables or on skins of animals but in the hearts of man'. The expert's evidence was therefore relatively worthless, for even if it contradicted the views of some ignorant laymen, the laymen might well be proved to be ultimately correct.

This attitude, which became more and more noticeable as the Lollard movement left the university halls and became a social revolt, is also embodied in the *De Veritate Sacrae Scripturae* which was written in the spring of 1378. In this book Wyclif attacked the scholastic theologians of his day with his usual vehemence as 'perversi, novelli aut moderni doctores, truncantes et lacerantes scripturas...pseudologi lolium in universitatibus seminantes'. In another work he said that we should not follow glossators like Johannes de Deo, Johannes Andraeae or Johannes Monachus, for they know nothing of the essentials of theology.[2] Earlier ex-positors of the Bible have not approached it with the eye of faith, for it is faith and faith alone which enables the Christian to inter-pret the Divine Message.

It was then an integral step from the Lollard emphasis on scrip-ture to the Lollard emphasis on faith. The Lollards have reverted to the Augustinian position, for although, like St Augustine, they do not under-estimate the importance of the reasoning faculties,

---

[1] *Repressor*, 1, 54. Cf. 'Thei seien thus, that what euer man or woman wole be meke in spirit and wole preie god helpe him, schal withoute faile vndir-stonde ech partie of holy scripture' (*Reule*, 17).

[2] *De Potestate Pape* (ed. J. Loserth, 1907).

they inevitably make everything subordinate to faith. Reason (*ratio*), Wyclif himself admitted, is with revelation or authority one of the bases upon which the body of divine truth is built. In his earlier works he had identified reason with the innate moral law of man, the *lex naturae* on which indeed all other laws, including some of the commandments of Christ Himself, must implicitly rest.[1] This viewpoint is, however, not only overshadowed in his later works by his emphasis on the inspired authority of scripture, which overrides all human traditions and to which all laws are inescapably subordinate, but it is also qualified by his theology. Faith and reason do not contradict each other, but the efficacy of man's reason has been lessened by his fall from grace. Reason is, therefore, a less sure means of arriving at divine truth than the revelation which is imparted to men through the scriptures. It has the *certitudo adhaesionis* of which medieval theologians were accustomed to speak when writing on faith. Thus although Wyclif's view of reason is not dissimilar to the view put forward by the scholastic theologians of his time, he differed from them in making the Bible—and implicitly faith—the rule and standard of belief and conduct.

His followers, educated in a less intellectual environment, laid their whole emphasis on faith and the scriptures. The law of scripture was for them an absolute law:

In this trowing and holding thei ben so kete and so smert and so wantoun, that whanne euer eny clerk affermeth to hem eny gouernaunce being contrarie to her witt or pleasaunce, thouȝ it ligge ful open and ful sureli in doom of resoun, and therfore sureli in moral lawe of kinde, which is lawe of God, forto to be doon; ȝit thei anoon asked 'Where groundist thou it in the Newe Testament?'

If the answer is 'no' 'thei it dispisen and not receyuen as a gouernaunce of Goddis seruice and of Goddis moral lawe'.[2]

The Bible was, then, an absolutely infallible book, inspired and

[1] *De Civili Dominio* (ed. J. Loserth, 1900), II, cap. 13: 'De quanto aliqua lex ducit propinquius ad conformitatem legis naturae est ipsa perfectior. Sed lex Christi patiendi injurias propinquius ducit ad statum naturae quam civilis. Ergo ista cum suis regulis est lege civili perfectior.'

[2] *Repressor*, I, 5–6. Cf. *id.* I, 7.

unerring, all sufficient and all embracing, which should be taught to the people in the language that they know best. It was the only law, so they argued, which the Church possessed, and it should therefore be believed by all Christians in simplicity of faith and heart. Even the Old Testament writers can claim to have an 'objective' authority because they have spoken the word of God by an *interna inspiracio*. Where it seems to err, the fault lies not in the text but in the expositor—*falsitas non est in scriptura sed in falsa intelligente*. In fine, the Lollard argument was based on the supremacy of faith over reason.

Pecock's answer to these Lollard arguments turned on the relative merits of faith or the scriptures and the 'doom of reason'. He believed that faith and the scriptures must be subordinated to the 'doom of reason' or the law of kind:

The hool office and werk into which God ordeyned Holi Scripture is forto grounde articlis of feith and forto reherce and witnesse moral trouthis of lawe of kinde groundid in moral philsophie, that is to seie in doom of resoun, that the reders be remembrid, stirid, and exortid bi so miche the better and the more and the sooner forto fulfille hem.[1]

Thus from the very start we have a fundamental answer to Wyclif's theology in Pecock's 'doom of reason'.

(*c*) FAITH AND REASON IN THE MIDDLE AGES

Before we analyse Pecock's reply to the Lollard arguments, we must interpolate a reference to the history of faith and reason in the Middle Ages. For it is clear that if Pecock's reply to Lollard arguments cannot be rightly understood without first analysing the Lollard point of view, it is equally clear that his importance in the history of European thought cannot be rightly adjudged without some reference to what had gone before.

The conception of faith and reason in the earlier Middle Ages was completely dominated by the thought of St Augustine and, through Augustine, of Plato. St Augustine's religious thought

---

[1] *Repressor*, I, 35.

was directed to the 'Vision of God',[1] and his ideas can only be rightly understood within the compass of his religious mysticism. God is the highest being of which we can think.[2] He contains the highest virtues and the noblest ideas. He is the eternal reason. Man can approach the fount of life by faith—the assenting to an idea[3]—and by reason. St Augustine implied that faith rather than reason was the key to divine knowledge,[4] but he did not neglect to assign the reasoning faculties to their proper place in the search for truth. The human reason perceives that there is something greater and nobler than itself. He further agreed that if we believe certain things we believe them because they are essentially reasonable. Yet all the sciences, including dialectic, are only of value in so far as they serve man's final end. He also explained that there are many ignorant men who can answer questions relating to matters of faith correctly. They were enabled to do this by participation in the divine illumination, the *lumen increatum*. St Augustine's influence was so great in the Middle Ages as to be almost incapable of definition, but he remained above all, in words which Thomas Bradwardine used, 'the true apostolic logician and philosopher'.

The rise of rival schools of thought, of realists and nominalists, in the tenth[5] and eleventh centuries, led to a dialectical treatment

---

[1] 'Deum et animam scire cupio. Nihilne plus? Nihilomnino' (*Solil.* 1, 7). This is also the teaching of the *City of God*.

[2] *De Vera Rel.* 57; *De Trin.* VIII, 3. Cf. *De Div.* qu. 46; *De Ideis*, 2: 'Sunt namque ideae principales formae quaedam vel rationes rerum stabiles et incommutabiles, quae ipsae formatae non sunt atque per hoc aeternae ac semper eodem modo se habentes, quae in divina intelligentia continentur, et quum ipsae neque oriantur neque intereant, secundum eas tamen formari dicitur omne, quod interire potest et omne, quod oritur et interit.'

[3] 'Cum assensione cogitare' (*De Praedest. Sanct.* 5).

[4] *On the Gospel of St John*, xxix, 6 (trans. H. Browne, J. H. Parker (Lib. of the Fathers, 1848, 1, 440)): 'Understanding is the reward of faith. Therefore seek not to understand that thou mayest believe, but believe that thou mayest understand.' Cf. 'Aderit enim Deus, et nos intelligere quod credidimus, faciet. Praescriptum enim per prophetam gradum, qui ait Nisi credideritis, non intelligetis (Isaiah viii, 9) tenere nos, bene nobis conscii sumus' (*De Lib. Arb.* 1, 4).

[5] John Scotus Erigena in the ninth century is a solitary but important figure. He affirmed the identity of true philosophy and theology on the

of fundamental dogmas of the Church and necessarily opened up
the question of the relationship between faith and reason. Many
of the writers of the period, like the monkish reformer Peter
Damian,[1] were suspicious of the use of dialectic and tried to dis-
courage their pupils from applying it to matters of faith. Thus
Bishop Hildebert of Tours (1057—*c.* 1133) emphasised faith as
opposed to reason which he, like his other contemporaries,
identified with dialectic. God willed that He might be only partly
comprehended in order that some merit might be attached to
faith. He defined faith as 'voluntaria certitudo absentium, supra
opinionem et infra scientiam constituta'.[2]

The realist school of thought, with its belief in universals, was
less likely to challenge the authority of the Church, for it treated
logic and dialectic as, in Damian's words, 'the useful but docile
handmaid'. The nominalists, on the other hand, were far more
inclined to give an important place to reason. The danger of pay-
ing too much attention to dialectic in opposition to authority is
seen in the life of Berengar of Tours (999–1088), whose zeal for
logic led him to formulate heretical views on the Eucharist and to
an unhappy controversy with Lanfranc.[3] But in fact the dialecti-
cians themselves never thought of giving faith and reason an equal
potency. The extraordinarily learned Gerbert, who mounted the
papal throne as Pope Sylvester II, wrote a book on the use

authority of St Augustine. Influenced by his reading of Greek philosophy and
by the opinions which he based upon it, he made very much more use of
reason than any of his contemporaries. He pays due respect to authority, in
the form of the Fathers and the Bible, but reason is superior to revelation, in
the sense that it is the truer interpreter of revelation. It must be remembered
that John's thought was powerfully coloured by a kind of mystic pantheism.
Cf. 'Intellect...and the rest of things that are said to be, are theophanies, and
in theophany really subsist; therefore God is everything that truly is, since he
makes all things and is made in all things' (*De Div. Nat.* cap. IV, p. 103 ff.
Cited in R. L. Poole, *Illustrations of Medieval Thought and Learning*, 59).

[1] 'Quae tamen artis humanae peritia si quando tractandis sacris eloquiis
adhibetur, non debet jus magisterii sibimet arroganter arripere, sed velut
ancilla dominae quodam famulatus obsequio subservire, ne si praecedit,
oberret' (*Opusc.* XXXVI, 5).

[2] *Opera*, ed. Beaugendre (1708), 1010.

[3] A. J. Macdonald, *Berengar of Tours* (1930).

of the reason,[1] but his discussion was dialectical rather than theological.

Thus the Augustinian conception of faith, which subordinated reason to faith, dominated medieval theology until the end of the Renaissance of the twelfth century. There was as yet no clearly defined demarcation between the provinces of philosophy and theology, of reason and faith. The famous formula 'credo ut intelligam'[2] gives the clue both to the thought of Anselm and his contemporaries and to their debt to St Augustine. Following Augustine and indeed surpassing him Anselm believed that all knowledge must be based on faith. He argued that as experience can only be based on faith, so understanding can only be based on experience.[3] One must therefore proceed from faith in order to arrive at understanding. The root of faith, he said in the *Monologium*, is 'credere in Deum'. There were of course distinctions between Anselm and Augustine, in their definition of reason and the reasoning faculty. Anselm and his followers identified reason with logic, the use of dialectic with syllogistic thought. Reason was to be chiefly used to examine the reasonableness of the faith. Yet his very emphasis on reason as seen in the famous ontological argument, in which Anselm tried to put forward a strictly philosophical argument for the existence of God, shows the way in which dialectic was making an inroad into theology. He tried to establish the dogmas of faith and of the existence of God, the Trinity and the Incarnation by means of natural reason or dialectic. Thus while scripture was still the foundation and faith the house of God, reason or dialectic was employed to interpret and to ascertain the truths which faith revealed.

There were, however, signs that reason was beginning to tire of its subordination to faith; yet we must not over-estimate the process. Abailard[4] is the outstanding figure, for although 'it would

---

[1] *De Rationali et Ratione Uti.*

[2] Anselm, *Proslogion*, I, I.   [3] *De Fide Trinitatis*, 3.

[4] Abailard has been compared to Pecock (Jeremy Collier, *Ecclesiastical History*, ed. Barham, III, 391), but beyond a very vague likeness their careers and thoughts have nothing very much in common and the comparison is misleading.

be a mistake', as Dr Harris says, 'to regard him as a rationalist in the modern sense of the word',[1] he did aim, in the words of his biographer, 'to use dialectic both as an instrument by which he could disprove the errors of contemporary heretics and as a method of explaining to his students the meaning of the Catholic faith'.[2] Abailard deals with faith and reason in three of his books, the *De Trinitate*, the *Theologia Christiana* and the *Introductio ad Theologiam*. The views which he puts forward in the first two books are pre-eminently orthodox. He emphasises the inability of human reason to explain sacred mysteries and quotes with approval Gregory's famous words: 'faith hath no merit to which man's reason gives sure proof'.[3] Human reason was a god-given means for the refutation of logicians and heretics. The third of the books in which he treats of the problem of faith and reason is less conciliatory, for he attacks ultra-conservatives like St Bernard who

---

[1] C. R. S. Harris, *Duns Scotus* (1927), I, 47.

[2] J. G. Sikes, *Peter Abailard* (1932), 45. Mr Sikes pointed out that Abailard was only trying to justify the reasonableness of Christianity, viz.: 'unde etiam cum per insigne rationis imaginis Dei specialiter homo comparetur, in nihil aliud homo pronius eam figere debuerat, quam in ipsum cujus imaginem, hoc est expressiorem similitudinem, per hanc obtinebat et in nullam fortasse rem percipiendam pronior esse credenda est, quam in eam cujus ipsa amplius adepta sit similitudinem' (*Introd.* iii, col. 1086 C, cited Sikes, *op. cit.* 48). Abailard had great faith in the efficacy of logic, which, he said, quoting Augustine, 'potest facere scientia', and again 'disciplina disciplinarum...haec docet docere, haec docet discere'. He suggested that the dignity of logic was made manifest by its etymological connexion with the divine Logos (Sikes cites Ep. XIII, col. 355 BC).

[3] 'We know that very often in his writings St Gregory used to teach the resurrection to those who had doubts about it, by reasoning with suitable examples and analogies; yet he said in the foregoing that "nec fides habet meritum, qui humana ratio praebet experimentum". Those whom he wished to build up in the faith of the resurrection were not able to refute his reasoning according to his own opinions, by which indeed he is said to have taught that matters of faith must never be discussed by human reason, although the very man who is said to have taught this, did actually use reason. But he did not say that the faith ought not to be reasoned about, nor that it should be discussed and investigated, but only that faith has no merit with God, when it is not the testimony of divine authority that leads us to it, but the evidence of human reason that completes our assent' (*Introd.* col. 1050 CD, cited in Sikes, *op. cit.* p. 53). The reference is to Gregory I, *Homil. in Evang.* XXVI, Migne, *P.L.* LXXVI, 1197 C.

rely on authority and authority alone. Yet Abailard's position remained orthodox, even if there were some indications of a critical spirit. This, for instance, is seen in the *Sic et Non* where he reveals his independence of patristic writers and implies that the canon of scripture itself is the only ultimately true authority. It is also seen in his statement that we must understand the faith before we believe it. 'Dubitando enim ad inquisitionem venimus, inquirendo veritatem percipe.'[1] It is, concludes Dr Poole, 'his general attitude towards the study of philosophy and of theology that demands our examination, far rather than those technical points in which he was suspected of departing from catholic Christianity....It is not that he doubts that the two roads, of reason and authority, must ultimately converge: only he will not start from any but the direct questionings of his own mind.'[2]

The position remained, however, pre-eminently Augustinian right up to the rediscovery of Aristotle's works. At the end of his *Metalogicon*, John of Salisbury compares and contrasts the Eternal Reason, which is infallible, with the human reason which has been weakened by man's fall from grace. In his *Entheticus* he pointed out that man's reason partook to some extent at least of the divine reason.[3] The mystical writers, of whom St Bernard of Clairvaux was the most characteristic, scorned knowledge unless it was associated with edification or devotion, and relied on the Augustinian 'divine illumination'. Thus Hugh of St Victor (1096–1141) held that the 'uncorrupted truth of things cannot be discovered by reasoning'. He believed that profane knowledge must neces-

---

[1] *Sic et Non* (ed. Henke and Lindenkohl, 1851), prol. 17.
[2] R. L. Poole, *Illustrations of Medieval Thought and Learning*, 116.
[3] *Id.* 196: 'Est hominis ratio summae rationis imago
    Quae capit interius vera docente Deo.
    Ut data lux oculis tam se quam cetera monstrat
    Quae sub luce patent et sine luce latent,
    Claraque fit nubes concepto lumine solis,
    Cum dependentes flatus abegit aquas:
    Subdita sic ratio formam summae rationis
    Sordibus expulsis induit, inde micat.'

                    (*Entheticus*, ver. 629–36.)

sarily subserve sacred knowledge. Faith itself is a form of certitude relating to beliefs or things not present which is more than opinion, and less than knowledge, and although it is cognitively speaking less satisfactory than knowledge it conveys more merit. Both he and his pupil Richard St Victor held that mystical contemplation is superior to *imaginatio* and *ratio*. The Franciscan order in particular inherited the Augustinian tradition. One of their greatest representatives, Roger Bacon, had little patience with syllogistic reasoning, but he held that faith and reason were interrelated sciences and that philosophy was subordinate to theology.[1] St Bonaventura's conception of the nature of knowledge was entirely mystical and may be summed up in the words of Isaiah, 'nisi credideritis non intelligetis'. Thus he postulates three definite approaches to knowledge, simple assent (i.e. faith), rational evidence (i.e. understanding), and simple intuition (i.e. purity of heart), but all three are definitely subordinate to the divine illumination, the *lumen intellectuale*.

The Augustinian tradition was also represented in the heterodox mysticism of the curious Spanish writer and missionary, Raymond Lull. His ideas on faith and reason were pre-eminently orthodox. Faith, he said, 'ascendit super intellectum, sicut oleum ascendit super aquam', and is necessarily in agreement with the understanding, for they together form the two feet of a man's mind, each being equally necessary to the other.[2]

The rediscovery of Aristotle's works and the use which the rationalising Averroists[3] made of them led to the great synthesis of philosophy and theology, of reason and faith, in the *Summa Theologica* and *Summa contra Gentiles* of St Thomas Aquinas. The

---

[1] He held that 'a knowledge of the Bible in the original' was the 'true foundation for a fruitful study of theology' (Rashdall, *Univ. Mid. Ages*, III, 245). Hence his attitude to the study of Greek and Hebrew: 'Theology and philosophy must be studied philologically and historically.' He was a great believer in the verbal inspiration of the Bible, holding that every new discovery had been anticipated in the Bible (Little, *Roger Bacon*, 25).

[2] *Ars Magna*, cap. 63, cited in F. Allison Peers, *Ramon Lull* (1929), p. 403.

[3] *Vide* E. Renan, *Averroès et l'Averroïsme* (Paris, 1852); P. Mandonnet, *Siger de Brabant et l'averroïsme latin au xiii siècle* (1911).

Church was at first very suspicious of the new Aristotelian thought. The Council of Corbeil, which met in 1210, forbade anyone to read the writings of Aristotle and the *Commentaries* of Averroës. In 1228, Pope Gregory IX writing to the masters of theology at Paris reproved them for making too much of reason and quoted the famous dictum of Gregory the Great with approval; but the floodgates of knowledge were open and the Church was unable to withstand the inrush. By 1240 the Church had acquiesced in the introduction of Aristotelian thought in the universities, for within a decade many of his books were presented as text-books for the teachers in the university.

Thus the old theory of knowledge, with its doctrine of innate ideas and divine illumination, was gradually replaced by Aristotelian empiricism and the doctrine of the *intellectus agens*, both of which were derived from Aristotle's doctrine of *nous* as laid down in the *De Anima*.[1] The provinces of theology and philosophy were now made distinct and carefully defined. Albertus Magnus excluded certain fundamentals of faith from 'the sphere of things knowable by the light of reason',[2] and in this he was followed by his great pupil, St Thomas Aquinas. St Thomas himself naturally affirms that there are certain fundamentals which can only be based on revelation and which cannot be approached by natural reason. 'It is impossible', he says, 'for the natural reason to arrive at the knowledge of the divine persons. By natural reason we may know those things which pertain to the unity of the divine essence, but not those which pertain to the distinction of the divine persons, and he who attempts to prove by the natural reason the trinity of persons, detracts from the rights of faith.'[3] These truths do not contradict the natural reason and reason can indeed play an important part in refuting arguments which are opposed to the truths of faith, and, in confirming, so far as logical

[1] The *De Anima* was translated from the Greek in the twelfth century, from the Arabic, with Averroës, by Michael Scot.

[2] 'Et ex lumine quidem connaturali non elevatur ad scientiam trinitatis et incarnationis et resurrectionis' (*Summa Theologica*, Opp. XVII, 6).

[3] *Summa Theologica*, I, qu. 32, art. 1.

arguments are capable of being so used, the truths delivered to man by divine revelation.[1] The reason acquiesces in these truths and itself plays a notable part in building up the structure of Christian doctrine, because the *preambula fidei* are certainly contained within its province. Reason is supreme in the world of sense and feeling and can itself prove the existence and entitative attributes of God. Thus whilst rational knowledge is humanly speaking more certain than faith, faith has the merit of being guaranteed by God Himself. In these ways 'naturalis ratio subservit fidei'. The careful synthesis of theology and philosophy[2] which St Thomas achieved in his *Summae* has never entirely lost its relevance, but it was unlikely that the harmony between faith and reason which had been achieved should go unchallenged for very long.

The reaction to Thomist thought, the nominalist or quasi-nominalist movement embodied in the thought and philosophy of Duns Scotus and William of Occam, reaffirmed this emphasis on faith and was inclined to divorce faith from reason. Duns Scotus was one of the earliest writers to challenge the Thomist solution. He identified the *lumen intellectuale* with the *intellectus agens*. In his *Opus Oxoniense* he affirmed that man needed a supernatural form of knowledge, which could not be vouchsafed by the natural light

[1] Cf. '"The light of reason within us is able to show us good things, and guides our will, in so far as it is the light of Thy countenance." It is therefore evident that the goodness of the human will depends on the eternal law much more than on the human reason, and when therefore human reason fails we must have recourse to the Eternal Reason' (*Sum. Theol.* IIa, qu. 19. art. 4. Resp.).

[2] The following quotation from M. Etienne Gilson is to the point: 'In Thomism alone we have a system in which philosophic conclusions are deduced from purely rational premisses. Theology remains in its proper place... at the head of the hierarchy of the sciences; based on divine revelation, from which it receives its principles, it constitutes a distinct science starting from faith and turning to reason only to draw out the content of faith or to protect it from error. Philosophy doubtless is subordinate to theology, but, as philosophy, it depends on nothing but its own proper method; based on human reason, owing all its truths to the self-evidence of its principles and the accuracy of its deductions, it reaches an accord with faith spontaneously' (*The Spirit of Medieval Philosophy*, 6).

of reason, to achieve his end, the *beatitudo Dei*. He describes theology as a practical science, and while he concedes that belief has, cognitively speaking, less certainty than knowledge, he shows that faith is more intrinsically important than reason for the realisation of divine truths.

William of Occam takes Duns Scotus's arguments very much further. He held that all knowledge which transcends the sphere of experience cannot be approached by reason and is therefore comprised within the meaning of the word 'faith'. He denied that either the unity or existence of God can be demonstrated by the natural reason. He also added that theology cannot be strictly speaking called a science, at any rate for human minds. He rejected the cosmological arguments put forward by Thomas Aquinas in the *Summa contra Gentiles*, and so far eradicated the sphere of natural theology that we are left with the theology of revelation alone. His theory is additionally imperilled by the voluntarism which characterised Scotist and Occamist thought. Religious truths must therefore be grounded on faith to such an extent that they are meaningless to those 'pro sapientibus mundi et praecipue innitentibus rationi naturali'. Faith was then the only guarantee of religious certitude.

Thus although it was the Lollard emphasis on faith which evoked Pecock's reaction and peculiar philosophy of 'faith and reason', Pecock's thought is intimately related to the intellectual development in these matters in medieval Europe and can only be rightly understood and properly adjudged against the particular, and Lollard, and the general, and scholastic, backgrounds.

(d) FAITH IN THE WORKS OF BISHOP PECOCK

Pecock agreed with the Lollards that scripture was essentially the basis of faith or revelation. 'Dyuynyte', he says in the *Repressor*, 'groundith articles of feith . . . trouthis and conclusions reuelid and affermed bi God to be trewe.'[1] Pecock did not under-estimate the

---

[1] *Repressor*, I, 33.

importance which scripture must naturally have in the Christian religion. A citation from his *The Reule of Chrysten Religioun* indicates his viewpoint:

the text of holy scripture in the bible, to which with herte and mouth and werk y wole ʒeue reverence and to whom y wole goodnes ʒeve and ascrive aboue alle othere mennes writingis into the eende and purpos oonly into which he was principaly ordeyned and writen, that is to seie into denouncing, teching, reueling and schewing to vs tho trouthis and articlis into whos knowing men mowe not come bi laboure of natural resonyng, whiche trouthis and articles ben therfore knowun of vs bi feith oonly. But certis this excellent reuerence wole y not ʒeve to holy scripture above alle othere writyngis of men for the tretyng or techyng or declaracioun of eny article or of eny trouthe in natural lawe of kynde or in moral lawe of kinde of which mencioun and remembraunce is maad in holy scripture.[1]

Thus he qualified his opinion by saying that in general scripture was subordinate to the 'law of kind'. In one place[2] he suggests that the fundamentals of faith are less subordinate to the law of reason than other biblical matters, but the general inference to be gained from Pecock's writings indicates that the scriptures must be entirely reasonable if they are to be believed. Where the Bible is dealing with supernatural matters 'so hiʒe and digne and harde that to hem natural resoun may not atteyne, thouʒ noon of hem ben aʒens resoun',[3] the interpretation must be in accordance with reason.

Scriptural truth may itself be divided into two sections, that which teaches and reveals truths of faith and that which teaches and confirms truths of reason. The first section cannot be wholly subordinate to reason—so, too, St Thomas Aquinas and other orthodox writers—but it must be interpreted reasonably. The second section marks the complete subordination of scriptural truth to reasonable truth: 'of al thi now seid moral seruice of God, Holi Scripture is oonli a witnesser and a rehercer, and takith it out

[1] *Reule*, 9–10.   [2] *Id.* 462.   [3] *Id.* 461.

and fro moral lawe of kinde and out of moral philsophie.'[1] It ought to 'be drawe to resoun and not resoun to it, for certis the lawe of kynde is in thilk maters souereyn aboue it and the lawe of scripture in thilk maters was ordeyned to be seruaunt and helping or ellis remembring into the lawe of kynde'.[2] Such is the preface to Pecock's discussion on faith.

Faith is defined by Pecock as that species of knowledge which a man does not gain from his 'natural witt', but from 'another person which may not lie, or who is God',[3] or as he defines it in the *Donet* 'a knowing of thingis and trouthis denouncid, affermed, reuelid and schewid to vs fro god and bi god, what god is, and what othire thingis ben longing to god, and that for as moche as thilk knowing may not be had of vs bi natural power oonly, without such denouncing and certifying from aboue'.[4] Faith is therefore different from 'other kindis and spicis of kunnyngis, which a man gendrith and getith into his understonding bi bisynes and labour of his natural resoun, bi biholding upon the causis or effectis or circumstauncis in nature of the conclusioun or trouthe, and withoute eny attendaunce maad to eny sure teller or denouncer, that thilk conclusion is a treuthe'.[5]

Faith like the scriptures on which it is based plays an important part in the religion of the Christian man because the fundamentals of our belief, the birth of our Lord 'ȝitt man and God' through the Virgin Mary, for instance, must inevitably rest upon it.[6] 'The thre persoonys in godhede, y brynge forth auctorite of feith writun in holi scripture, of whiche scripture alle cristen ouȝten take her feith.'[7] Reason, he admits, is mainly concerned with our behaviour in this life, and cannot, for instance, prove the immortality of the soul, which is an essential element in the Christian religion re-

---

[1] *Repressor*, 1, 79. Cf. 'Forwhi alle tho trouthis and conclusions Holi Writt takith and borewith out of moral lawe of kinde, and ben not hise as bi grounding, and founding, and prouyng, but oonli bi rehercing, witnessing, and denouncing' (*id*. 82).   [2] *Reule*, 464.
[3] *Id*. 425: 'Feith is a knowing as alle men witen.' Cf. *Book of Faith*, 123, 163.
[4] *Donet*, 108. Cf. *Folewer*, 168.
[5] *Book of Faith*, 124.   [6] *Id*. 123.   [7] *Reule*, 23.

vealed by faith.[1] He deals with certain specific fundamentals of
the Christian religion which are based on revelation in the *Reule*:
the creation of the world in six days, the fall of man, the redemption of man through Jesus Christ and the use of the sacraments.
But he differentiates between these truths by calling some of them
reasonably certain and some probable truths.[2] Thus Pecock does
not at any time deny the necessity of faith but he beats the bounds
with certain qualifications which challenge its importance and
even reduce its significance.

Thus faith is either opinional or sciential, that is, it is either
based on opinion or science, but the difference is really one of
degree of verity rather than of principle. Thus if it is opinional
it is a likely truth based on evidence which may be assumed to be
true, whereas if it is sciential it is founded on evidence which is
almost bound to be true.[3] Sciential faith must exist in Heaven,
since opinional faith, which was the form of faith held by the
Apostles, will no longer exist inasmuch as opinion has been replaced by assured fact. Pecock distinguishes between sciential
and opinional faith as follows:

If a treuthe be knowe sureli and sikirli, thanne thilk kunnyng
or knowing is woned be clepid intellect, science, craft or prudence.
And if a treuthe be knowun oonli bi probabilnes and likelihode
and not sureli, thanne thilk kunnyng or knowing is woned be
clepid opinioun vpon the mater of science, craft or prudence.…
If a treuthe which we mowe not knowe in the now bifore seid
maner bi doom of resoun, withoute assercioun of an other trewe
persoun, be knowen in mannys vndirstonding bi the seid assercioun or witnessing of a trewe persoun, which assercioun is the
ground of feith; thanne it is knowe bi assercioun or witnessing
of God doon bi his Holi Scripture, or bi eeldist and lengist vce of
bileeuyng in the Chirche, or bi godli myracle doon into witnessing of it, or bi speeche of God doon bi him silf, or bi his suer
messanger withoute writing; and in ech of these caasis the
knowing is holi feith or goostili feith.[4]

---

[1] *Reule*, 26.   [2] *Id.* 203 ff.
[3] *Folewer to the Donet*, 63. Cf. *Book of Faith*, 140–4.
[4] *Repressor*, 133.

Such faith must in any case be essentially reasonable or as Pecock calls it 'feith allowable bi resoun'.[1] So far there is nothing very much to differentiate Pecock from previous writers on this subject. They too would have agreed with what he had to say on excessive and unreasonable faith, but some of Pecock's conclusions were of a far-reaching nature. He urges that many of the deeds which have been done by holy men, the vow of 'jepte, the slauȝtir of sampson, the fiȝt of dauid aȝens goly, the lesing of jacob to his fadir, the thombe kuting of seint Mark...and the goyng of maure vpon the ryuer'[2] are not morally virtuous deeds, and must not be followed by men because they are therefore essentially unreasonable. He says in extenuation of this that if we were aware of the circumstances, the actions might appear more reasonable, but, lacking that knowledge, we must conclude that they were based on an unreasonable faith.[3] 'Whanne euere eny seyntis teching or exaumpling sowneth or semeth aȝens thi lawe maad of lawe of kinde and of feith reuelat in scripture, thou forbede, lord, but that we refuse it.'[4] For this reason scripture passages[5] which would seem to warrant exceptional faith of this nature are liable to misinterpretation. It is true that Christ tested the disciples' faith, but their faith was guaranteed by Christ's direct command[6] and by the miracles which they had witnessed with their own eyes. In itself, our faith is therefore all the greater because we have not these self-same guarantees,[7] and we must accordingly exercise our faith according to reason. The reason for excessive faith is partly psychological, the presence of 'sum vnkinde humour...domynacioun of malencolie in sum notable membre of mannys body'.[8]

---

[1] *Donet*, 14.   [2] *Reule*, 449.

[3] He suggests that although God may not have approved of their actions, they were pardoned by him: 'thei mowe wel be considerid, wondrid and examyned, but not folewid' (*id.* 450).   [4] *Id.* 450.

[5] E.g. Matt. viii, 10; Matt. xv, 28; Matt. xvii, 20; Mk. ix, 23, etc.

[6] E.g. Matt. xvii, 27—when our Lord commanded St Peter to fish, promising him that he would catch a fish with a golden piece in its mouth.

[7] *Reule*, 452.

[8] *Reule*, 459. He also said that an unreasonable faith cannot be founded on 'allegorik or tropologik' exposition of scripture (*id.* 457).

Human decisions on matters of faith can be safeguarded from error by the body of faith enshrined in the Catholic Church, 'the comoun faith...clepid catholik'.[1] It is the lack of this which Christ censured and which must immediately arouse our suspicions; 'alle suche singuler feelingis in the vndirstonding and movingis in the affeccioun whiche ben not vniuersal in summe men of alle maner complexioun ben to be hold suspect and not liȝtli to be folewid'.[2]

But reason is an even surer test of the truth of revelation. In contradistinction to St Gregory[3] he holds that the nearer faith approximates to the 'law of reason' the more certain becomes the evidence for its truth,[4] the greater the merit of belief. To 'bileeve withoute evydence is unresonable, and therfore unvertuose and so demeritorie'.[5] True faith is dependent then in the first instance on adequate evidence.[6] Thus St Thomas Didymus was not rebuked because he saw fit to criticise but because he continued to be credulous in the face of perfectly adequate evidence. Faith must be tested before it can be believed 'by the natural sensitive wittis and oure natural resoun', for such credulity would otherwise be an insult to our intellect.

If thou seie that thou hast noon euydencis sufficiently mouyng thee forto so bileeue, certis thanne thou maist not it bileeue, fforwi oure vndirstonding or resoun may not consente to eny thing it to be trewe but if therto be euydencis forto so consente mouyng, ȝhe and compeling.[7]

The clergy, as Pecock avers, have neglected to gather such evidence together into a persuasive testimony, with the result that

---

[1] Id. 453.   [2] Id. 460. Cf. Book of Faith, 170, 181.

[3] Gregory I, Homil. in Evang. XXVI; P.L. LXXVI, 1197 C.

[4] 'It folowith herof that a man schulde labore aftir to have manye evydencis to eche article of the feith, rather than to stoond to oon or tweyne evydencis oonli' (Book of Faith, 144).

[5] Book of Faith, 149.   [6] Cf. id. 128–9, 140–4.

[7] Reule, 444. Cf. 'The examynacioun...ouȝte not to be maad go and falle upon the natural meenys...as ben natural causis,...effectis...circumstauncis of the same article...but...to be maad go and renne upon tho meenys whiche witnessen so likli God to haue schewid, or have affermed thilk article to be trewe, that no meenes ben had or likeli ben hopid to be had forto schewe so likli the contrarie' (Book of Faith, 134).

a great many Mohammedans and Jews have for a long time remained unconvinced of the truths of the Christian faith.[1]

The cause whi jewis and hethen men bileeuen not the feith of cristenhode is that thei haue not tho now spoken off argumentis to hem mynystrid and not to her resoun representid with sufficient tariaunce vpon hem.[2]

Peter Alfonso, a Spanish Jew who became a convert to Christianity through his examination and comparison of the truths of Jewish, Saracenic and Christian literature, is the one exception to this rule.[3]

Thus 'all werkis doon for feithis sake muste also be doon bi sum maner doom of resoun'. This phrase is constantly and even monotonously repeated by the bishop in all his books.[4] Whatever is accepted by faith must be proved acceptable to the reason, so that 'oure natural resoun hath such an interesse to feith that without doom of oure natural resoun feith may not in vs be gendrid neithir contynued, neithir eny article of the feith may of vs be knowe or take for trewe'.[5]

In conclusion, Pecock would admit that reason is the more certain form of knowledge and provides a basis for the judgement by which faith is both accepted and interpreted, but this need not, so he would say, diminish the significance of the truths vouch-

---

[1] *Book of Faith*, 130 ff.   [2] *Reule*, 429. Cf. *Book of Faith*, 138.
[3] *Book of Faith*, 136.
[4] Cf. 'Doom of resoun muste trie, examyne and iuge bi argument of open sure sillogisme, takyng euydencis from the significacioun of the wordis and from the circumstauncis of the processe bifore goyng and aftir folewyng, or from othire placis of scripture therto biholdyng' (*Folewer to the Donet*, 66). 'Whether eny of these poyntis or eny othir such poynt or article ou3te to be bileeuyd of vs bi feith or no, oure resoun muste deme' (*id.* 74).
'Law of kinde is oure lawe, and if ne were the reuelaciouns of articlis it schulde be al oure hool lawe' (*Reule*, 448).
'Natural resoun' is the 'most conuenient exposicioun' of scripture (*Reule*, 464).
'How schulde or my3te we wite that this article or thilk article is of vs to be taken and to be allowid for feith' or alternatively disallowed unless 'the doom of oure resoun hadde place to juge in sum maner aboute the maters of oure feith, whether thei ben trewe or no' (*Reule*, 425).
[5] *Folewer to the Donet*, 74.

safed by faith. Faith is well-nigh supreme in its own province. In matters of pure revelation 'we schulen ȝeue wel nyȝe ful credence to the precise literal pretencioun of holi writt, and drawe oure resoun and compelle our resoun into obeischaunce of it, and noon exposicioun therupon make but if it be to make accordaunce bitwene thilk party and othere parties of holi writt'.[1] It is possible, even probable, that in the eternal life all will be known by the 'light of reason', for faith can never subsist side by side with the certainty which is so much more satisfactory than mere probability. On the other hand, it is not possible to deny that Pecock puts very much more store by the 'light of reason' than by faith. Like St Thomas Aquinas he has attempted to synthetise reason and revelation into a single strand, but the synthesis does not really form a true harmony. Pecock thought of faith and reason as the two sides of a single whole. Man was created by God to live 'after the doom of resoun or of feith allowable bi resoun', so that he may obtain everlasting life.[2] The moral virtues by which he governs himself are 'iugid and deemyd of resoun or feith', whether they are commandment or counsels. But in the long run it is reason which outstrips faith in the argument.

(e) REASON IN THE WORKS OF BISHOP PECOCK

Pecock not only rebuffed the Lollard emphasis on faith and the Bible. He went one step further, and in so doing not only prepared the way for his own fate, but made a small niche for himself in the history of fifteenth-century thought. This is clearly what differentiates his thought from that of the other adversaries of Lollardy. He has undermined and even controverted the fundamental strength of the Lollard position, i.e. their confidence in

---

[1] *Reule*, 461. Cf. It 'folewith that oure resoun may not iuge and deme and telle to vs that this or thilk article is to be taken for feith more than eny other poynt or article is to be taken for feith and that we ouȝte beleeue thilk article and so ech other article, withoute this that oure resoun haue stronge euydencis for thilk side and therwith that tho be strengir euydencis than he hath to the contrarie side' (*id*. 426).

[2] *Donet*, 14 ff.

the primary importance of the scriptures and of faith.[1] Having undermined that position, he supplied a different, carefully argued philosophy based on that reason which is well-nigh if not completely inclusive of faith, and which is the true guide in matters of conduct and belief. This is not to say that the 'doom of reason' was wholly evoked by his opposition to the Lollard movement. It may well have arisen naturally as part of his intellectual development, but that intellectual development itself was largely conditioned by the fact that he was engaged in writing a *summa theologica* against the Lollards.

The 'doom of reason' is the central feature in his thought. It is the thread running through all his surviving books, but it is perhaps most apparent in the *Repressor*. It is therefore only natural that we should examine Pecock's 'doom of reason' in connection with the Lollardy which he was endeavouring to refute. What did he mean by the term 'doom of reason'? What were its limits? How did it compare with faith as a basis for the religious life? What were its implications? These are some of the questions with which we shall have to deal.

The 'doom of reason' formed a primary absolute, the basis of God's law, and is in some sense identical with that law; it is the 'Moral lawe of kinde, which is lawe of God'.[2] It therefore includes nearly everything that the scripture teaches mankind, with the important exception of certain fundamentals of revelation. 'Al the leerning and knowing', as he puts it, 'which Holi Scripture ȝeueth vpon eny bifore seid gouernaunce, deede or trouthe of Goddis moral lawe mai be had bi doom of natural resoun.'[3] The evils with which his age was afflicted might well be the result of man's stubborn refusal to give due attention to the inward 'scripture of reason' and to man's insistence on the teaching of

[1] He refers his readers to the *Repressor* and *Book of Faith* as evidence of this (*Book of Faith*, 114–15).

[2] *Repressor*, I, 6. Cf. Friar John Bury in the *Gladius Salomonis*: 'Quod non est officium Sacrae Scripturae fundare regimina, actus, leges, et veritates quae natura vel ratio adinvenire potest.'

[3] *Id.* I, 12.

the Bible. Modern clerks themselves are far too inclined to say
'fy in resoun, fy in argumentis', and 'summe othire wolden lauȝe
and calle "sophym", whanne it was alleggid that a trouth was
prouyd bi sillogisme'. For the syllogism, according to Pecock,
was the most valid means of proving a given conclusion. Such
contempt was worthy of the severest censure.[1]

But it would be quite wrong to call Pecock a rationalist in the
modern sense of the word. He did not, for instance, exclude the
fundamental truths of revelation. He believed that he had found
a more satisfactory intellectual method of approach to the truths
of the Christian religion, a method that by its very implications
challenged the maxims of an all too popular Lollardy. Divinity
was an intellectual science in which religious feeling played very
little part. 'The groundis of dyuynyte ben the domes, with and bi
discurses of resoun maad bi silogisme reulid in sum maner of the
thre figuris, bi and at the surest open craft ȝouun in logik therupon.'[2] The greatest divinity scholar is the man who 'is hiȝest
leernyd man in argumentis of resoun and in assoilyng which
ouȝte be assoiled'.[3]

In accordance with normal medieval practice Pecock supported
his conclusion by references to biblical texts. Thus he referred to
the thirty-first chapter of the Book of Jeremiah (*v.* 33): 'I will put
my law in their inward parts and write it in their hearts', and to
appropriate texts from the Epistle to the Romans (c. ii) and the
Epistle to the Hebrews (c. viii) among others. The interpretation
of these texts naturally depended on the use of reason; 'the textis
and processis of sum parti of hooli scripture...doom of resoun
muste trie, examyne and iuge bi argument of open sure sillogisme.'[4] In any case such assurances counted less with Pecock
than the application of reason-judgements to experience and

---

[1] *Folewer to the Donet*, 10. Cf. *Reule*, 32, where he censures clerics who have
neglected 'treuthis of vniuersal philosophie comprehendyng lawe of kynde
and lawe of feith'. Cf. *Book of Faith*, 138, where he talks of the danger to
faith caused by 'defaute of sad and wel leerned divinis'.

[2] *Folewer to the Donet*, 66.

[3] *Id.* 10.   [4] *Id.* 66.

perception, by which it should be possible to reach heights identical in all but name with those vouchsafed to mankind through the truths of revelation.

The study and employment of this natural reason are therefore 'more necessarie to Cristen men, and...more worthi than is the outward Bible and the kunnyng ther of'.[1] It is sufficient, for instance, that the worship of images should be proved necessary or harmless by the use of reason without taking into account what scripture has to say on this matter.[2] Reason rather than scripture would make the pagans more likely to accept Christian beliefs.[3] In fact, then, 'the more deel and party of Goddis hool lawe to man in erthe, and that bi an huge gret quantite ouer the remanent parti of the same lawe, is groundid sufficiently out of Holi Scripture in the inward book of lawe of kinde and of moral philosphie, and not in the book of Holi Scripture clepid the Oold Testament and the Newe'.[4]

For Pecock, then, the 'doom of reason' constituted a philosophy. He specifically says that that part of divinity which does not deal with faith is no more and no less than philosophy, and by philosophy he therefore means the 'doom of reason'. 'Doom of reason' has three characteristics, an analysis of which helps us to understand what Pecock means by this phrase. In the first place reason is a unique possession of man, a distinctive faculty which the animals do not possess.[5] Every educated man who has a training in logic may reach the ultimate reality of human truth and approach the ultimate realities of divine truth by the 'doom of reason', providing of course that he applies his reason to the truths he has learned from the scriptures. 'Oure natural resoun bi his owne liȝt and labour may fynde and gete the knowing of ech treuthe being withynne lawe of kynde without eny outward persoon, enformer and techer or affermer that the

---

[1] *Repressor*, I, 52. [2] *Id.* I, 171–2.
[3] He brings forward arguments based on reason, sometimes 'withoute eny therto presupposid feith', so that 'paynemys, hethene men' 'schulden haue noon horroure or abhomynacioun to cristen feith' (*Reule*, 29).
[4] *Repressor*, I, 39. [5] *Donet*, 12.

principal thing whereaboute the resoun in this li3t labourith in his cours and arguyng is trewe.'[1]

In the second place, the doom of reason is, as we have seen, epistemologically superior to faith or revelation. Faith is a subsidiary element, even if it remains the basis of many of the fundamentals of the Christian religion. The 'law of kind' is a far more efficacious and salutary force in Christian thought and practice since it is not only a better key to the door of knowledge than faith, but it also includes a great deal of teaching on matters that his contemporaries would have based entirely on scripture. Thus his own teaching on matrimony and usury, which is, he says, a hundred times more enlightening than the few brief references to these and other questions which are to be discovered in the Bible, shows that man's reason is more adequate than Holy Scripture in giving 'miche more leernyng and kunnyng'.[2] He adds later: 'if eny semyng discorde be bitwixe the wordis writen in the outward book of Holi Scripture and the doom of resoun, write in mannis soule and herte, the wordis so writen...ou3ten be expowned and be interpretid and brou3t forto accorde with the doom of resoun in thilk mater.'[3] This argument is clinched by a final, definite assertion, 'al this kunnyng my3te be had bi labour in doom of resoun, thou3 no biholding were maad into Holy Scripture'.[4]

Then, in the third place, he declared that the 'doom of reason' was identical with the law of God, for with the will it constitutes a natural virtue. It is the 'lawe of conscience' which the will must perforce follow.[5] 'If a coral stoon schal staunche blood, he must have a qualite in him, which qualite muste be a power and a ground wherbi the coral schal do the deede of staunchyng blood.'[6] In the same way the natural virtues, of which reason is the chief, are the real potentials of human action, the commanders

---

[1] *Reule*, 435.   [2] *Repressor*, I, 12 ff. Cf. *Folewer to the Donet*, 143.

[3] *Repressor*, I, 25.   [4] *Id*. I, 17.

[5] *Folewer*, 46: the 'wil folewe resoun' (*Reule*, 228). Man's service to God, he says, is to 'live aftir the doom of oure resoun, that is to seie the use of oure wil and the use of alle oure othere powers under wil in all the deedis' (*id*. 227).

[6] *Folewer*, 45.

of the 'kunnyngal' and moral virtues which in themselves cover most aspects of thinking and acting.[1] It is, therefore, the same thing to live according to the 'doom of reason', to live according to the law of God and to live 'morally virtuously'. These three characteristics give one some indication of the importance which Pecock attached to reason.

Thus it seems fairly clear that by the 'doom of reason' he means the natural law based upon the innate moral feeling of man. He refers to the natural conscience of man, but he does not mean by law of nature the same thing as his contemporary, Raymond of Sebonde, meant. It is not a physical but an instinctive moral law with which he is dealing, a law which partakes of the nature of the Kantian categorical imperative. He himself speaks of it as the 'resoun of men, which is the ynner iȝe of the soule and the ynner iȝe of men'. He commences by saying that it is the 'natural witt and natural liȝt which thou lord god hast sett in her soulis', and goes on to say that 'it cannot be idil, but that aftir men ben come into sufficient age of resonyng forto vse' it.[2] Again he urged that man's 'parfiter' service to God is to live 'bi natural liȝt, which doom is callid lawe of mannys kynde'.[3] Although this phrasing may recall the Augustinian theory of divine illumination to mind, there is no real comparison with it. When man's reason is expressed in written law, that law becomes natural law; thus the law against usury, one of the few references to economic affairs in Pecock's works, is clearly a law of man's natural reason. Reason is, in fact, the continually active eye of the soul, an attribute of God Himself and therefore, in point of time, it is not only prior to scripture[4] but is of the essence of the uncreated Creator, the *primum mobile* of the universe. It is additionally unchangeable

---

[1] *Folewer*, 3.

[2] *Reule*, 225. There are, he says, three 'lawis of kynde' in this world, 'oon propre to man, which is forto folowe resoun in his wil', the second proper to beasts, and the third is common to animals and plants (*id.* 229–31).

[3] *Id.* 227.

[4] Which even if unwritten Pecock believed to date from the early days of creation. Yet oral tradition in itself is inadequate (*Book of Faith*, 250).

and eternal and 'more cleerli kept in heuene than it may bi vs be kept in erthe'.[1]

It was therefore possible that primitive man could, had he so used his capacities, have found out all the truths of religion except those which are directly based on revelation, 'bi strengthe and liȝt of her natural resoun without eny affermyng or teching maad to hem from thee, god'.[2] Adam's fall from innocence had deprived man of the clearest reasoning faculty so that 'he must haue now labour to encerche and fynde the trouthis of thi lawe'.[3] Thus it might be surmised that in Abraham's time men and women were living by natural law although they were naturally circumscribed by their environment from translating the 'doom of reason' into an active reality. In an interesting discussion on image worship and its origin Pecock declared that 'soone aftir the bigynnyng of the world' there were some that 'lyueden in doom of resoun oonli and receyueden not such now seid bileeue delyuered to the world bi God and bi aungelis',[4] and that some had had better reasoning powers than others. This accounted for the more spiritual and correspondingly less material aspects of image worship, so that finally 'ech such man was moued bi doom of resoun forto chese to him such a spirit to be to him his Souereynest Lord and so to be to him his God'.[5] It is clear then that the law of nature, of kind, of reason, was 'writen in mennis soulis with the finger of God as it was so groundid and writen bifore the daies of Abraham and of Iewis',[6] for it was in the 'grete see of lawe of kinde in mannis soule eer Crist or hise Apostlis were born into

---

[1] *Reule*, 463.   [2] *Id.* 430.   [3] *Id.* 463.

[4] Pecock meant by a state of reason in early society more or less the same thing as Wyclif meant by *status innocentiae*, for both agree that the fall of man weakened man's power of reason. In his *De Statu Innocenciae* (ed. J. Loserth and F. D. Matthew, 1922) Wyclif asserted that faith was superfluous because man witnessed God and had a clear insight, in so far as time, state and age would allow, of the Christian doctrines. The primitive society was free from sin, was immortal, feared nothing except God, spoke one language and lived communal-wise in the state of Paradise which, Wyclif quaintly added, possessed a fertile soil and a good climate.

[5] *Repressor*, I, 244.   [6] *Id.* I, 20.

this lijf'.[1] If the law of nature had not been established before the scriptures it would imply that it received its being as a result of their compilation. This is untenable: 'which no wijs man wole graunte.'[2]

In order to prove his point, he contrasts the illogicality of those who would say that the scripture was the basis upon which the law of nature was founded by two picturesque similes, by one of Christ and His Apostles selling fish from the sea, and by an account of the way in which the Londoners gaily decked their houses with greenery and flowers brought in from the countryside on Midsummer Eve. Those who had but 'litil witt' in 'her hedis' would presumably declare that the fishes had their origin in the 'panyeris or dossers' or 'out of the hondis of Crist' and that the branches and flowers grew out of the 'cartis or the hondis of the bringers'.[3] 'And thus ouȝte be avoidid', he adds, 'this obieccioun, riȝt as thouȝ a man were a knyȝt and a preest; ȝit knyȝthode in thilk man is as fer a twynne fro preesthode in the same man, (as bi her bothe naturis and beingis, thouȝ not yn place or persoon,) as ben knyȝthode in oon persoon and preesthode in an other persoon.'[4] Reason and reasoning, for in one place he shows that he realises the linguistic confusion which results from indefinite linguistic practice,[5] are then identical with the law of God, of the essence of God's personality and of the essence of the true man, His creation. They therefore existed from the beginning of the world and even before the scriptures began to be compiled.

Pecock also concluded that heathen philosophers had reached the truths embodied in the words: 'Thou shalt love the Lord thy God with all thy heart and mind and thy neighbour as thyself' independently of revelation, and solely through 'her studie in naturall witt'.[6] Many previous writers, including Abailard,[7] had recognised that pagan thinkers had come to the knowledge of

[1] *Repressor*, 1, 30.
[2] *Id.* 1, 24.
[3] *Id.* 1, 28–30.
[4] *Id.* 1, 51.
[5] *Donet*, 12.
[6] *Repressor*, 1, 14.
[7] Abailard, *Introd. ad Theol.* 1, 25, col. 1034 CD. Cf. *Epist. ad Romanos* where he speaks of God working 'per rationem quam Deus contulit'.

certain truths which were fundamental to the Christian faith through an unconscious but none the less divine revelation. Pecock did not deny the necessity for such a revelation but he emphasised the fact that the potentialities for arriving at these truths were naturally inherent in every man's natural reason.

Pecock delimited the range of 'doom of reason' by certain qualifications.[1] In the first place a reasonable faith, even the 'doom of reason' itself, must necessarily be dependent on satisfactory evidence. 'Whanne a thing is deliuered to resoun with euydence', he says, 'it is liȝter receivid and perceivid than if the same or an othir thing be delyuered to oure resoun with oute evidence or with not so greet evydence.'[2] In another place in *The Reule of Chrysten Religioun* he writes:

And sithen mannys resoun bi his vncessable kinde muste needis be moued to consente or discente this or so more or lesse aftir that the euydencis to hym mynistrid ben forto so consente or discente him moving, and he may not consente or discent saff bi strengthe of euydencis to him mynistrid or presentid, and not other wise consente or discente than as euydencis to him presentid moven—riȝt as it is of the bodili iȝe withoutforth or of the ymaginacioun withynforth—bicause that the resoun is not a power of free worching as is the wil, and ellis resoun were a free worcher as is the wil which noon wel leernyd man in philo[so]phie wole or may for schame graunte no more than of the iȝe or of the taast or smelle—therfore it muste nedis bifalle that what euer jew or hethen man or cristen man parfiȝtli heere the argumentis to be maad into this present purpose in the 'book of feith' and wole attende sufficientli how thei proceden, he muste needis consente to the conclusiouns of hem rather than to the contraries of tho conclusiouns.[3]

[1] In the *Reule* he affirms that 'natural reason' can make an absolute judgement: 'And also ther may no man make comparisoun bitwixe his worthines in godis and an other mannys worthines in godis but if first and bifore he haue an absolute judgement, feeling and knowing of his owne worthines in it silf.'
[2] *Id.* 91.
[3] *Id.* 428. Cf. 'our resoun may not knowe eny trouthe and consente therto withoute this that oure resoun haue euydencis forto so consente' (*id.* 426).

Thus sufficiency of evidence is the real clue to persuasion—'god amende alle defautis and among alle othere these defautis that clerkis han not laborid to fourme out cleerli suche now seid argumentis'—of all 'witty hethen men'.[1]

Evidence itself must vary according to its nature and its quality. In the first place Pecock mentions the evidence of experience, 'grettist evydence', which thereby gives 'the grettist certeinte which mai be had in oure knowing'. The Lollards, he says, teach that no member of the ecclesiastical hierarchy 'cometh into the trewe and dew vndirstonding of Holy Scripture', and that their own views based on their interpretation of the Bible *ipso facto* lead to salvation. But such teaching, he goes on to suggest, is contradicted by the evidence of experience, for it is clear that there are many good Christians who are members of the hierarchy and many evil livers among the Lollards.[2] A more positive example is afforded by St Paul's conversion, 'forwhi, in that that Poul hadde the gospel revelyd to him bi Crist, Poul hadde this sillogisme in his resoun', a case where 'sure experience' was accompanied by 'ful certeynte'.[3] In another place Pecock hazarded that 'whateuer experience techith we ouȝte holde, but if [*i.e.* unless] resoun or Scripture or sure revelacioun schewe other'.[4]

In the second place, certain axiomatic truths, by which men cannot possibly be deceived, may determine the judgement which the mind makes in the light of the natural reason.[5]

In the third place, the judgement of the natural reason is safeguarded by the syllogism, for which as we have seen Pecock had the very greatest veneration[6]. In so far as the syllogism was

[1] *Reule*, 429.

[2] *Repressor*, I, 103. Many of the Lollards are 'greet leechouris...avoutreris in greet haunt and contynuaunce...theefis, euen aȝens her owne leernyng and aȝens her owne holding and doctrine'.   [3] *Book of Faith*, 179.

[4] I owe this reference to the Rev. G. F. Nuttall, B.D.

[5] E.g. *Reule*, 39–40: the *summum bonum*.

[6] See pp. 15–16 of this essay. *Repressor*, I, 76: 'Sotheli, if a man wole reule him thus, he schal neuere be bigiled aboute maters of resonyng; forwhi ther is noon conclusioun or trouthe in the world, but that into proof, of it mai be had a sillogisme weel reulid.'

demonstrative it was well nigh infallible, for it 'geueth sure and vndoubtable kunnyng'. Pecock's trust in the syllogism—'sotheli, if a man wole reule him thus, he schal neuere be begiled'[1]—is singularly interesting from the historical point of view because it reflects the medieval aspect of Pecock's intellect, but it is more or less philosophically valueless and philologically wearisome. The most important fact which emerges from what Pecock has to say in regard to evidence and the primary significance of reason is the fact that the natural reason makes judgements.

Thus from the evidential basis of reason we come to the reason-judgement, the crown and peak of Pecock's 'doom of reason'. 'Fforwhi', he writes at the commencement of the Reule, 'the natural office of resoun is forto schewe what the wille ouȝte chese or refuse, comaund or forbede to be doon in outward deedis or in inward deedis in eny other power of the soule dyvers from the wil, and the natural office of the wil is forto conforme hym to thilk schewing of resoun.'[2] The essence of reason is judgement, judgement to know what is to be 'pryncipaly and fynaly to be reuerencid, louyd and servid', and to estimate what is and what is not sinful.[3] Such judgements themselves are of two

[1] 'Suerte of knowing is had bi ech other of the xix maners or chaungis of sillogismes tauȝt in logik bi opene reulis. Lete therfore ech man abide in his resonyng in what euer mater of resonyng he hath to do, in to tyme he be sure that he hath suche seid sillogismes; and he schal neuere be deceyued. So that al the cause whi men ben deceyued in resonyng is her hastynes, that thei wole iuge bi schorte argumentis, eer tho argumentis ben reducid into formes of sillogismes; or ellis for that thei trusten and trowen the premisse be trewe, eer that thei seen the premisses sufficientli proued bi sillogizing, into tyme it be come up into premissis so open in sure trouthe or ellis so open in probabilite, that noon nede is that eny other premisse be take forto proue hem; or ellis for that thei knowen not bi reulis ȝouen therto whanne an argument is a formal sillogisme, and whanne he so is not' (Repressor, I, 76). Cf. Book of Faith, 126, 175. He defines the difference between a 'demonstrative' and a 'probable' syllogism: 'this difference here now touchid is the difference bitwix a demonstratijf sillogisme and a probable sillogisme...a sillogisme which ȝeueth sure and vndoutable kunnyng and a sillogisme which ȝeueth probable kunnyng oonli' (Repressor, I, 77).   [2] Reule, 24.

[3] Id. 25: 'that wherbi a man knowith the partie that is riȝt, he may knowe the partie which therto is vnriȝt.'

kinds, 'knowen or sureli and sikirli' and 'probable and likeli'.[1] This distinction is, however, merely a distinction between two kinds of truth, not between two alternatives or opposites. Thus Pecock cannot give demonstrative proof of God's existence or of God's creative power, but he can use reason to try to prove the likelihood of these two truths. Therefore there is really little actual difference between 'probable kunnyng' and 'sure kunnyng', for each in itself is 'sufficient forto reule and dresse and move mannis wille into choicis withinforthe and into comaunds and outward deedis'.[2]

Although these reason-judgements are not infallible they actually approach as near to infallibility as possible. Most of Pecock's opponents urged that his reason-judgements were defective, and that his whole argument was therefore based on a false premiss. 'Mannys resoun', so they argued, 'is a thing whiche in hise doomys and iugementis ofte failith, as experience ofte schewith.'[3] As the senses with which God has endowed mankind do not always or necessarily perceive the truth, they must therefore form a fallible basis for reason to exercise a judgement. This is in itself, Pecock replies, no reason for refusing to obey the law of kind, any more than if we should refuse to obey our hands or feet after they have made a false action.[4] He acknowledges that reason cannot be infallible but he shows clearly enough that the judgement which reason operates is as infallible as human mechanism will allow. Thus one may well answer, says Pecock, that the 'doom of reason' is the most trustworthy agent of truth yet discovered and to that extent may be termed infallible. Even if it should so happen that man acts by an 'erroneous doom' he is not in danger of falling into sin, for God realises that he is unconsciously acting against his real intention. 'Sithen, whanne resoun and wil not failen, and thou bi hem doist riȝtli, thou art medid and rewardid, and whanne resoun and wil failen, whilis thou it not causist, neither it knowist, or desirist, thou art not oonli excused, in the dedis comyng therbi, but also thou art for hem medid and rewardid, as thouȝ resoun and wil in tho dedis not faileden.'[1]

There is finally the experience of the Catholic Church itself, which has been very rarely deceived in its application of the 'doom of reason', an experience guarded by the reasoning powers of its thinkers and its councils. Therefore, whether the 'doom of reason' errs or not remains with Pecock an entirely academic point, which should not affect one's decision either way, providing the intention to judge by the light of the natural reason remains paramount in the individual mind.

Thus by making themselves the interpreters of the scriptures the Lollards have misunderstood the Catholic faith. 'Thei wolen not fecche and leerne her feith at the clergie of Goddis hool chirche in erthe', but 'thei wolen fecche and leerne her feith at the Bible of Holy Scripture, in the maner as it schal happe hem to undirstonde it.'[2]

It must be said finally that Pecock never says that the authority of the Catholic Church itself is infallible, as it is also dependent on the authority of the 'doom of reason'. 'Forwhi al this kunnyng

---

[1] *Book of Faith*, 218.

[2] *Id.* 110. By the same reasoning Pecock proved that the Lollards were mistaken when they said that the best man, morally speaking, was the best interpreter of Holy Scripture. They are like women who 'puttiden al her affeccioun or motyue in her wil...and not in her intelleccioun or resoun', since holy scripture is no more a self-sufficient guide to the life of a Christian man than honey is 'al cheer, al the coumfort, al the thrift which is in al othere mete' (*Repressor*, 1, 67). Why, he asks, should the good expositor be the good man? Exposition is an intellectual function, unaffected by the morals of the expositor. 'Wherfore folewith that thouȝ God wolde not suffre eny man to haue the dew vnderstonding of Holi Scripture bi his natural witt, but bi ȝifte of God, ȝit herwith stondith weel that a bad man haue as plenteuosely thilk ȝifte as a good man, and that sum bad man haue thilk ȝifte more plenteuouseli than sum good man, riȝt as sum bad man or sum lasse good man hath ȝiftis of helth and of miraclis doing more plenteuoseli ȝouen to him than a good man or than a more good man' (*id.* 1, 95). Even the gift of prophecy and of revelation has sometimes been granted to the morally vicious: 'Verili to seie in myn experience, ful manye passyng meke men y haue knowe, which han be ful lewid in the knowing of moral vertu and han be ful of doutis' (*id.* 1, 96).

myȝte be had bi labour in doom of resoun, thouȝ no biholding
thereto were maad into Holi Scripture, or thouȝ Scripture were
distroied and brent, as summen trowen that it so was, with al the
writing of the Oold Testament in the tyme of the transmigracioun
into Babilony...wherfore needis folewith that Scripture is not
ground to eny oon seid vertu...but oonli doom of natural resoun,
which is moral lawe of kinde and moral lawe of God, writun in
the book of lawe of kynde in mennis soulis, prentid into the
ymage of God, is ground to ech such vertu, gouernaunce, deede,
and trouthe.'[1] Such was Pecock's answer to the Lollard arguments and such was the fundamental principle of his own
thought.

[1] *Repressor*, I, 17–18. Cf. *Book of Faith*, 282: 'For certis it may be that sum
oon symple persoon as in fame, or in state, is wiser forto knowe, iuge and
declare what is the trewe sense of a certeyn porcioun of Scripture, and what
is the treuthe of sum article, and that for his longe studiyng, laboring and
avising therupon, than is a greet general conceil.'

CHAPTER XI

PECOCK'S REPLY TO THE LOLLARDS (2)

THUS PECOCK had, to his own satisfaction, demolished the bases upon which Lollard teaching was founded by reference to the relative merits of faith and reason. He now proceeded to review other characteristic elements in Lollard teaching and to refute them by reference to scripture and the 'doom of reason'. His arguments have only an incidental originality, as when for instance he touches on the relation of the law of reason to the Ten Commandments, but for all that they remain important because he embodied his argument in a general scheme based on the fundamentals which we have analysed, and because an analysis of his arguments throws light on later Lollard ideas. Finally, Pecock replies to the Lollard charges in the English language, and if for no other reason than this, his argument is deserving of analysis.[1]

He turned first to the question of image worship and pilgrimages. Wyclif had at first approved of reverence being paid to images in so far as they formed the poor man's bible,[2] but he later condemned them root and branch.[3] His followers were equally or even more stern in their condemnation of image worship.[4]

[1] Lollard opinions represented in this chapter are taken from a general consensus of Wyclif's own books and those of his followers where they are not explicitly quoted from the *Repressor*. Although many of the Lollard tracts contain views which had nothing in common with those of Wyclif, it has not been thought worth while to differentiate between the arguments used by Wyclif and by his followers, for Pecock was replying to Lollard views as a whole, from his own experience and probably from the two tracts previously mentioned (pp. 89–90).

[2] Wyclif, *Sermones*, ed. J. Loserth, II, 125.

[3] Wyclif, *Liber Mandatorum*: 'therefore must we preach against all such costliness, beauty and other arts, which are employed more for the purpose of extracting money from deluded strangers than to promote the religion of Christ among the people.'

[4] *Apology of the Lollards*, ed. J. H. Todd, 85 ff.; the author urges that image worship leads to idolatry when a man 'setteth in his affection anything before God' by giving a creature what is God's due alone, thus treating God

Pecock's own work in the *Repressor* throws light on the Lollard attitude to pilgrimages. They argued that the pilgrimages were in the first place unnecessary and in the second place evil in themselves. They were unnecessary because no 'rememorative signe' would be needed if the clergy carried out their duty and preached the gospel as they should. 'Vein and waastful occupacioun it is forto make myche labour and cost forto haue and vse the sympler and vnperfiter and lasse representing ymage of a thing, whanne with lasse labour and cost mai be had the perfiter and fuller and better representing ymage of the same thing. But so it is, that ech lyuyng man is verier and perfiter and fuller and better representing ymage of Crist and of ech seint, than is eny vnquyk stok or stoon graued and ourned with gold and othere gay peinturis.'[1] Further, as God is everywhere present, there can be no possible justification for making pilgrimages to specific places where God is supposed to be specially present. 'Wherfore it is vein waast and idil forto trotte to Wasingam rather than to ech other place in which an ymage of Marie is, and to the rode of the north dore at London rather than to ech other roode in what euer place he be.'[2]

Finally, apart from the scriptural proofs[3] which necessarily played a large part in every Lollard argument, pilgrimages are evil in themselves inasmuch as they are a temptation from the Devil. Images have that 'form' of evil of which St Paul speaks and present an admirable opportunity to Satan for the working of false miracles.[4] They do not even induce godly behaviour in the

---

irreverently and making the creature resemble God, 'for many believe the image to be God and many believe God's virtue to be in the image subjectively'. Cf. Gower, *Vox Clam.* II, 520, 541; *Confess. Amant.* 1501, where he bewails the failure of the common people to distinguish between heathen gods and Christian images (ref. B. L. Manning, *The People's Faith in the Time of Wyclif*, 99). For other Lollard views *vide* Wyclif, *Sel. Eng. Works*, ed. Arnold, III, 462-3, and *Remonstrance*, ed. Forshall, 23 ff.

[1] *Repressor*, I, 193.   [2] *Id.* I, 194.

[3] E.g. John iv, 21 ff.; Joshua xxiv, 14, 19 ff.; Exodus xxii; Ps. cxv, 4 ff., etc.

[4] Pecock replies to this argument by saying that it is no proof of the wickedness of images. The Devil has spoken to men and women, but we do

pilgrims. On the contrary, these become conceited and vain through the attention paid to them. The money spent on pilgrimages is thus ill-spent and could be much better used in the 'visiting of poor men, and teching of vnwise men, and bisie studie in deuoute bookis and in othere bookis of goostli leernyng'.[1] Again, the images so venerated are worshipped idolatrously, as the service books used at certain festivals, the 'Vexilla Regis prodeunt', the Feast of the Invention of the Cross and the Feast of the Exaltation of the Cross clearly indicate. 'And open it is that to Crist him silf (if he had be there present) thei myȝten not haue mad more lowȝli knouleching that he was her God, than thei at thilk tymes and placis maden to the baar crosse or to the chest of relikis in which the eukarist was not.'[2] Pecock replied to these arguments against image worship and pilgrimages by arguments based on reason and on scripture.[3]

His discussion centred around two problems which he asserted the Lollards had entirely misunderstood: what do we mean by 'image' and what do we mean by 'worship'? The Lollards have confused image worship, which is veneration for holy saints and martyrs represented by their symbols, the images, with idolatry or worship of the images as gods. Reason condemns idolatry completely: 'that sum godli vertu is in tho ymagis, or that the ymagis doon myraclis, or that thei ben quyk and seen, heeren, or speken at sum while, or that thei sweten at sum while.'[4] An image is a 'creature' made by man which cannot possibly be worshipped as a god because God was uncaused and 'made al thing and which was euer withoute bigynnyng'. No man who had 'come into ȝeeris of discrecioun and is passid childhode, and which is

not therefore conclude that all men and women are evil. In every case where the miracle is thought to be false, a thorough investigation should be ordered so that the truth may be made known (*Repressor*, 1, 226–7).

[1] *Id.* 1, 195.

[2] *Id.* 1, 205. The Lollard attack on the Palm Sunday and other Easter ceremonies is interesting.

[3] E.g. *Donet*, 121 ff.

[4] *Repressor*, 1, 148. Thus the true purpose of image worship was to direct Christians to real religion, a book for the 'leude peple' (*Dives and Pauper*, 113).

not a natural fool' can possibly dissent from this vital distinction between an image as a picture or representation and an image as an idol or god.[1] It is true that we speak of an image as St Anne or St Peter, but this does not mean that we believe the image to be actually St Anne or St Peter any more than we believe King Arthur or Hector of Troy in pictures of Arthur and Hector to be real persons; and yet we may well speak of all of them as such. He does not deny the abuses to which image worship may give rise, but the prevalence of such abuses is no justification for a wholesale attack on image worship itself. Worship implies no more than reverence or veneration, and if the veneration is excessive the fault does not lie in the image but in the men who worship the image. 'If I haue a fruyteful tre which in oon or in summe of hise braunchis hath a canker, schal y therefore hewe down al my tre?' The use of incense or the placing of lights before an image is not excessive veneration, since incense and lights are used before a plain white wall in a church. Therefore we are very much more justified in using them before a pictorial representation of the abstraction which we are worshipping. It is important, however, that we should worship before and not to the image. Even for a scholar the 'iʒe siʒt schewith and bringith into the ymaginacioun and into the mynde withynne in the heed of a man myche mater and long mater sooner, and with lasse labour and traueil and peine, than the heering of the eere dooth'.[2] If such pictorial representations are a means of edification for the learned man, they must be even more efficacious for the unlearned and illiterate.

The evidence of scripture supports the conclusion arrived at by 'doom of reason'. God, who may not act contrary to his own attributes, commanded two images of the cherubim to be made to adorn the ark.[3] The brazen image of the serpent was also made by

[1] Cf. 'Hethen men and also Iewis weren neuer so lewid that thei passiden in lewidnes children of x. ʒeer age now lyuyng, or suche persoones whiche in these daies ben clepid and take for foolis' (*Repressor*, I, 241).

[2] *Id.* I, 212.

[3] *Donet*, 121; *Repressor*, I, 137 ff.

the Israelites with the express approval of God. The first commandment, Pecock explains, does not condemn all images but the worship of such images as 'goddis' by the people.[1] If God had wished to prohibit images altogether, He would have made a special commandment to that effect, and that one of the first, but He only forbids the use of images as gods. All the other passages in the Bible which superficially condemn image worship give voice to the condemnation of the false gods which the Lollards have identified with images.[2]

Therefore whilst he agrees that 'ymages mowe leefulli be broke whanne thei ben vsid in ydolatrie irremedili', Pecock sees nothing wrong in the use of images as 'rememoratijf or mynding signes'. The sacraments, whose validity is unimpeachable, are themselves reminders of Christ's life and activities,[3] and images are just as valid and indeed as vital memorials of Christ's life and passion.[4] We do not, he goes on to say, reproach a man when he makes 'a ring of a rische and putte it on his fynger, or that he write sum seable cros or mark or carect with cole or chalk in the wal of his chaumbre or hal, or that he hange vp bifore his siȝt sum hood or girdil or staf' in order to remind himself of something which he wishes to remember or to do.[5] Why then should we refuse to allow the worship of images, which serves much the same purpose, especially when it has been clearly proved that scripture does not condemn the practice? An additional proof, if needed, can be found in Christ's approval of the money which bore the imperial image, 'wherfore nedis folewith that Crist approued weel hem forto haue and vce a graued ymage of the Emperour, as of her souereyn lord in erthe. An whi not thanne Crist schulde allowe and approue men forto haue and vse a graued ymage of the Emperour in heuene, as of her Souereyn Lord in heuene?'[6] This is not only an excellent example of the micro-macrocosmic trend of medieval political theory—the monarchism of heaven and

[1] *Donet*, 125.   [2] *Repressor*, 1, 143 ff.   [3] *Id.* 1, 163, 209.
[4] Juliana of Norwich averred that 'paintings of Crucifixes' were a part of her creed (*Comfortable Words*, 18).
[5] *Repressor*, 1, 166.   [6] *Id.* 1, 140.

earth—but it is also a curious example of the triviality and subtlety of much medieval thought. So he concluded that image worship is a 'plesaunt seruice', 'a merytorie and weel done dede', justified by the arguments of reason and scripture which obviously refuted the Lollard viewpoint.

Pecock used very similar arguments in relation to Lollard attack on pilgrimages. They too are a 'rememoratijf or mynding signe' of the 'holi lijf and passioun of Iesus Crist' which are justified by scripture and reason. 'Sithin it is not resonable and conuenient that suche bodies or bonis or relikis be left withoute in the baar feeld, (and that bothe for it were aȝens the eese of the peple whiche schulde come therto in reyny and wyndi wedris, and for that thei myȝten thanne be take awey bi wickid men not dreding God,) therfore it is ful resonable and worthi forto bilde ouer tho bodies and bonis and othere relikis chapellis or chirchis.'[1] Such places, of which there seem to be a certain number in each country, are fit objects of devotion. Devotion is the main reason for making a pilgrimage, 'forto be quykli and deuoutli remembrid in the place of pilgrimage vpon Goddis worthinessis, hise benefetis and punyschingis, his holi lijf and passioun, or upon summe Seintis holi conuersacioun, or forto to haue quietnes and soolnes to preie to God or to a Seint'. In addition to this the pilgrim, providing he reveals his task by some medal or other token, gives a godly example to the towns and villages through which he passes on his way to the journey's end.

A discussion on the holding of landed estates by the clergy and the endowments which made them possible ensued. The Lollards argued that they gave rise to vicious living, simony and avarice, that they diminished charity, weakened the authority of the state and caused dissensions and wars.[2] These charges were justified, they affirmed, by the experience of past history. St Jerome said that the more powerful the Church grew the more it decreased in virtue.[3] They also made much of the supposed reaction of an

[1] *Repressor*, I, 182.   [2] E.g. *De Blasphemia*, cap. IV.
[3] S. Hieronymus, *Vita Malchi*, Migne, *P.L.* XXXIII, 53: 'postquam ad Christianos principes venerit, potentia quidem et divitiis major sed virtutibus minor facta sit.'

angel to the Donation of Constantine: 'Hodie venenum ecclesiis Dei infusum est.'[1] Although Wyclif never challenged the authenticity of the Donation, he never tired of reiterating the disastrous consequences of Sylvester's acceptance of the Emperor's gift. The Lollards, and Wyclif, further argued that the secular authority could remedy this evil state of affairs by depriving the clergy of their endowments when they were obviously exercising a *dominium* that was based on sin.[2] The endowments of the Church must be purged away by the secular authority just as Jerusalem was despoiled by Titus in ancient time if the Church is to return to its pristine purity and to rid itself of corruption.[3] It is, moreover, the duty of the king, who is God's vicar and actually of greater importance than the priest, to see that the clergy live frugally and do not attack the temporal power.[4] The people themselves could refuse to pay the tithes of bad priests.[5]

The Lollards' attack was closely bound up with incipient national feeling. They made much of the alien character of the Roman see

---

[1] 'Sprott', *Chronicle*, ed. T. Hearne (1719), 43: 'Anno iii^c. xv. Constantinus baptizatur a Sancto Silvestro, et tunc ditavit ecclesiam Romanam libertatibus, praediis, et possessionibus, et dedit sedem suam imperialem Sancto Petro et suis successoribus. Et illo tempore Diabolus in aere volando clamavit, Hodie venenum ecclesiis Dei infusum est.' Hearne's indiscriminate appreciation of 'morsels of antiquity' (*vide* D. C. Douglas, *English Scholars* (1939), 235) led him to attribute the chronicle to Sprott, a monk of St Augustine's, Canterbury. Another chronicle (edited by Dr W. Bell, Liverpool, 1851) also bears Sprott's name but again on insufficient evidence. This does not mention the episode of the angel but speaks of Sylvester's cure of Constantine.

Wyclif: 'Narrant chronica quod in dotatione ecclesiae, vox audita est in aere angelica tunc temporis, sic dicentis, Hodie effusum est venenum in ecclesia sancta Dei' (*Dialogus*, lib. IV, cap. XVIII, cited in Babington, II, 324 n.). Cf. *English Works*, 374. The author is not Wyclif.

Pecock says that the original authority was Gerald of Wales in his *Cosmographia Hiberniae* and that even if it were true the fact that it was a 'Diabolus' that gave the message completely invalidates it. The passage occurs in *Libri de Invectionibus*, VI, cap. XXVII (*Opera*, ed. J. S. Brewer, R.S. 1861, I, 192).

[2] *De Blasphemia*, cap. IV; *Opera Minora*, 226. He also says that Sylvester was acting honestly and was therefore forgiven by God. Cf. *Trialogus*, IV, 18, 311.

[3] *Opus Evangelicum*, ed. J. Loserth, 1895; *De Blasphemia*, cap. I, 'Purgatio gloriosa ecclesiae ab antiqua blasphemia'; *De Civili Dominio*, 'Ecclesiae ad primam perfectionem restitutio', etc.

[4] *De Officio Regis*, ed. A. W. Pollard and C. Sayle (London, 1887), *passim*.

[5] *De Blasphemia*, cap. VI; cf. *De Civili Dominio*, I.

and of the way in which England, 'a garden of delights that never failed', sent her treasure to Rome.[1] An economist might term such a view 'pre-mercantilist' because it rested on the assumption that prosperity at home was induced by the amount of gold in the country's coffers. 'It was simony to give the pope gold for his lead, and first fruits for the gift of a church. When a lord hath the gold for presenting, the gold dwelleth still in the land, but when the pope hath the first fruits the gold goeth out and cometh never again.'[2] This opened the way to the Lollard attack on firstfruits, provisions and so forth.

Pecock's justification, which is a reply to attacks of the nature described above, is both ingenious and interesting. After replying at length to the scriptural arguments, which had been put forward by the Lollards in defence of their thesis, he examined their position in the light of reason. 'Forwhi, ben not alle the lawis of the Iewis reuokid bi Crist, ech oon, except what is lawe of kinde?'[3] Admittedly Christ seems to have recommended the life of poverty, but there is no indication as to whether this was a commandment or a counsel. In virtue of this lack of evidence and direction from both the Old and the New Testaments, there remains a third possibility, the reference to the final authority, arguments based on the 'law of kind' or 'doom of reason'.[4] He first argues, referring in passing to the history of the Apostolic age, that the perils of poverty are quite as great as, if not greater than, those of great riches. The communism, which was practised by the Church of Jerusalem in its early days, was caused by the dangers which surrounded it, and was incidentally as applicable to laymen as to priests. Indeed, since the Church has been so well endowed, there have been more learned and more saintly prelates than there

[1] This sentiment was found in perfectly orthodox works, e.g. the poem 'John of Bridlington' in T. Wright, *Political Poems*, I, 123 ff.

[2] *De Eucharistia*, 223: *Sel. Eng. Works*, I, 282; II, 395; III, 281, etc.

[3] *Repressor*, I, 291.

[4] *Id.* II, 310–12. 'The ensaumpling of Cristis greet pouerte in abstenyng fro temperal vnmovable possessiouns lettith not preestis forto hem take, receyue, holde and weel demene into gode vsis' (*id.* II, 312).

were in the days before its endowment.[1] Similarly, alms have been more plentifully distributed and there have been more rather than less martyrs and confessors since the days of Constantine.[2] Wealth has been an impetus rather than an impediment to the spread of Christianity. In any case although riches may well be the occasion of sin, they are not necessarily its causes, for these are dependent on the use that man makes of his own free will and of the riches at his command.[3] Both good and evil are occasioned by riches just as they are caused, for instance, by the use that a man may make of his own tongue. No one, however, would think of cutting out a man's tongue merely because it was a potential occasion of evil.

Although Pecock acknowledges that there are abuses,[4] his chief complaint at the moment is that if, indeed, there is any evil, the evil arises from the fact that the endowments of the Church are insufficient.

And perauenture this cause moued deuoute temperal lordis in the oold daies forto so richeli endewe bischopis and othere statis of the chirche; and therfore noman may argue and proue that, as bi strengthe of her riche endewing, that the statis of the chirche ou3ten or schulden be lad into wors plijte than thei schulde be, if thei were porelier endewid; or if thei were not endewid with immouable godis at al. Wold God the bischop writer of this book hadde so sure knowing of his saluacion as he hath experience vpon the trouthe of this now of him affermed sentence.[5]

----

[1] 'For, who euer can schewe that bifore the daies of Hillari, Ambrose, Ierom, and Austyn, and Gregori weren in the Latyn chirche so worthi techers with holi lyuyng to gidere as thei weren and as her successouris weren, y schal 3eue to him myn arme' (*Repressor*, ii, 335).

[2] He says that there were numerically more martyrs before Constantine but that the spirit of martyrdom was none the less vigorous in the later days (*id.* ii, 336).   [3] *Id.* ii, 325.

[4] He complains that Lollardy spreads because the clergy 'more labour aboute worldli kunnyng of lawe, and of wynnyng, and aboute beneficis and worschipis, than aboute the kunnyng of substancial scole of dyvynite, other than myche such as serveth for sermouns in pulpit, which laymen trowen al to be substancial divinitie' (*Book of Faith*, 138).

[5] *Repressor*, ii, 307; cf. *Reule*, 259.

Founders of convents and colleges should therefore make certain that they have endowed their foundations sufficiently to safeguard them against beggary.[1]

It is equally necessary that every cleric should have a fixed, regular stipend, for if he is dependent on the good will of his parishioners, he may refuse to denounce vices of his flock for fear of offending them. Besides their 'wittis and willis schulden be infirmer than ben hise, and also for freelnes thei wolden grucche ofter than thei schulden aȝens correpciouns and reulingis, as experience ofte in suche maters schewith'. He puts forward another objection to slender incomes, as sophisticated as it is full of common sense, declaring that if the incomes of the clergy were reduced as the Lollards wished, no one would be ordained priest. It is not therefore only a matter of morality, but a matter of policy for the endowment of benefices to be as secure as that of the chantry priest.[2]

Finally, allowing for the moment the misuse of wealth by certain of the clergy, he refers to the remedies which the Lollards advocated and shows how unfair such a movement as they wanted would be to the Church as a whole. If the clergy did not perform their duties properly, Wyclif had argued that their incomes and the offerings of the faithful should be stopped. But, says Pecock, the clergy have not been guilty of misusing property conferred specifically upon them, but of misusing property conferred on the Church of which they are the agents. Wyclif's remedies are both irrational and absurd.[3] He says once again that we do not cut down the tree itself if an apple tree does not bear much fruit in any single year. Therefore if the clergy who are guilty of such misdemeanours are deprived of their endowments their successors who 'ben not ȝit founde in wijte or defaute' would suffer for offences of which they were clearly quite innocent. 'If I trespass

---

[1] *Repressor*, II, 346–7.
[2] *Id.* II, 392 ff.
[3] *Id.* II, 381. 'Who is to judge when the tithes or offerings should be withheld? No man should be a judge in his own cause.'

against the king', says the bishop, 'why should my heirs suffer?'[1] People should not say that a man's successors will misuse his goods because he and his predecessors have done so.

The real remedy for the evils occasioned by endowment is simplicity itself, but it is necessarily difficult to achieve in practice. 'Lete oonli good men and weel proued men in vertues be takun into preesthode and into prelacie, wherynne ben riche possessiouns.' There would then be no need to reproach the Church for her misuse of endowments, since her wealth would be used for the profit of all mankind and she would then be exercising a true *dominium*. There are certain other remedies which could be taken to prevent the recurrence of such abuses, the possibility or the actuality of which Pecock does not attempt to deny. He urged that wicked clerks should be brought before the ecclesiastical courts and tried under the regular forms. If they were found guilty, either a fine or a penance should be imposed, and if the charge warranted it, they should be deposed from office.[2] Pecock's discussion of the endowment question is certainly fairer and more logical than those of many medieval writers on this topic, and his reply to the Lollard arguments is notable for its intellectual vigour and shows his awareness of the realities of the situation.

It was but a short step from a vindication of the endowments of the Church to a justification of its officers. The Pope of Rome was necessarily the main target for Wyclif's attacks, but there is a progressive development in his arguments. In his earlier writings he regarded the Pope as the head of the Church if he is an 'evangelical man' living in conformity with the law of Christ.[3] Then he spoke of him as a man of whose ultimate salvation he cannot, by reason of his predestinarian views, be at all certain,[4]

---

[1] *Repressor*, II, 414. 'Would anyone condemn Christianity because Judas Iscariot was a member of the Church?' (*id.* II, 490).

[2] *Id.* II, 396.   [3] *De Blasphemia*, cap. III.

[4] 'Nullus papa debet presumere se esse caput ecclesie...non sic assereret quod sit predestinatus, eo quod non est de substancia fidei quod iste sit predestinatus' (*De Ecclesia*, ed. Loserth).

and finally as Antichrist himself. In the *De Potestate Pape*, written in 1379(?), he seemed to maintain a definitively modified Gelasian position in relation to the spiritual and secular functions of man, emphasising the purely spiritual nature of the clergy's authority—for the secular authority itself has spiritual responsibility—and urging that the two powers must work together in harmonious co-operation. But he not only rejected the Gelasian position as interpreted by Hugh of St Victor. He went further and so whittled down the power of the Pope, even in spiritual matters, that the latter seemed an impediment to spiritual progress rather than the chief Christian pastor. His general conclusion is that Peter's headship was not temporal but spiritual, a headship in humility and meekness but not in power and renown.[1] The Pope is only a Pope in so far as he imitates Christ,[2] refuses endowments and temporal power and does not formulate unchristian traditions for the sake of gain. Even in this work there are definite signs that Wyclif, influenced by the great schism, the 'felix dissensio', which was revealing the true nature of Petrine authority, not only thinks that it would be better to have no Pope at all, but also equates the Pope with *Antichristus*.[3] In *De Blasphemia*, a book which contains a particularly violent attack on papal authority, he argued that it would be just as well if the English people renounced their allegiance to the Pope on the death of Urban VI and returned to the primitive Christianity of the 'Golden Age of the Church', the mirage which has deceived so many reformers.

His final view, leaving out of account the violent words of many of his English works, is represented by the *Opus Evangelicum*, an essay in abuses and abuse, in which he argues that the Pope is the man of whom Christ said 'he will come in my name saying I am Christ and will seduce many'. In both the *De Potestate Pape*[4]

[1] *De Potestate Pape*, cap. VII.
[2] *De Blasphemia*, cap. I, II, and other works, *passim*.
[3] *Supplementum Trialogi*, cap. IX, 450: 'Manifeste patet, quod uterque istorum pseudopaparum tanquam membrum diaboli in causa stultissima provocat homines ad pugnandum.'
[4] *De Potestate Pape*, cap. VI, 103-35.

and the *Opus Evangelicum*, he contrasted the virtues of Christ with the vices of the Pope. While Christ represents the truth, the Pope is the master of lies. To his worldly power and riches, Wyclif opposed the poverty of Christ, to the canon law of the Church the teaching of the Bible, to the hirelings fighting for temporal dominion the persecution and suffering which greeted the Apostles. While Christ forbade his disciples to take the sword the Pope wages fierce wars, not sending his emissaries to preach the Gospel but to further his own selfish aims. It is ironical to call this man, whose house is a den of thieves and a nest of diabolical simony, Holy Father. Indeed, the Church does not really need a visible head, especially when that head so clearly opposes the will of Christ.[1]

It was this latter, vigorous, vehement point of view which Wyclif's later disciples emphasised in sermon and pamphlet. The Curia had from the earliest days met with Wyclif's scorn, not only as it was the college of electors, but because it also formed the papal court. The cardinals—CARior DIaboli NAtus Licium Seminator or Custos Apostatorum Regni Diaboli Iuvans Nequissimum Ad Legem Iudicis Sopiendam—form a sect unknown in scripture which wallows in dirt at the foot of its master, the Pope.[2] Bishops, archdeacons and other members of the hierarchy were not less responsible for the evil state of the Church. They do not live according to scripture, for they have lost their 'apostolic status' through evil living, lust for temporal power and allegiance to their master, the Pope. 'Dumb fools in the realm of hell' instead of preachers of the gospel word, they draw Wyclif's anger upon themselves still more when they are absentees. Absentees who hold offices in plurality—it should be remembered that Wyclif himself was not quite innocent of this offence—and in particular foreigners

[1] E.g. 'Videtur multis ex fide Scripturae et facto hominum, quod in Curia romana sit radix hujus blasphemiae, quia homo peccati antichristus insignis loquitur, quod sit summus Christi vicarius, in vita et opere inter mortales sibi simillimus' (*De Blasphemia*, cap. 1).

[2] Thus he refers to papal legates as 'legatos cum bullis missos ab latere antichristi'. Cf. *De Blasphemia, passim; De Officio Pastorali, passim.*

appointed to high office by the Pope in virtue of his 'blasphemous' pretension to be lord-in-chief of all benefices,[1] receive especial condemnation. Archdeacons are attacked for their pride and luxurious living, for the fines which they inflict in order to increase their revenues, for their abuse of the powers of excommunication and absolution.[2] In particular, he attacked the 'Caesarean' clergy, those who occupy high offices in the state and give more of their attention to politics than to religion. The cure for such prelates in every case is obvious; they should be deprived of their riches.

Pecock's replies are based on the twin pillars of scripture and reason. The argument based on scripture is largely one of analogy. Because the Jews had a High Priest who was the chief figure in the Jewish world, the Pope must occupy an analogous position in the Christian world.[3] He then reverts to the Petrine arguments —'*thou art Symount, the sone of Iohanna, thou shalt be called Cephas or heed*'—an argument too well known to call for discussion here. It was perhaps a little more difficult to prove the existence of bishops and archdeacons from scripture, but Pecock ingeniously evades the point by suggesting that since the 'cuntre in which the Iewis in tho daies dwelliden was not but litil, (for it was not so large as is the rewme of pure Englond)', there was no need for a hierarchy.[4] Further, it was necessary from the point of view of natural law that there should be some authority to whom individuals could refer for judgement on vexed questions. It was for this reason that 'God...ordeyned...bischopis aboue the lou3er preestis, and archebischopis aboue bischopis, and the pope to be aboue alle the othere'.[5]

The argument is interesting because it soon leads to the question of *dominium*. Pecock has little to say on this matter but he rejects the egalitarianism of the Lollard. There is every reason for a hierarchy in which the Pope not only has authority over the Church but the archbishop is the master of bishops—so Pecock

---

[1] See G. Barraclough, *Papal Provisions* (1935).   [2] *De Blasphemia*, cap. VII.
[3] *Repressor*, II, 436.   [4] *Id.* II, 436.   [5] *Id.* II, 381.

found to his cost—the bishop of priests, the priests of deacons and the deacons of the laity.[1] Such a conception as this was almost integral to medieval society. Of the revolts against this theory of *dominium* Wyclif's is the most interesting. In his *De Civili Dominio* he concluded that everyone in a state of grace has lordship over the whole universe whilst the wicked man has no right to it at all.[2] Wyclif, who followed FitzRalph's *De Pauperie Salvatoris* very closely, differentiates *dominium* from *usus*. Society as it is at present constituted is contrary to the law of nature, and is in effect the result of sin, of the Fall which upset man's state of primitive innocence. It would therefore no longer be true to affirm that a 'man is lord over his servant just in so far as he is the servant of his neighbour' in this present degenerate state of society. Wyclif's argument is therefore very largely a matter of theory, and as far as the practical side of affairs was concerned, it was only 'when the power of the spiritual and the temporal lord crossed one another that Wycliffe's strict principle came into play'.[3]

Such authority as Pecock gave to the clergy and laity is also ideally dependent upon their virtuous conduct.[4] The *dominium* of the clergy is very real in every sense but it is a *dominium* with responsibility. '3it y feele not thus, that the clerkis ben free therbi forto expende tho godis in eny point a3ens ri3t doom of resoun in pride or in glotenye or in leccherie or in waast, and ben not

---

[1] *Repressor*, II, 417 ff.

[2] 'All human dominion, natural or civil, is conferred upon him by God, as the prime author, in consideration of his returning continually to God the service due unto him; but by the fact that a man by omission or commission becomes guilty of mortal sin, he defrauds his lord-in-chief of the said service, and by consequence incurs forfeiture: wherefore...he is rightfully to be deprived of all dominion whatsoever' (cited in R. L. Poole, *Illustrations of Medieval Thought and Learning* (ed. 1920), 256). Dr Poole's discussion is most useful. He says of Wyclif's theory of dominion: 'There is a feudalism here, but a feudalism in which there are no mesne lords; all men hold directly of God, with differences no doubt in accidentals, but in the main fact of their tenure all alike. It is this principle of the dependence of the individual upon God and upon none else that distinguishes Wycliffe's views from any other system of the middle ages' (*id.* 255).

[3] *Id.* 265.

[4] *Repressor*, II, 426.

worthi blame of God.'[1] The *dominium* which is condemned in St Matthew's Gospel is not the real *dominium* which Christ exercised over His apostles but tyranny. If ecclesiastical dominion is to be abolished, then secular authority must quickly follow suit. Pecock infers that secular authority is as equally divinely ordered as the hierarchical authority of bishop or archdeacon. In fact a little later on he argued that a monarchical form of government among the laity is a justification for the same form of government among the clergy.[2]

Thus basically the difference between FitzRalph, Wyclif and Pecock is not so very great. The riches of the Church are the 'patrimony of the poor' and the rich man's goods are at the disposal of those who need them, since, as St Bernard said, 'to not ʒeue to poor man the godis of poor men is even synne with sacrilegie'.[3] *Dominium* as Wyclif argued in his *De Dominio Divino* and his *De Civili Dominio* depends on grace and sin alone makes it forfeit. The real distinction rests on the interpretation which each of the writers puts on the method of fulfilment. Thus Pecock refused to carry his thesis to its logical conclusion because 'it wolde folewe, if princis weren customabili mys vsers of tho godis, that the comoun peple schulden take fro hem tho godis hem abiding in her statis of princehode. And if this schulde be doon, manye myscheefis wolden thereof folewe.'[4] This quotation is doubly interesting because it suggests that Pecock knew that he could not conscientiously carry his argument to a logical conclusion, and whether Wyclif himself would have demurred at this conclusion in practice is very doubtful. Pecock has little idea of the contractual nature of some medieval theories of *dominium*.

Pecock has not very much to say on the canon law, but he differentiates it from the divine law and from the 'law of reason'. It is based, like the civil law of which it is the ecclesiastical

---

[1] *Repressor*, II, 412.   [2] *Id*. II, 443-4.

[3] *Id*. II, 409. Wyclif agreed that obedience should be paid to tyrants unless the tyrant could be compelled to relinquish his rule through passive disobedience.

[4] *Id*. II, 415.

counterpart, on human authority and is purely concerned with the good government of the Church. It has therefore in all likelihood been in existence since the Church itself was founded, so that all objections, whether based on scripture, reason or history, which might be adduced against canon law, are proved to be groundless. 'It is leeful lawis be mad bi man and be sett for to be in vce with the comoun Cristen lawe ȝouun and mad immediatli bi God.'[1]

Another topic which is intimately connected with Pecock's survey and defence of the episcopate is the duty of preaching. The Lollards asserted that preaching was one of the most important duties of any cleric and of a bishop in particular. William Sawtre reiterated the all too frequent Lollard injunction: 'I saw that each deacon and priestis held to preche the word of God... algatis beware that the peple vndirstonde wel, and so vse comoun speche in their owne persone.' It was with this in mind that Wyclif had instituted the lay preachers, 'simple men and women and those accounted ignorant laymen...to confounde the pride of the worldly wise',[2] who were sent out to preach the rudiments and fundamentals of the Christian faith, the Paternoster, the Ten Commandments and the Seven Deadly Sins to the common people of town and village. The Lollards were not, however, alone in emphasising the duty of preaching, and of preaching that was based on the Gospels. 'Alle doctoures', says an anonymous writer, 'shuld lat owte in to the worlde holy techynge of Godes lore, forto cache sowles fro synne into the wey of salvacion.'[3]

---

[1] *Repressor*, ii, 461. He refers to Gratian's *Decretum* elsewhere.

[2] Dr H. B. Workman (*John Wyclif*, ii, 202) says that many of the poor preachers were probably laymen after Wyclif's death but that in his lifetime they were mostly 'unbeneficed clerks without a bishop's licence'.

[3] MS. Roy. 18 B. xxiii, fol. 150 (cited in G. R. Owst, *Preaching in Medieval England*, c. 1350–1450, 3). Cf. MS. Harl. 2398, fol. 91 b (Owst, *op. cit.* 4): 'Yf thou be a prest and havest kunnynge and auctoryte, preche and teche Godes worde to his peple; and yf thou be no prest thenne bysy the in the halyday to here prechynge of Godes worde and be aboute with thy goede spekyng and styrynge to brynge thy neyȝebores to betere lyvynge.' Preaching was, legally speaking, a duty of the clergy (*Lyndwood's Provinciale*, ed. J. V. Bullard and H. Chalmer Bell (1929), 26).

Bishops and doctors might reprove the sins of humanity and be listened to,[1] whereas the 'pore mens wordes ben sett on syde'. The obligation of doctors and bishops, 'dumb idols' and 'waterless clouds' to preach was all the greater. Gascoigne is as emphatic on this point as earlier orthodox writers and as the Lollards themselves had been.

Pecock, however, did not believe that preaching was the most important, even a necessary duty, for a bishop, as it must in any case be subordinate to his other obligations. The evidence suggests that Pecock himself did not neglect his duties in this respect despite the fact that he thought that teaching was so much more important than preaching. He is distrustful of the eloquent doctor:

And in special be waar that thou not accepte, chese, and take a clerk forto be sufficient to thee into the now seid purpos bi this aloon, that he mai were a pilioun on his heed; neither bi this, that he is a famose and a plesaunt precher to peple in a pulpit; neither bi this, that he is a greet and thikke rateler out of textis of Holi Scripture or of Doctouris in feestis or in other cumpanyingis.[2]

But one of his own sermons, as we have seen, provoked a hornets' nest, whilst other sermons which he delivered were, according to his own account, equally provocative.[3]

In fact the fifteenth-century sermon was an imperfect production, even judging it by the standards of an earlier age.[4] Here and there a preacher of eminence like Pecock's adversary, Dr William Lichfield, rector of All Hallows and reputed author of no less than 3083 sermons all written in his own hand, or John Felton of

---

[1] Dr Lichfield said that a man 'herynge holy sermonys is ofte by such herynge stirid in his herte to repentaunce and gode lyvynge' (Owst, *op. cit.* 191).

[2] *Repressor*, I, 88. On the 'pileum' see Rashdall, *Med. Univ.* III, 390-1.

[3] E.g. *Donet*, 104-5. See pp. 34-7 of this essay.

[4] Dr Owst writes of the university sermon, 'fulsome self-depreciation, fatuous metaphors, lavish titles of honour for his auditors, stilted Latin verses' (*op. cit.* 262). In addition to Dr Owst's two books, *Preaching in Medieval England* and *Literature and Pulpit in Medieval England* (1933), Chapters II and III of Canon C. H. Smyth's *The Art of Preaching* (1940) contain some useful material.

Oxford, another of his contemporaries, or in an earlier age, Bishop Brunton of Rochester or Master Rypon of Durham, stand out. But in general the subject-matter of the most eloquent preachers of the day, the friars or 'clamatores in pulpitis'[1] as Pecock called them, was often entertaining but neither mentally nor spiritually satisfying. The material for the sermons was not only unsatisfactory but the parish priest too often neglected his duty:

> It were a travail for to preche
> The feith of Christ, as for to teche
> The folke painim.[2]

In one way then Pecock was not only defending but he was also attacking abuses, putting forward the more rational view that good grounding was necessary for good preaching.[3] Master Robert Rypon, sixty years previously, had emphasised the good preacher's need of knowledge,[4] but he had noticeably less circumspection than Pecock.

After this lengthy discussion on the hierarchy and all that was

---

[1] John Bale's catalogue of Carmelite authors numbers more than 40 for the period 1350–1450. Cf. Richard de Bury: 'for there grows up among your promiscuous flock of laity a pestilent multitude of creatures, who nevertheless the more shamelessly force themselves into the office of preaching, the less they understand what they are saying, to the contempt of the Divine Word and the injury of souls' (Owst, op. cit. 84).

[2] Gower, Confessio Amantis. Cf. Hoccleve, Regement of Princes:

> 'The oynement of holy sermonynge
> Hym loth is upon hem for to dispende.'

Cf. 'How wolt thise gret clerkes answere and thise gret persons that dwellen in lordes courtes, that preche not one in three ȝere or foure? I trowe ful harde' (MS. 18 B. xxiii, fol. 63 b—cited Owst, op. cit. 43).

[3] The difference between teaching and preaching is examined by Roger Byrde in MS. Harl. 6580, fol. 2 (Owst, op. cit. 4): 'A grete differens es betwene prechynge and techynge. Prechynge es in a place where es clepynge to gedyr, or foluynge of pepyl in holy dayes, in chyrches or othe places and tymes ordeyned therto. And it longeth to he tht been ordeyned therto, the whyche have jurediccion and auctorite, and to noon othyr. Techynge es tht eche body may enforme and teche hys brothyr in every place and in conable tyme, es he seeth tht it be spedful: ffor this es a godly almes dede to whych every man es bounde tht hath cunnynge.'

[4] 'Restat quod scientia est curato necessaria' (Owst, op. cit. 28 ff.).

connected with it, Pecock proceeded to speak of the Lollard attack on the monks and friars. Wyclif's barbs were first aimed at the endowed orders, the 'religiosi possessionati', but later the friars, whose efforts he had at first championed, became the chief targets of his attack. His attack was in reality a combination of the hostile viewpoints of William of St Amour and William of Occam. The monks are hypocrites who act as spies on behalf of the Papal Curia, who live like leeches on the riches of the realm, who form so great a financial and moral burden to the English people that they should be disendowed and expelled.[1] He could not conceive of a universal church which was characterised by an intricate hierarchy and a system of monastic and mendicant orders living a life different from that of the other members of the Church. He regarded their perpetual vows—and here Pecock agrees with him, if for a very different reason—as unlawful, but his main attack centred on their way of life and their allegiance to an extra-national sovereign, the Pope. He also complained, like Gascoigne[2] and other orthodox writers, that the system by which they appropriated vicarages was evil. Finally, he asserted that both monks and friars were most certainly not appointed by Christ, and that they did not even keep to their vows of poverty. They are in fact the parasites of the English nation.

Pecock's reply to the Lollard argument is perhaps the least satisfactory of his answers, partly, perhaps, because Pecock was himself not over-sympathetic towards the friars. Some of their number were among his most persistent opponents. After refuting the suggestion that the religious orders are false teachers and 'flaterers and enviers and ypocritis and bacbiters' of which the

---

[1] De Blasphemia, cap. XIV–XVII, 201 ff.

[2] Loci e Loco Veritatum, 3, 5. Gascoigne says that it was one of the causes of the ruin of the kingdom of Bohemia. Pecock incidentally put down the 'wepeable destruccioun of the worthi citee and vniuersite of Prage and of the hool rewme of Beeme' to the strife among the 'bible men', who 'trustith to his owne studie in the Bible aloon' (Repressor, 1, 86–7). Dr R. A. R. Hartridge's History of Vicarages in the Middle Ages (1930) contains some useful information on appropriations.

Epistles[1] and St Hildegarde speak,[2] he refers to the positive reasons
for their existence. Christ may not indeed have appointed them
directly, but neither did he appoint the Lord Mayor of London.
That certainly does not prove that either the religious orders or the
Lord Mayor are condemned by Him or by His followers.[3] It may
be admitted that monasteries contain bad monks, but even such
monks do less evil than the soldiers fighting in France, possibly a
justifiable but certainly a remarkably tactless statement considering the fact that France and England had been engaged in hostilities for over thirty years:

Take me all the religiose men of England, whiche ben now and
han ben in religioun in Englond this thritti ʒeeris and mo now
eendid, in which XXXti ʒeeris hath be contynuel greet werre
bitwixe Englond and Fraunce; and lete se what schulde haue
worthe of the men in these ʒeeris, if thei hadden not be mad
religiose...whether not thei schulden haue be...gileful artificers,
or vnpiteful questmongers and forsworn iurers, or sowdiers
wagid into Fraunce forto make miche morther of blood, ʒhe, and
of soulis, bothe in her owne side and in the Frensch side? Who
can seie nay herto, but that riʒt likeli and as it were vnscapabili
these yuelis and many mo schulden haue bifalle to tho persoones,
if thei hadden not be religiose?...And sotheli this skile (as me
semeth) ouʒte move ech man ful miche forto holde with such
religiouns, if he be wijs forto considere how synful it is welnyʒ

[1] E.g. Colos. ii, 8, 18; I Tim. iv, 2; Titus i, 10; II Pet. ii, 1–2; II Pet.
iii, 3; Jude i, 4.

[2] The Lollards like many other writers made much of the writings of the
learned abbess Hildegarde: 'And among the prophecies and reuelaciouns
spokun bi the seid holi maide Seint Hildegart sche spekith that aftir hir daies
schulde rise iiii ordris of beggers' and that 'thei schulden be flaterers, and
enviers and ypocritis and bacbiters' and 'of wijse and trewe men this ordre
schal be cursid' and 'that for her synful and gileful lyuyng the comoun peplis
hertis schulden falle awey from hem, and thei schulden falle and ceese and that
her ordre schulde be alto broke for her bigilingis and her wickidnessis'
(*Repressor*, II, 483–4). On Hildegarde see Migne, *Pat. Lat.* CXCVII.

[3] Dionysius Areopagiticus tells us that: 'he makith mensioun that the grete
dukis of the chirche, whiche lyueden with the Apostlis, maden and ordeyneden
the religioun of monkehode to be had and vsid in the chirche' (*Repressor*, II,
459). He says that it is a great pity 'lay peple' have not the epistles of St Ignatius
and Denys's 'book of Goddis Namyngis' 'in her modir tunge', for they would
then reverence the hierarchy as they ought (*Book of Faith*, 189).

alle persoons lyuyng out of religioun; and into how comberose
plijt the world is brouȝt, that tho synnes (as it were) mowen
not be lefte...thouȝ thei ben men and not aungels and kunnen
not lyue without al synne.[1]

His replies to the Lollard attacks on monastic buildings and the
Franciscan habit of counting money with a stick were equally
evasive.[2] In numerous writings and especially in the *De Apostasia*,[3] Wyclif had attacked the monks, their ships on the seas,
their treasures of jewels and money as well as their palatial buildings. These attacks were repeated and expanded by his followers.
Pecock tried to justify the building of great mansions and churches
by the monastic orders by referring to the use which the upper
classes of society[4] made of them and the subsequent patronage or
reward so gained, which ultimately redounds to the benefit of the
poor. A previous opponent of Wyclif, unknown by name but
termed by his enemies 'pseudofrater, idiota et nimis ignarus',[5]
had used much the same plea when he urged that disendowment
would mean that monasteries could no longer offer hospitality.[6]
So Pecock writes:

It is alloweable, profitable, and procurable bi therto strecching
meenis that lordis and ladies, whanne thei schulen come to citees,
be loggid out fro the myche entermeting of the world in suche
placis where the world schal be myche holde out of her siȝt and

---

[1] *Repressor*, II, 516–17, or as he puts it more succinctly: 'and that tho lyuers
in religioun han lyued ther yn so vicioseli ȝit myche more vicioseli thei
wolden haue lyued, if thei hadden lyued out of religioun.'

[2] *Id.* II, 544: 'thei ben not weerned bi the same religioun forto telle such
money with a stik holdun in her hond, neither forto kepe it in her cofris,
neither thei ben weerned for to holde, bere, touche, and handle cuppis and
dischis, knyfis and iewelis of siluer and of gold, how euer preciose and
delectable to the siȝt tho iewelis ben.'

[3] *De Apostasia*, II, 23, 32, 34, 42, 44.

[4] This was not an idea entirely confined to the medieval period, viz. when
$36,000 were spent on a building site and $8500 for chimes by the Michigan
Avenue Baptist Church it was urged that 'in a region of wealth and fine
houses, you must have a fine church' (*Standard*, April 20th, 1871).

[5] *Sermones*, III, 37.

[6] It had been one of Wyclif's complaints that the friars visited the homes
of the great but 'deign not to come to poor men's houses for stink and filth'
(*Sermones*, III, 194).

out of her cumpeyning, that he ʒeue not to hem occasiouns of yuel...it is alloweable, resonable, and profitable that religiose persoones of whateuer religioun thei ben, haue freendis and menteyners and defenders...aʒens wrongers and diffamers of the synful and wickid world.[1]

In addition to this, large churches admit large congregations more comfortably than small churches and offer opportunities for people to go there to

here theryn prechingis to be mad in reyne daies...whilis the grete multitude mowen come thider in reyne daies after mydday, for to counceile with her freendis and with her wise counseilers aboute making of accordis and aboute redressing of wrongis and aboute other vertuose deedis.[2]

The least impressive of his arguments is that with which he justified the Franciscan attitude to money.[3] The method which they employ, he urges, is really a reminder of the abuses to which excessive love of money can give rise. When the Lollards assert that the Franciscans show but little scruple about touching jewels, Pecock can only reply that 'iewelis ben not in so manye kindis so redy and so niʒe to the vce in which the hauer mai delite him synfully, as is money'.[4]

Although Pecock's arguments are superficial and evasive—he himself cannot have been ignorant of the vast extent of monastic property, the great abbey of Osney, for instance—his concluding point is not without interest. He does not deny that many of the monks and friars, indeed many of the clergy, are fallible, but he

---

[1] *Repressor*, ii, 548–9.   [2] *Id.* ii, 553–4.

[3] The difference between *usus laxus* and *usus pauper* with all its attendant implications was one of the causes of the rise of the Spiritual Franciscans (*vide* D. L. Douie, *The Nature and Effect of the Theory of the Fraticelli*, Manchester, 1932). At first all purchases were made through a third person, a 'spiritual friend', but by 1250 spiritual friends had become legal representatives or business agents. 'As the proctors were entirely dependent on the friars, the formality of acting through them was often disregarded in practice and the Franciscans' claim to be the observers of evangelical poverty rested solely on the theory that the ownership of their goods, both real and personal, was vested in the Holy See' (A. G. Little, *Studies in English Franciscan History*, Manchester, 1917, 32). For Pecock's views on 'wilful pouerte' see *Donet*, 51.

[4] *Repressor*, ii, 557.

asks his opponents to show some understanding, to realise that the clergy were not only officers of an institution but human beings as well. 'Weel y wote that in summe thingis prelatis synnen and amys doon. For, thouʒ thei ben prelatis in the chirche, thei ben men and not pure aungels, and therfore thei ben suche, and muste needis be suche, that han the natural temptatyue wrecchidnessis whiche other men han.'[1] Or again: 'preestis ben born vndir coniuncciouns and constellaciouns stiring and moving into as greet freelnes and badde maners as othere laymen ben born, and also preestis ben of as badde kindeli complexiouns moving into badde and scharpe passiouns as ben laymen; and so al freelnes, which is naturali and strongli and fersly in lay men, ben lijk miche in preestis.'[2] This curiously human touch has something of the Renaissance humanism about it, despite the scholastic mould into which Pecock's thought had been forced.

This did not end his controversy with the Lollards, but as the manuscripts containing his arguments on other topics with which he intended to deal have been lost we can only just touch on some of his arguments. The *Filling of the Four Tables*,[3] the *Book of Worshipping* and the *Book of Sacraments* probably contained the substance of his refutation of the other Lollard propositions in greater detail than does the material which we now possess.

The first of the remaining five points concerned the invocation of saints and the intercessions which priests offered up on behalf of particular people. 'The lay peple erren...That the preestis and othere clerkis preien to God and to Seintis, and thei so preien bothe for hem silf and for her neiʒboris; and thei graunten to summe othere persoones forto be partyners in sum kinde of her preiers, and of her abstinencis, of her wacchis, and of her othere gode deedis and suffrauncis.'[4] Pecock once again attacks the individualism of the Lollard argument: 'ech man schal fare weel goostli oonli bi hise owne gode deedis.'

[1] *Repressor*, I, 105.   [2] *Id.* II, 450.
[3] This book must be identical with the *Spreading of the Four Tables*.
[4] *Repressor*, II, 561.

In the second place he turned to the Lollard condemnation of 'bellis, baners and suche othere...ymagis and crossis...relikis kissid of men' which the Lollards asserted 'myȝten be solde and be delid to poor men' and which often became the objects of superstitious veneration.[1] When he had been dealing with the question of image worship, Pecock had touched on this question and his reply must have been of a very similar nature to the Lollard argument against the worship of images. The following quotation gives an outline of his argument. They, he says,

be dressid to remembre vs of tho thingis whiche thei ben ordeyned to signifie and bitokene. Of whiche signes summe ben ordeyned of the clergie with consent of the comoun peple, as ben the bodili hous of the chirche with alle the ornamentis therynne, with liȝtis, encensis, hali watir, gay and riche clothis and garnementis, crossis, ymagis, peyntingis, bellis, organs, myrie songis, stipelis, gay corven roofis with craftiose windowis, dyuersite of deedis to be doon after reule and ordre of the ordinal.[2]

He further mentions that 'al thin holy wordis, lord, reding, heering or remembring, ben more speedful into this purpos of gendring welwilling...than ben the othere signes in her beste maner vsing'.[3] If these symbolic rites and articles do not serve to recall the objects for which they stand then they 'ben vsid rudely, and vnfrutefully...and waasten greet cost of almes and expensis'.[4]

He then came to Wyclif's attack on transubstantiation:

That in the chirche ben had grete signes and sacramentis, and her vsis; as ben baptem, confermyng, hosil of Cristis bodi and blood, and othere mo; whiche sacramentis and her vsis summe of the lay peple holden to be pointis of wicche craft and blindingis, brouȝt into Cristen men bi the feend and the anticrist and hise lymes. And in special thei abhorren aboue alle othere the hiȝest and worthiest signe and sacrament of alle othere, the sacrament of the auter, the preciose bodi and blood of Crist for us hangid in

[1] *Repressor*, II, 562.   [2] *Reule*, 244.   [3] *Id.* 244–5.
[4] He stipulated that in any case 'ouer myche cost' must not be expended on symbols and tokens, e.g. 'thre hundrid mark for oon sewt of vestementis in a tyme of myche derthe whanne peple were in poynt to deie for hungir, or forto make a belle of ii hundrid mark'.

the cros and for us out sched; in so miche that thei not oonli scornen it, but thei haaten it, mys callen it bi foule names, and wolen not come her thankis into the bodili chirche, whilis thilk sacrament is halewid, tretid, and vsid in the masse.[1]

Pecock's reply, as we can gather from his allusions in *The Reule of Chrysten Religioun,* followed closely along the ordinary orthodox lines.[2] The Lollard attacks on oaths[3] and on war[4] were the concluding points with which he intended to deal.

The significance and value of Pecock's reply to the Lollards should by now be fairly clear. His replies to the Lollard attacks

---

[1] Pecock's defence was not only published in his—lost—*Book of Sacraments* but also in two other books which he wrote, the *Book of Baptism* (*Repressor,* II, 564) and the *Book of Eucharist* (*Repressor,* II, 564; *Reule,* 96). In the *Reule* he says in regard to salvation through the sacraments: 'he muste receive or haue wille to receive if he may bi his age, the sacrament of baptym with feith of crist, of his lijf and of his passioun...in repentaunce of his old synys afore doon if he haue eny afore doon, and in wille to lyue riȝtfully...and also thanne may he be eftsoones confermed and strengthid to stonde bi grace to be receivid in deuout receivyng [of the] eukarist' (*id.* 206). Cf. *Donet,* 34–5.

[2] 'Riȝt so out of this article of bileeue which is that aftir crist had takun breed in his hondis and hadde blessid it and hadde seid, "this is my body which schal be takun for ȝou", the chirche drivith out and concludith forth bi labour and avises in resoun that ther was no bodily breed in cristis hondis but the breed ceesid to be, And that the whitnes, gretnes, roundenes, figure, fauour and othere qualitees and accidentis whiche weren bifore in the breed and cleeving to the breed weren in thilk tyme withoute eny bodili substaunce hem supportyng, And also that into how manye euer parties crist brake and hadde brokun what he heelde in his hoondis, in ech of alle thilke parties, how litil euer it hadde y-be, schulde haue be al the ful and hool, long and greet cristis body, and that in lijk maner it is whanne euer a preest hath maade consecracioun of breed at the auter, and al this the chirche deliuereth to the lay peple and makith no counseil ther of...but certeyn open ynouȝ it is that the lay peple wold be as redy forto resone, drive and labore in her vndirstonding vpon the seid maters touching the sacrament of the auter now deliuered to hem bi the chirche' as they would on the Holy Trinity itself (*Reule,* 94–5; cf. p. 96, where he mentions 'namelich Johan Wiccliffe' by name).

[3] 'That the clergie in certein causis and maters swerith and makith othere persoones forto swere...' (*Repressor,* II, 564).

[4] 'That men for her trespacis ben doon into her deeth. For summe of the lay partie holden that no man schulde be slein of eny other man for eny trespace, cause or perel; but al slauȝter vpon man is reserued to God. And also thei holden that in no wise and in no caas bateil is leeful, neither bitwixe Cristen and Cristen, neither bitwixe Cristen and hethen' (*id.* II, 564–5).

on the orthodox position give a remarkably good picture of the
views which the mid-fifteenth century followers of Wyclif maintained. In the second place, the reply itself was based on a philosophy which Pecock summed up in the phrase 'doom of reason'.
The conjectures with which he was dealing and with which both
the Lollards and their opponents were concerned, the conception
of natural reason, the authority of the scripture, and of ecclesiastical tradition, had long been commonplaces in the medieval
schoolroom. Pecock's significance was that 'he arranged', as a
recent writer has put it, 'the familiar stock in trade of the scholastic theologian in a strikingly fresh order'.[1] It was this which
led to his being charged with disbelieving the infallibility of the
Church and of general councils.

Then thirdly this discussion throws light on Pecock's own
character. Although his personality was essentially medieval, his
emphasis on the necessity for persuasion is suggestive of the
humanism of later eras. He definitely says that the clergy will be
blamed at the last judgement if they have used fire, sword or
'hangment'—although he does not doubt the validity of these
methods—rather than 'cleer witt' to draw men to the true faith.[2]
It shows too, and this is markedly important, that Pecock had
great gifts as a critic, and in one sense it is as a critic that he stands
out in the ecclesiastical history of fifteenth-century England.
Indeed, the *Repressor* is more than a *livre de circonstance*, and the
reply to the Lollards which it contains will, in the words which
Babington has used, 'be regarded as a masterly performance'.

[1] The late Mr B. L. Manning.   [2] *Book of Faith*, 139.

CHAPTER XII

BISHOP PECOCK AS A CRITIC

Pecock's reply to the Lollard arguments together with his reliance on the 'doom of reason' have already disclosed his critical ability. There are many illustrations in his works, some of them mentioned in the charges brought against him at his trial, of that critical ability at work. Such criticism was certainly not without parallel in the Middle Ages, but the way in which Pecock worded his criticisms, even of St Thomas Aquinas from whom he at times explicitly disagrees,[1] disclosed an insidious, even if an unconscious attack upon the 'medieval ethic' of authority. He was constantly at pains to justify his attacks upon traditional authorities, especially as he realised that such indiscreet criticism aroused angry comment from his opponents.

His contemporaries were particularly irritated by the superior attitude he adopted towards Aristotle and the Fathers of the Church, whose writings, he declared, were not more inspired than his own. Aristotle's opinions should only be accepted when they have been proved to be true by the 'doom of reason', for his authority does not carry greater weight than that of any other philosopher. 'It likith not to me forto so reuerence and folewe Aristotil aȝens treuth, ffor wel y wote it was neuyr Aristotilis wil that eny man schulde so do.'[2] He himself said that a great friend is Plato but a greater friend is truth. He, no less than others at this present day, failed to elucidate many points of natural and moral philosophy.

---

[1] 'Thouȝ thilk doctour hadde be my fadir, y wolde and muste needis varie from him in this now towchid poynt' (*Folewer*, 100).

[2] *Folewer to the Donet.* Cf. 'What was Aristotil othir than a louer of trouth, and therfore a laborer bisi forto fynde the knowyng of treuth, bothe for him silf and for othire? Many, forsothe, of oolde philesofris passiden him in the mathematik sciencis and in astrologie, and many passiden hem in methaphisik, and many passiden hem in medicinal philosofie. Oonli in logik and in comoun natural philosofie and in moral philosofie he passide the othire oolde clerkis' (*id.* 151–2).

His attitude to the Church Fathers is well summed up in this quotation from the *Repressor*:

Writingis of Doctouris in greet plente and noumbre myȝten be brouȝt into witnessing of this present purpos, and greet multitude of her writingis myȝten be brouȝt sownyng into the contrarie; but for as miche as her feelingis and her writingis neither binden neither vnbinden in eny mater more or ferther or otherwise than thei [ben] taken out of lawe of kinde or of Holi Scripture or of mannis lawe,[1] neither to hem it is to trowe ferther or more than thei kunne hem grounde in eny of these now spoken groundis or fundamentis....Ech of hem seide and wroot, as he trowid for the tyme to be trewe; thouȝ ful ofte thei seemen among hem to discorde and ful ofte redili thei discorden.[2]

He says of St Jerome, for instance, that 'his tunge was not the key of heuen or of erthe, neither had power to make eny thing to be trewe or fals'. Doctors of divinity cannot be called creators because they are merely students of divine truths.[3] The truth of their own views is dependent on their approximation to the axioms of divinity or to conclusions deduced from the 'doom of reason'. The biblical exegesis of famous doctors is always liable to correction, for there is constant 'amending and encresing of resoun and newe fynding of thingis afore hid'.[4] He goes on to say that to refer important questions to doctors or to scripture without thinking about the questions themselves 'schendith our verry scole leernyng and clergie and kunnyng'.[5] It is only right that the laity should realise that the teachings of Aristotle and the Doctors are not necessarily infallible, because if they do this they will not be so quick to attack Pecock when he differs from them.[6] Yet we must not carry Pecock's challenge too far; he himself disowns any attempt to disparage their works which are 'ful profitable, namelich if thei be take into vse bi a good discrecioun'.[7]

It is not only Aristotle, the Fathers or the scholastic thinkers of

---

[1] 'Mannis lawe' = civil law of nations and canon law of the Church.
[2] *Repressor*, II, 320. Cf. *Book of Faith*, 146.
[3] *Folewer to the Donet*, 65.   [4] *Reule*, 464.
[5] *Id.* 465.   [6] *Folewer*, 68.   [7] *Id.* 11.

the medieval period who suffer discomfiture at his hands, for dogma and historical tradition are similarly criticised. 'Alas', he observed in relation to faith, 'the Cristen clergie laboren not as ȝitt forto considere clerli what feith is in his owne kinde, and whiche ben the evydencis wherbi it schulde be proved, and forto dispose tho evydencis in cleer formal maner of silogisme, and to have hem redi at mynde.'[1] It is shameful to argue that faith, the substance of salvation, may not be examined in order to see whether 'it is worthi to be allowid for trewe faith or no'. Such 'prisonyng of thi faith'[2] is a denial of the Church's right and should in consequence be denounced by the clergy. Certain other suggestions which he put forward concerning biblical and credal questions are significant in view of the trial. He had not the critical exactitude which impelled Abailard to compile *Sic et Non*, but the general intelligence of his mind obliged him to ask questions and to formulate suggestions as to the answers.

Although there can be little doubt that he would not have challenged the 'divine inspiration' of the biblical writers had he been pressed on this point, he once again subordinates the Bible to the 'doom of reason'. It is in many ways no more sacred than any other book, 'writun and schapun vnder dyuerse figuris in parchemyn or in velim', and accordingly no more holy than any other volume which 'hath lijk good ynke, and is lijk craftili figurid'.[3] He treated the contents of the Bible in a similar fashion, exposing them to the eye of inquiry and criticism. The most interesting example of Pecock's critical method is his investigation of the origin of the Book of Genesis. Moses, he suggests, compiled the book of Genesis by editing a number of traditions which had been handed down through the centuries. 'Forwhi, soone aftir the flood of Noe, ther was leernyng of the vii sciencis, and writing maad in ii pilers, oon of bras, and another of erthe, and also in the same tyme ther was leernyng and writyng of wicchecraft, or of nycromancie, as the Maistir of Stories writith,

---

[1] *Book of Faith*, 131.   [2] *Id.* 133.
[3] *Repressor*, I, 81.

in the chapiter of the toure of Babel.'[1] As Enoch was the inventor
of writing, he might have been the first chronicler of the tradition
which forms the basis of Genesis. It was not unlikely, he adds
with a happy inspiration, that Noah kept such records and made
'ghostly' reckonings in his ship. These traditions were handed
down through his sons to Abraham and so on to Moses who
'gaderide al this togidir, and made a book therof which is clepid
Genesis'.[2]

The few references which he makes to the writing of the
Gospel stories are interesting but far less effective instances of his
critical ability.[3] He follows medieval authority in making the
Gospels synoptic in the real sense; Matthew wrote seven years
after the Crucifixion, Mark seventeen, and Luke and John later
still.[4] The attention which he pays to oral tradition is certainly suggestive in its implications: 'O my sone', he addresses an imaginary

[1] *Book of Faith*, 262–4. Petrus Comestor is the Master of Stories. A
reference to witchcraft in the *Donet* (206) is not irrelevant here. Witchcraft is
condemned, he says, because 'that thilk craft puttith vertu in wordis and
countenauncis and dedis more than bi resoun can therynne be founde'.

[2] *Id.* 264; cf. the views of Andrew of St Victor (B. Smalley, *The Study of
the Bible in the Middle Ages*, 105).

[3] Pecock's reference to Miracles. While there is no doubt as to the general
orthodoxy of Pecock's views on miracles, it is interesting to note that he carried
his 'reason-judgement', his emphasis on necessary evidence, into his discussion
on this subject. Thus: 'to privey myraclis we schuden not renne, forto defende
oure opinioun or oure answere bi hem, without that sufficient evydence therto
serveth' (*Book of Faith*, 270). Miracles must be 'wel tried and examyned bi
sufficient trewe witnessing, or bi open at fulle schewing' (*id.* 293). There are,
he adds, many 'pretense myraclis and pretense inspiracions', and he continues: 'Thomas of Cantilbiri is a seint; Joon of Bridlington is a seint, in the
seid dew undirstonding of this word seynt, and so forth of othere, whos
lyvyng, and for whom the myraclis doon ben weel examyned, and tried bi
witnesssis sworne;...Forwhi, certis among hem a diligent wise ensercher
schal fynde, sumtyme supersticiouns, sumtyme errouris aʒens sure knowen
trouthe, sumtyme heresies aʒens the feith, and sumtyme contrariete bitwie hem
silf.' There is, he also says, a little earlier in the *Book of Faith*, a mass of evidence to suggest that truth gets very deformed in the process of narration:
'al the tyme of werre during these xl ʒeer bitwixe Ynglond and Fraunce, wist
y not scant iii or iiii men, whiche wolden accorde thorouʒ out, in telling how
a toun or a castel was wonne in Fraunce, or hou a batel was doon there' (*id.*
252).   [4] *Book of Faith*, 255.

interlocutor, 'if thou woldist take hede, hou a tale or a tiding, bi the tyme that it hath runne throuȝ iiii or v mennys mouthis, takith pacchis and cloutis, and is chaungid in dyvers parties, and turned into lesingis, and al for defaute of therof the writing.'[1]

But there is much more to Pecock's critical faculty than this. One of the charges which had been levelled against him at his trial had accused him of having written a new creed, *novum symbolum*,[2] and an examination of the truth of this charge is a fruitful indication of the critical working of Pecock's mind. It is clear that he did not regard the Creed as the epitome of the Christian faith so much as a supplement to those truths ingrained in man's mind by natural reason. The Creed must not be regarded as an all-inclusive statement of faith,[3] but as an authoritative declaration of belief which should be accepted by all Christians.[4] The New Testament, which is of far greater importance than the Creed, may much more justifiably be called the Apostles' Creed.[5] There is little or no direct evidence that Pecock ever fabricated a new creed in his own words.

The cumulative evidence, however, that he used the Apostles' Creed, omitting the Descent into Hell, is extensive, and it was around this omission that the theory of the new creed centred. Whetehampstead says that Pecock added a fourth creed in the vernacular from which the article 'de Descensu Christi ad Inferos' was omitted.[6] The creed which Pecock published in the *Donet* certainly omitted this article,[7] and implicit recognition of the omission was given in the *Book of Faith*. It is possible that the latter part of this book might have given us some useful information on this point as the bishop proposed to treat of the Apostles' Creed in it, but—perhaps for that very reason—it has disappeared. In the fifth chapter he argued that Duns Scotus's[8] statement that

---

[1] *Book of Faith*, 250-1.   [2] Whetehampstead, *Chron. Monast. S. Albani*, 1, 280.
[3] *Donet*, 158.   [4] *Book of Faith*, 248.   [5] *Donet*, 104.
[6] Whetehampstead, *op. cit.* 1, 280.   [7] *Donet*, 103-4.
[8] *Opus Oxoniense*, 1, dist. 11, qu. 11: 'Dico quod Christum descendisse ad inferna non docetur.' Cf. 111, dist. xx11, qu. 1. *Vide* Seeberg, *Die Theologie des Duns Scot* (Leipzig, 1900), 268 ff., 281 ff.

belief in Christ's descent 'into hellis' was a necessary fundamental of Christian belief was not warranted by scripture and, presumably, by natural reason. For 'in the tyme of Austyn, and of othere holi clerkis aboute Austyns tyme, the comune crede hadde not withynne him this seid article'.[1] This proves, first, that the Apostles were not the authors of the Creed which goes by their name, and, secondly, that the Creed is not a full, nor as far as this article is concerned an accurate, statement of Christian doctrine. Both these statements constitute an implicit denial of the beliefs of contemporary theology and have a significance rarely recognised by past students of Pecock.

The Descent into Hell was a belief which played an important part in medieval theology, especially in popular theology. An examination of the writings of Pecock's time is some indication of this. Thus the author of *The Lay-Folks Mass-Book* writes:

> Tho soul of him went into helle,
>   tho sothe to say;
> vp he rose in flesshe and felle
>   tho thryd day.[2]

Similarly John Myrc writes:

> How he wente to spoyle helle,
> In soule and godhede wyth-owte nay
> Whyle the body in towmbe lay.[3]

We have the same attestation in three very dissimilar authors:

> Was in a ston byried,
> And descended a-doune to the derk helle,
> And fet oute our formfaderes & hy full feyn weren.[4]

and

The seuenthe article is of his descendynge into helle, wherof we say, only in the comon crede Descendit ad inferna. He descended in to helle, that is to say, when hys soule departed from

[1] *Book of Faith*, 304–5.
[2] *The Lay-Folks Mass-Book*, ed. T. F. Simmons (E.E.T.S. 1879), 20.
[3] *Instructions for Parish Priests*, ed. E. Peacock (E.E.T.S. 1868), 16.
[4] *Pierce the Ploughmans Crede*, ed. W. W. Skeat (E.E.T.S. 1867), 30.

the body by dethe on the crosse, then the same soule vnied to the godhed, went downe into helle. Ther the holy sowles of fathers were, the body abydynge on the crosse and afterwarde taken downe and buryed, vnyed also to the godhed for the godhed departed neuer from the soule ne from hys body...the soulle and the body were departed by dethe. Also ye shall vnderstande that oure lorde delyuered not all that were in helle.[1]

Finally Wyclif:

His sowle went to helle, and toke owt the sowlys that he ordeyned to save before this world was made.[2]

This belief was accepted unquestionably by both scholarly and popular writers as well as by professional theologians.[3] Perhaps Duns Scotus's view is less dogmatic than say the view of Wyclif or Aquinas,[4] for he allows that Descent into Hell is not narrated in the Gospels, but neither he nor other theologians questioned its validity as an article of faith.

Therefore the way in which Pecock challenged its authenticity is very striking, especially when all the manifold implications of

[1] *The Myroure of oure Ladye*, ed. J. H. Blunt (E.E.T.S. 1873), 317.

[2] *Select English Works*, ed. T. Arnold (1871), III, 116.

[3] The significance of the belief may be gathered from the following references: Alcuin, *Commen. super Eccles.* 3; *Adv. Elipand.* 2, 2; Paul. Diacon. *Pat. Lat.* Migne, XCV, col. 1328, 1330; Paulin. Aquileia, *Poetae Latini aevi Caroli.*—'Claustra gehennae fregit', ed. P. Dümmler; Hincmar, *de Predestinatione, Pat. Lat.* CXXIV, cols. 283, 299; Haymo of Halberstadt, *Pat. Lat.* CXVIII, col. 445; Rabanus Maurus, *Pat. Lat.* CXII, *Homil.* 16 *in sabb. sanct. Pasch.*; Druthmar of Corbie, *Pat. Lat.* CVI, *Expos. in Matth.*; Atto of Vercelli, *Exp. in ep. ad Eph.* col. 566; Petrus Alphonsus, *Pat. Lat.* CLVII, col. 643, *tit.* 10; Anselm, *Pat. Lat.* CLVIII, *Hom.* 3 *in Matth.* 14, *Hom.* 4 *in Matth.* 17; Abailard, *Pat. Lat.* CLXXVIII, *Expositio symbol. Apost.* col. 626; '*Sic et Non*', col. 1468; St Hildegarde, *Pat. Lat.* CXCVII, col. 1076; Rupert of Deutz, *Pat. Lat.* CLXX, *De divinis officiis*, 1.7. c. 15, col. 195, 571; Peter Lombard, *Pat. Lat.* CLXXXVI, *Sententiarum*, 1.4. c. 16–26; 1.5. c. 1. For a non-theologian cf. Jean de Joinville, Natalis de Wailly, Paris (1874), 278. A slightly critical note is sounded by Durand de Saint-Pourcain in an interpretation of a phrase used by Abailard in *In Sent. Comm.* 1. iv, dist. 22, q. 3, 2 (Lyons, 1569).

[4] Append. qu. 1, art. 2: 'Sancti patres ante adventum Christi fuerunt in loco digniori, quam sit locus in quo nunc purgantur animae post mortem, quia non erat ibi aliqua poena sensibilis; sed locus ille erat conjunctus inferno, vel idem quod infernus.' Cf. Part III, 2. n. q. 1. ii, 395 ff.

that challenge are considered. First, it was an attack on the acceptance of this article of the creed as a necessary doctrine of belief. Secondly, he suggested that the Apostles had not actually compiled the Creed which went by their name, another challenge to an accepted view. It was not only believed by St Thomas Aquinas, for instance,[1] that the Apostles themselves had written the Creed which goes by their name, but it was believed that the Creed could be analysed by pointing to the sentences which each of the Apostles had contributed to it. Thus St Peter wrote the phrase 'Credo in deum patrem omnipotentem creatorem celi et terre'; St Andrew, 'Et in Iesum cristum filium eius unicum dominum nostrum'; whilst St Thomas was responsible for the 'Descendit ad Inferna'.[2] It should be noted that Pecock bases his criticism on history, that the 'Descent into Hell' was unknown to 'holy clerkis' living about the time of St Augustine.[3] If this were a genuine product of his own spontaneous critical faculty, it would be yet another proof of his importance in the fifteenth century, because he is again challenging something that was everywhere admitted to be true. This is, however, very uncertain. In any case, when he comes down to details he is inaccurate, for although the origin of the 'Descent into Hell' clause is obscure, it seems to have originated at Aquileia at the end of the fourth century,[4] and to have slowly percolated through to the West.[5]

In the third place, Pecock's denial of this article is important because of its close association with the widely spread belief in

---

[1] *Opusculum VII in Symbolum Apostolorum*, scilicet 'Credo in Deum' Expositio, XVI, 135 ff.

[2] *The Myroure of Our Ladye*, 312.

[3] In actual fact St Augustine himself does admit the Descent into Hell—*Ep.* CLXIV, 5.14; 2.3; 4.12.

[4] E.g. Hahn, *Bibliothek d. Symbole*, Breslau (1897), 22 ff.; Caspari, *Quellen* (Christiana, 1869), II, 46; F. Kattenbusch, *Das Apostol. Symbol* (Leipzig, 1900), II, 895 ff.

[5] A clause of a similar nature is found in the formulae of Sirmium (359), Nike in Thrace (359) and Constantinople (360)—Sanday, *Journal of Theological Studies*, III, 17.

the 'Harrowing of Hell', the significance of which we must appreciate if we are to understand the full import of Pecock's challenge. It is usually believed that the idea of the 'Harrowing of Hell' originated in the so-called *Gospel of Nicodemus* or *Acta Pilati*, which dates from the fourth century, but the actual story of the Descent into Hell is a later appendage, very rarely found in the Greek and never in the Syriac, but nearly always in the Latin, in itself an interesting consideration.[1] Its origin is, in fact, exceedingly obscure, nor did the late Dr M. R. James think it was appended to the *Acta Pilati* until the fifth century. In any case the idea itself, of the delivery of the Patriarchs from the shades of Sheol, dates as far back as the second century,[2] but it is more frequently found in later centuries after various dramatic additions had been made to the text.[3]

As we have it to-day the story of the Descent into Hell is as follows: Karinus and Leucius, two citizens of Arimathea whose resurrection to life Jesus had procured, write of Jesus' coming to Hades. They tell how Satan told Hades: 'Make thyself ready to receive Jesus who boasteth himself that He is the Son of God', and of how the Lord of Majesty appeared in the form of a man and lightened the eternal darkness and broke the bonds that could not be loosed. Then the 'succour of his everlasting might visited us that sat in the deep darkness of our transgressions and in the shadow of death of our sins'. Finally, the Lord 'holding the hand of Adam delivered him unto Michael the archangel, and all the saints followed Michael the archangel, and brought them all into

---

[1] M. R. James, *The Apocryphal New Testament*, 95.

[2] *Vide* references in the article on 'Descent into Hades' in Hastings, *Encyclopaedia of Religion and Ethics*, IV, 660.

[3] *Vide*, e.g., the *Homilies* of Eusebius of Emesa. It is possible to trace the developments in this belief from Ignatius to Tertullian who with Irenaeus implies that all that Christ did was to transfer the O.T. saints to a pleasanter part of Hades—'limbus patrum'—but for Ignatius the O.T. saints have been brought to salvation without the intermediate residence in Hades. Similarly, Christ's victory over Satan is probably in itself an expansion of the original version of the *descensus ad inferos*. Loofs traces it as far back as Origen in *Gen. Hom.* 17, 5 (ed. Lommatzsch, 1831–48, VIII, 290) basing it on Acts ii, 27.

the beauty (grace) and glory of Paradise', and at the same time thrust Satan, who wished to keep Jesus in Hades, into Tartarus.[1] In the medieval version,

> then jheus sone toke satanas
> that are was lore and sire,
> and him in thraldom bunden has
> to brin in endles fire.

Now this—the most extended version of the harrowing of hell which originally arose from the phrase 'was buried'[2]—had the very widest circulation and the deepest theological implications during the medieval period, when, from the very fact of human nature, hell was of more topical significance than heaven. Full treatment of the belief, for instance, is found in Caedmon's and Cynewulf's poems, whilst the *Gospel of Nicodemus* received the blessing of the Church and, indeed, the tenth-century Homily for Easter Day is derived almost entirely from the second part[3]—the Descent into Hell. There is little need to trace its further history, for by the twelfth century it had already become a favourite subject, in view of its dramatic possibilities, for the mystery plays, which in many ways represent better than anything else can the common beliefs of the ordinary man.[4] The 'Harrowing of Hell' was certainly a popular subject for the playwright; it appears frequently in the York Plays, the Wakefield (Towneley) Plays, the Chester and Coventry Plays, as well as in many others. Its

---

[1] M. R. James, *The Apocryphal New Testament* (Oxford, 1924), 118–43. Cf. also the 'Book of the Resurrection of Christ' by Bartholomew the Apostle (Coptic): 'Jesus...wrought havoc in Hell, breaking the doors binding the demons Beliar and Melkir and delivered Adam and Holy Souls' (*op. cit.* 167 ff.) and the Gospel of St Bartholomew.

[2] 'Christ went to Hades according to the beliefs of the age precisely because He died and was buried' (*E.R.E.* 660—ref. Tertullian, *de Anima*, ed. Reifferscheid, 1, 388), for Jews and Greeks believed that Hades and the grave were identical.

[3] *Blickling Homilies* (E.E.T.S.), 82 ff. *Vide* also the medieval version of the *Gospel of Nicodemus* by W. H. Hulme. The Gospel was first attributed to Nicodemus in medieval times by Vincent of Beauvais in the *Speculum Historiale* and by Jacob de Voragine in the *Legenda Aurea*.

[4] K. Young, *The Drama of the Medieval Church* (Oxford, 1933), 1, 149–77.

popularity is also seen in the constant use which was made of it by other writers and poets; perhaps the most famous example comes from Dante's *Divina Commedia*:

> rispose: 'Io era nuovo in questo stato,
>   quando ci vidi venire un possente
>   con segno di vittoria coronato.
>
> Trasseci l' ombra del primo parente,
>   d' Abel suo figlio, e quella di Noè,
>   di Moisè Legista, e ubbidiente;
>
> Abraam patriarca, e David re,
>   Israel con lo padre, e co' suoi nati,
>   e con Rachele, per cui tanto fe',
>
> ed altri molti; e fecegli beati:
>   e vo' che sappi che, dinanzi ad essi,
>   spiriti umani non eran salvati.'[1]

The invention of printing still further enhanced the popularity of the belief, which retained its hold on men's mind in the days of the Reformation.[2]

Thus the belief in the delivery of the Patriarchs from Hades, a confirmation in a sense of the inspiration of their writings by Christ, was an essential feature of orthodox medieval Christianity. Pecock's denial in fact constituted a theological *faux pas* of the first order, more especially as he supported his denial with historical criticism, however inaccurate. It should be understood that the medievalists divided Hell into four particular parts:

For there is one helle where dampned soules and fendes are and there came not oure lorde for to dyleuer any of them. Aboue that helle ys purgatory. And aboue that ys helle where chyldren are that dye wythin age vncrystened. And them our lorde delyuered not. But aboue all thys ys the helle of fathers where all they that dyed in trew faythe and charyte abode the comynge of cryste & all them he delyuered.

---

[1] *Divina Commedia*, Inferno, Canto IV, ll. 52–63. Cf. XII, l. 38.
[2] Luther believed that the Descent into Hell should be accepted as an article of faith. See J. Monnier, *La Descente aux Enfers* (Paris, 1905), 248 ff.

Babington says in reference to this: 'Pecock would without much scruple have admitted it to be an article of faith *in general terms* (taking hell as "the state of the dead, in general, without any restriction of happiness or misery"), though not in the *particular sense* in which it may have been ordinarily explained in his own age.'[1] But Pecock denied the descent of Christ into hell, into the *limbus patrum* and elsewhere, and he was too well acquainted with the different variations of hell to speak in the general terms postulated by Babington.

Thus if this omission did not in itself create the new creed of which Gascoigne, Whetehampstead and other of his adversaries complain, it did challenge a medieval belief on a fundamental point, and as significant was the critical bent of Pecock's mind which made such a challenge possible.

Pecock's examination of the Ten Commandments, and in particular of the third or Anglican fourth commandment, again reveal his critical faculty, for he affirmed that the Ten Commandments in themselves do not constitute an all-sufficient ethical system.[2] Those who urge that they do 'biwamblen so rudely and so vnredili, as thouȝ thei hadden forȝete hem silf to biholde into her clergye'.[3] Pecock's own 'four tables', which may, on the other hand, be called a full and inclusive exposition of God's will,[4] form a far more efficacious system of moral theology.

In particular he disputed the tendency to equate the Jewish Sabbath, the object of the third commandment, with the Christian

---

[1] Babington, Introd. lii n. He rightly says that 'Lewis, in attempting to wash Pecock clean, has somewhat dirtied his own fingers' (ref. Lewis, *Life of Pecock*, 180).

[2] The Ten Commandments cannot even pretend to contain all God's laws for the Jews, so that even logically speaking they cannot pretend to include all God's laws for the Christians (*Donet*, 135). Thus maiming, beating, fornication are not forbidden nor do the Commandments touch on the relationships between a superior and an inferior, the sacraments or repentance. They do not even teach God's laws clearly or sufficiently but in a 'hid, priuy, schort maner oonli' (*id.* 142).

[3] *Donet*, 142.

[4] *Id.* 119 ff., 147, 161.

Sunday.[1] The commandment is no longer binding on Christians because it merely aims to maintain the Jewish Sabbath, and it is therefore no more relevant to Christians than the command to eat the paschal lamb or to wear a cloth made of linen and wool, or the command not to use 'an hors and asse couplid togider'.[2] The Christian Sunday does not commemorate the day on which God rested from the creation of the world, but the day of our Lord's resurrection. Neither reason nor history indicate that Christ translated the Jewish Sabbath into the Christian Sunday.[3] It is far more probable that the practice of Sunday observance arose by will of the people's 'doom of reason', 'ffor that the peple in tho daies weren willi to do and holde such gouernauncis as were to her goostly profite', although they were in no way commanded so to do.[4]

Apart from this the Commandments do not form an all-inclusive system. When Christ, for instance, commanded the rich

[1] *Donet*, 148 ff. Pecock was disputing the opinions of certain doctors who maintained that the commandment was partly grounded in natural and partly in ceremonial law. The method of his argument is a good example of his syllogistic logic, viz. nothing was bidden in the third commandment save the hallowing of the Sabbath. The hallowing of the Sabbath (Saturday) is no longer binding on all Christians. Therefore there is nothing in the third commandment which is binding on all Christians. This is the rule of the general and the special mentioned by Aristotle in Book VII of the *Ethics*. He further argued that it cannot be proved that the Apostles made a law for its 'wilful deuout vse' though it was the custom in the Apostles' time to hallow it. It is probable that the people in those days made the law of their own free will. Sunday was chosen because 'Crist roos fro deeth to lijf the sundaie' (*Donet*, 132). It may be recalled that Puritan teaching was later very much inclined to equate the Sabbath with the Sunday, to such an extent that the M.P. for Shaftesbury was expelled by the puritan House of Commons in 1621 for asserting that Sabbath meant Saturday. *Vide* W. P. Baker's comments on seventeenth-century 'Observance of Sunday' in *Englishmen at Rest and Play* (ed. R. Lennard, 1931), 96 ff.

[2] It is fruitful to compare Dom John Gaytrik's sermon: 'The thirde commandement es, that we halde and halowe oure haly day, the sonondaye, and all other that falles to the ʒere, that er ordeynede to halowe thurgh Haly Kyrke' (*Religious Pieces*, ed. G. G. Perry (E.E.T.S. 1867), 5).

[3] *Donet*, 131.

[4] *Id.* 131. 'Bi doom of good pollitik resoun and profitable gouernaunce and good reule...withoute comaunding of the prelatis in tho daies' (*id.* 132).

man to keep the Ten Commandments if he was really desirous of obtaining eternal life, he did not mean the Ten Commandments alone, but all the commandments which came within the scope of Jesus' teaching. Gluttony is not forbidden nor are preaching and teaching commanded in the Ten Commandments, but both come equally within the scope of Jesus' commandments. 'And so, sone, thou maist se that manye thingis ben feynid about the x comaundementis of moyses tablis, which ben not trewe, or at the leest which ben lacking her groundingis.'[1] Thus like Richard Hooker in the next century, Pecock seems to have grasped that theology displayed not a static but a progressive revelation. It was his specific aim to deliver Christians from servile attachment to views and theories which were only held because they happened to be the view of certain venerated doctors. Christ, he pointed out in the same place, realised the importance of gradual enlightenment by means of which the teaching was adapted to those who were being taught.[2]

Finally, his critical faculties led him to challenge the authenticity of the Donation of Constantine. The *Donatio Constantini*—the supposed gift of temporal dominion over Rome, Italy and the 'provinces, places and *civitates* of the western regions' 'to Pope Sylvester I by the Emperor Constantine the Great in gratitude for his conversion'—which was embodied in the so-called Constitutum Constantini, a forged document dating from the ninth century or possibly earlier, was one of the theoretical bases on which temporal dominion and the far-reaching claims of the medieval papacy were founded.[3] Cited by Ado of Vienne[4] and Hincmar of Rheims[5] among other early writers, it was not put to any great use by papal propagandists until the times of Leo IX. From this time forward it became a weapon of ever greater im-

---

[1] *Donet*, 158.   [2] *Id.* 158.
[3] See my article on the 'Donation of Constantine' in the *Church Quarterly Review* (Dec. 1942), cxxxv, 39–64.
[4] 'De Sex Aetatibus Mundi' in Migne, *Pat. Lat.* cxxiii, 92.
[5] 'De Ordine Palatii' in Migne, *Pat. Lat.* cxxv, 98.

portance in papal hands, if very variously interpreted, and having been included in the Forged Decretals it became part of canon law.[1] Even the opponents of papal power did not challenge its authenticity, but they refuted the orthodox papal interpretations put upon it. Dante, for instance, writes:

> Ahi, Constantin, di quanto mal fu matre,
> non la tua conversion, ma quella dote
> che da te prese il primo ricco patre![2]

Although the significance of the Donation of Constantine is less than has sometimes been thought, there was little question as to the important place which it occupied in papal tradition. It did not go entirely unscathed—Leo of Vercelli, the imperial mystic, and Otto III, had questioned its authenticity, while the Arnoldists, the followers of Arnold of Brescia, had denounced it. In general both orthodox and heretical writers, papalists and anti-papalists, recognised its validity, however much they might differ as to the correct interpretation to be placed upon it.

The fifteenth century brought about a change in men's views about the Donation of Constantine, for it was challenged by three very different writers, by Cardinal Nicholas of Cusa, by Lorenzo Valla and by Reginald Pecock. Cusanus was the first of the three to challenge its authenticity, questioning its genuineness (together with that of the Forged Decretals) in the De Concordantia,[3] a work that was written about the time of the Council of Basle. Valla was a very different type of man, for although he was ordained to the priesthood he was certainly not concerned with proving how reasonable the Christian faith was for the benefit of deluded heretics. He was a scholar of great originality and critical skill, whose abusive attacks made him not undeservedly unpopular with his fellow-men. It was he who proved the falsity of the so-called letter of Christ to King Abgarus of Osrhoene.

---

[1] Decretum Gratiani, dist. XCVI, 13, 14. It was added as 'palea'.
[2] Divina Commedia, Inferno, Canto XIX, ll. 115 ff.; De Monarchia, III, c. x. Wyclif's view was not dissimilar—e.g. Wyclif, Trialogus, III, cap. 20; IV, cap. 17.
[3] De Concordantia Catholica (Basle, 1565), III, 2, 782–3.

Not content with that, he ridiculed the monastic life, accused St Augustine of heresy, and sneered at the Latin of the Vulgate—but withal became apostolic secretary to Pope Nicholas V in 1447. This spirited, abusive, scholarly humanist has little in common with Pecock except for his critical faculty. It is interesting to notice that he too questioned the attribution of the Apostles' Creed to the twelve apostles, and, but for the timely assistance of Alfonso of Naples, might have been tried by the Inquisition whither the attacks of the friars were leading him. Finally, he denounced the Donation of Constantine together with the papal dependence on it in the *De falso credita et ementita Constantini donatione declamatio*,[1] a well-reasoned exposure written in Valla's usual elegant, satirical style. With infinite sarcasm he pictured the Emperor Constantine alienating his territory, but his rejection of the authenticity of the documents is based on his examination of the evidence. Like Pecock, he urges that the claims of tradition are not supported by contemporary witnesses:

If any one among the Greeks, the Hebrews or the Barbarians were to say that such a thing were handed down by tradition, would you not ask for the author's name or the production of the record?

It has been urged that Pecock followed Valla but there is no real evidence to suggest that this statement is true.[2] In general the close-dating sequence,[3] the probability that Pecock had been working on the *Repressor* before 1449, the fact that this is not the only piece of critical work in the few remaining works of Pecock, almost certainly prove that he reached his conclusions independently of Valla, and Nicholas of Cusa. An examination of his attitude to the Donation certainly shows his critical faculty working vigorously. He begins by saying that 'in legendis ben

[1] *Opera* (Basle, 1540); W. Schwahn, *Laurentii Vallae de falso credita et ementita Constantini Donatione Declamatio* (Leipzig, 1928). Valla's work is fully treated in my article in *C.Q.R.* cxxxv, 47 ff.

[2] Canon Maynard Smith says 'Pecock had read Valla' (*Pre-Reformation England*, 422), but in response to my inquiries he kindly tells me that he had no direct evidence for this statement and that it was a statement by implication.

[3] Valla was writing c. 1439–40.

founde manie ful vntrewe fablis', and then in particular relation to the facts which led medieval scholars to accept the Donation of Constantine as a genuine document he continues:

in othere epistlis of Constantyn, which he wroot whanne he was in his moost rialte, is not such a stile of him as is in this now seid epistle...and sithen in the seid storie of Damase Pope is founde vntrouthe, which Ierom weel aspied....For whi...the seid Emperour Constantyn endewid not the Pope Siluester neither eny chirche in Rome with eny greet habundaunt immouable possessiouns, but oonli with possessiouns competentli and mesurabily, with sufficience seruyng for the fynding of the preestis and mynystris of the chirchis whiche he endewid...but al the habundaunt and riche endewing of the pope and his see chirche in Rome came bi othere persoones longe aftir Constantyn; as by Pipyn king of France, and by Charles king of Fraunce, and emperour, bi Lodowic king of Fraunce...and bi Matilde.[1]

He then proceeded to a more detailed analysis of his supposi-tions. In the first place, if the Donation of Constantine to Sylvester did not take place, the event has been shrouded in a conspiracy of silence, remarkable in any event, but even more surprising in view of the history of Sylvester's successors on the throne of Peter. Again, Pope Damasus did not mention the Donation although he told Jerome of far more trivial and less important endowments.[2] The editor of the *Historia Tripartita* forges another link in the chain of negative evidence by the account which he gives of Constantine's will and of the territory of succeeding emperors. The request which Pope Boniface IV made of Emperor Phocas asking him for permission to turn the Pantheon into a church is another fact which reveals the falsity of the Donation, for such a request would have been unnecessary had the Donation of Con-stantine corresponded with historical reality.[3] Finally,

by manye hundrid ʒeeris after the deeth of Pope Siluester the eleccioun of the pope mad at Rome was sende into Greke lond, where the emperour was oftir and lenger togidere than at Rome, forto be confermed or admittid of the emperour; as can be proued

[1] *Repressor*, II, 354, 358, 359.   [2] *Id.* II, 360.   [3] *Id.* II, 362.

bi sufficient credible cronicles and stories, and in special forto seie in the cronicle of Martyn,[1] where he spekith of Pope Vitilian. This y seie not for this, that it so doon was weel doon.[2]

Thus another plank from the floor of the medieval mansion vanished.

Pecock's critical faculty was, then, one of his most outstanding characteristics, the characteristic which, in spite of his medieval and scholastic approach to learning and of the defects by which that approach was marked, entitles us to regard him as a Janus-like figure, who, like so many of his contemporaries in this century, stands with one face looking into the past and one veering towards the future.

[1] I.e. Martinus Polonus.   [2] *Repressor*, II, 364.

CHAPTER XIII

BISHOP PECOCK AND THE
ENGLISH LANGUAGE

THE use which Pecock made of the English language in his writings is a further indication of his importance, and it is this aspect of Pecock's work which has been most closely studied.[1] Nothing so well suggests that Pecock, even if he was a distinctively medieval character, was an embryonic 'national' and Renaissance figure as his use of the English language. The fact that he wrote in English was probably even more irritating to his accusers than the views which his books contained. Champion of papal provisions and defender of the Church as he was, like Wyclif, possibly because of Wyclif, he realised that the use of the vernacular was the way in which contact between the Church and the people might be best maintained.

As yet Latin still remained the language in which serious books were normally written and which for generations to come was the language of the lawyer and the churchman. It was not, for instance, until 1459 that the indentures between the university and the city of Oxford were made out in the English language. The majority of English chronicles were written in Latin. Pecock's contemporaries, John Capgrave (1393–1464) and Sir John Fortescue (1394–1476?), both wrote the bulk of their work in Latin.[2] Wyclif wrote all his important philosophical and theological works in that language. Even Pecock wrote a not inconsiderable number of books in that language, possibly before

[1] E.g. Dr Hitchcock's introductions to the *Donet* and the *Folewer to the Donet*; F. Schmidt, *Studies in the Language of Pecock* (Upsala, 1900); B. Zickner, *Syntax und Stil in Reginald Pecock's 'Repressor'* (Greifswald, 1900); A. Hoffmann, *Laut- und Formenlehre in Reginald Pecock's 'Repressor'* (Greifswald, 1900).

[2] Capgrave wrote a life of St Katherine in verse and a life of St Gilbert of Sempringham in prose, a guide for pilgrims to Rome and a *Chronicle of England* in English. Fortescue wrote a book on *Monarchy*.

translating them into English,[1] including the *Book of Faith*, the *Proof of the Chrysten Feith*, *Just Apprising of Doctouris*, *Book of Penaunce*, *Book of Prestehode*, *Book of Sacraments*, *Book of Sentence of Cristen Religioun*, *Book of Questyouns*, *Book of the Chirch*, *Book of Lay Mennis Bookis*, *Just Apprising of Holy Scripture*, and possibly others.[2] Yet it was Pecock's aim to present his philosophical and theological treatises in definite, dry, dull but crystal-clear English prose, so that all his readers would be able to understand his writings. It was this aim, and its effects, which placed him head and shoulders above so many of his contemporaries.

It is true that his English style is of debatable significance, since it can hardly be maintained that it had very much influence on the development of English prose. His enemy, Wyclif, whose prose had naturally far wider circulation than his own, was also far more influential in moulding the future of the English language. Much that was once attributed to Wyclif cannot certainly be his but there can be no doubt of the influence of the Lollard movement on the development of the English language. Wyclif's prose has greater flexibility and is less cumbrous, but it must be remembered that Wyclif's English works, like those of his Lollard followers, were written essentially for an unlearned audience, and that he was therefore far less hampered by the difficulties facing Pecock.

Pecock's English was used for the presentation of a theological-philosophical treatise and had therefore to be definitive. His syllogistic method did not allow for false quantities or misrepresentation. The English language was as yet unformed and no real attempt had yet been made to write a work of the kind which Pecock was presenting to his public. He may therefore lament:

Langagis, whos reulis ben not writen, as ben Englisch, Freensch, and manye othere, ben chaungid withynne ʒeeris and cuntrees,

---

[1] E.g. *Reule*, 99. But this is not always the case—viz. *Folewer to the Donet*, 29.
[2] *Vide* Appendix II for more detailed references. The *Book of Faith* was, of course, a translation of the Latin edition of this book of the same name which may, however, have been rather more extensive (*Book of Faith*, 148). He also mentions a book in Latin called the *Lasse Book of the Chrysten Religioun* (*Donet* 26, 180, 181). This would almost certainly be part of the *Reule*.

that oon man of the oon cuntre, and of the oon tyme, myȝte not, or schulde not kunne undirstonde a man of the othere kuntre, and of the othere tyme; and al for this, that the seid langagis ben not stabili and foundamentali writen.[1]

But he grappled with the problem in a way that is the philologist's admiration and sometimes, it must be admitted, the modern reader's despair. His prose is monumental, heavy, massive, dull and sometimes, but not always, wearisome and lacking in originality. It must be borne in mind, however, that he was writing for his contemporaries and not for the delectation of the twentieth-century professor. The sentences are long and complex, but their form, syntax and style is accurate, and the general argument behind his different books has an amazing unity. It is true that he resorts to a number of devices which undoubtedly tax the modern reader's patience, but which enabled him to safeguard himself against misrepresentation. The pleonastic quality of his writings is, for instance, one of their chief drawbacks, but if one remembers both his aims and the general use made of repetition by contemporary authors such redundancy is understandable. Dr Hitchcock gathered together some examples in her admirable introduction to the *Folewer to the Donet*.[2] These included, 'forto forge and compowne or to settle to gedir in seemyng' (*Donet*, 10); 'accidentis or fallyngis' (*id.* 12); 'moost according or moost compendiose gadering to gider, that is to seie, moost sehort profitable gadering togider' (*id.* 19); 'obstynat and so vnouercomable and unaȝendressabli hardid' (*id.* 160); 'vnconsidered and vntobethouȝtvpon' (*id.* 161); 'nextnesse or immediacioun' (*Folewer*, 195); 'priuacioun or lak' (*id.* 148).

The dialect of his works is mainly significant because of its normality. It is easy, especially with the Lollard translators, to

---

[1] *Book of Faith*, 251.

[2] Hitchcock, Introduction to the *Folewer*, lxii. It was not wholly his desire to impress his meaning upon such of his readers whose intellectual capacity was limited which made him repeat himself. He also used it—e.g. 'gile and wijle' (*Donet*, 8); 'poynt and pricke of tyme' (*id.* 8)—for the 'sake of ornament and rhythm' (lxii, lxiii).

associate English works of this period with a particular part of the country, but there are no such outstanding features in Pecock's prose. His dialect is best defined as East Midland, rather different in a trivial way from the London dialect, and the product of a man who had lived in Oxford and London. Perhaps the most noticeable feature of his work, as it was of Wyclif's, is the large number of suffixes of the *i* as opposed to the *e* type,[1] e.g. *-is*, *-id*, *-ir*. Both Professor Skeat[2] and Professor Schmidt[3] thought that this was a characteristic of the Oxford district, but Dr Hitchcock has shown that this is a doubtful assumption, in that more frequent and noticeable characteristics, the *-ur*, *-us*, *-un*, *-ud* ending, the frequent present indicative plurals in *-eth*, do not occur in his works.[4] Another indication of the provincial nature of Pecock's prose is the use of the diphthong before *-sch*, the form 'waisch' for instance or the form 'swothe'.[5] In general, however, Pecock's prose is approaching the normal, standardised English.

The choice of words remained by far and away the most difficult of Pecock's tasks. His main aim was clarity, to make his reader understand what he had in his mind, even at the cost of redundancy and repetition, and knowing the minds of many so-called educated Englishmen, we may well sympathise with him in his task. He did not mean to entertain, and his work, like that of Wyclif and other medieval philosophers, is almost devoid of

[1] Prof. Wyld has only noted one form 'ungerd' (ungirt).

[2] W. W. Skeat, 'On the dialect of Wicliffe's Bible' in the *Transactions of the Philological Society* (1896).

[3] F. Schmidt, *Studies in the language of Pecock* (Upsala, 1900).

[4] F. Hitchcock, Introduction to the *Folewer*, xxv ff. The *u* spelling is the general characteristic, e.g. examples taken from the *Registers of Godstow and Oseney* (ed. A. Clark, E.E.T.S. 1905 and 1907), lattur, utturly, etc. Pecock never uses 'them' for the third person plural of the personal pronoun, always 'her' or 'hem'. Dr Hitchcock says that his verbal forms are normally East Midland but that there are occasional southernisms and south-westernisms— 'an occasional possible pres. indic. pl. in *-eth*, e.g. serueth, (*Donet*, 23); an occasional form with *gg*, the Southern development of OE. *cg*, as *ligge*, (*Donet*, 161), alongside the Midland development of the analogical form with single *g*, *seie*, *bie*, etc.; the occasional *i-*, *y-* prefix (OE. *ge-*) of the past participle, e.g. y-callid etc. (xxvii)'.

[5] H. C. Wyld, *History of Modern Colloquial English* (London, 1936), 81.

humour,[1] but to instruct and teach the fundamentals without which a Christian society could neither run smoothly nor righteously. Thus he is experimenting, feeling his way over new ground with the careful yet deliberate tread of the explorer. Therefore he endeavours to find and even coin words which most aptly translate his meaning. In some cases he uses words of recent importation, or anglicises foreign words.[2] In other cases he translates Latin words into their English equivalents[3] or extends or slightly changes the meaning of English words already in use.[4] Finally, he coins words of his own, some of which were far too cumbrous-vn-to-be-thouȝt-vpon-or vnaȝenseiabili-to endure, whilst others, as a quick survey of the *New English Dictionary* reveals, have come into lasting use.[5] He had a wide vocabulary which shows that he was not merely acquainted with theological literature. The complex sentence formation, which we have already mentioned, and the detailed explanation which he gives to minor points, makes his performance all the more astonishing even if at first sight it makes his prose more cumbersome.

Pecock massed a great deal of material into his books, and gave it a unity and a form. He may lack precision and brevity but he is rarely very obscure; even to-day the plan of the works stands out above the material. Dr Hitchcock suggests that in this as in much else he was not unlike Richard Hooker whose prose suffers from much the same defects as Pecock's. Infrequently he rises to real eloquence whilst his command of metaphor is noticeable throughout.[6] His illustrations are fresh and vivid, piercing the monotony

[1] The late Mr B. L. Manning mentions Wyclif's 'elephantine playfulness' (*Cambridge Medieval History*, VII, 495), but his wit is rare. Pecock has a dry witty aside now and again but they too are few and far between.

[2] Dr Hitchcock has the following examples: assumpt, defensory, discherid, excusatorye, explaying, inpressli.

[3] E.g. appetitis or lustys, accidentis or fallyngis.

[4] Ouerer = superior: rennyngli = cursim, etc.

[5] *Vide* Hitchcock, Introduction to the *Folewer*, lxi, n. 1.

[6] He does not use metaphors to any extent (this was typical of fifteenth-century prose—A. D. Greenwood, *Cambridge History of English Literature* (1908), II, 295), but where they are employed their aptness is not spoiled by any elaborate explanation.

of the syllogistic argument with a ray of real medieval sunshine. Time and time again his wording is abrupt, precise and telling; 'smel or smatche', or 'worldis wynnyng'. The prayers into which he breaks from time to time in the *Reule* are fresh and simple, if lacking the emotional piety which we have learned to associate with much medieval religion.

He himself has been charged with translating the scriptures into the English language.[1] In transcribing an anonymous chronicle of the fifteenth century, which has since been edited, Stow said definitely that Pecock 'had laboured for many years to translate the Holy Scripture into English'.[2] Pecock's biographer, Lewis, thought that there was no good authority for such a statement, and his judgement met with the approval of Churchill Babington.[3] But the claim was not entirely abandoned. A learned reviewer of Babington's works suggested that 'there can be little doubt that Pecock is not translating offhand and that his quotations, as they stand, are sufficiently distinct from either of the Wyclif versions. Take, for instance, the text from the Epistle to Timothy with which he heads his *Repressor*: the remarkable word "undernyme" has not been discovered in any extant version.'[4] Twenty years later an American scholar, Dr Charles A. Wager, on the basis of an analysis of Pecock's biblical quotations in the *Repressor*, asserted: 'in cases of minimum divergence, we have

---

[1] This discussion has appeared in an article of mine entitled 'Bishop Pecock and the English Bible' in the *Church Quarterly Review*, CXXIX, 281–96.

[2] Stow, *Annals* (ed. 1602), 666; *An English Chronicle*, ed. J. S. Davies (Camden Soc. 1856, LXIV, 75): 'And this same yere...master Reynold Pocock bysshop of Chichestre a seculer doctour of dyuynyte, that had labored for many yeres to translate Holy Scripture into Englysshe.' The name of the author is unknown, but it is possible that he may have come from Canterbury (*id.* 91–4). He was certainly a contemporary of Pecock, and probably wrote his chronicle between 1461 and 1471. Cf. also Holinshed, *Chronicle* (1808), 245; *Reg. Bekynton*, I, 303: 'books containing translations of the Holy Scriptures made by him and others from Latin into English.'

[3] John Lewis, *Life of Reynold Pecock* (2nd ed. 1820), 231; Babington, Introduction to the *Repressor*, lxxxiii.

[4] *Dublin Review*, N.S. (1875), XXIV, 45.

citations made *memoriter*, in some instances, at least, with the Vulgate in mind; in cases of maximum divergence practically a new translation based probably on Wyclif.'[1] What is the origin of Pecock's quotations? Are historians right in acknowledging or dismissing the possibility of a new translation by Pecock?

First, there can be no doubt that there was an extremely close connection between the Wycliffite Bible in its second and later form[2] and Pecock's citations. Babington makes this clear when he says that 'in the majority of Scripture citations, Pecock employs the version ascribed to Wyclif, in that form of it, however, which is the later of the two'.[3] Even leaving out of account the cases of more or less minimum divergence from the Wycliffite version, the number of exact quotations is impressive. There are some 88 quotations from Pecock's works which coincide with the text of the second Wycliffite version out of a total of 400 quotations in the six surviving works of Pecock. The greatest number of these quotations come, as one might expect, from the *Repressor*, where Pecock was dealing exclusively with the arguments which had been put forward by his Lollard opponents. It is, however, quite significant that there are also some twenty exact quotations in the lengthy and also earliest extant work of the bishop—*The Reule of Chrysten Religioun*. It is true that many of these citations are only short sentences: others are, however, very much longer, and Dr Babington's assertion that the longer citations were nearly all taken from the Wyclif Bible, which was challenged by Dr Wager,[4] may well be accepted. There is, for instance, a longish quotation—I Corinthians xiii, 4–8—in the *Donet*[5] which, among

---

[1] *Modern Language Notes* (1894), 197.

[2] I.e. the more successful work in which the translation is freer and less stilted, e.g. the Latin participles of the first version become finite verbs in the second. The main responsibility for this later version rested with Wyclif's lieutenant, John Purvey.

[3] Babington, Introduction to the *Repressor*, xxviii.

[4] Dr Wager estimated that the number of exact quotations from the *Repressor* was thirty-two, but analysis shows that this figure is inaccurate, for there are certainly as many as fifty accurate citations.

[5] *Donet*, 164.

others, is an accurate transcription from the second Wycliffite version, whilst there are many others in the *Repressor*[1] which bear testimony to Babington's thoroughness and scholarship. But it was, on the other hand, inaccurate for him to claim that exceptions to this rule were 'mostly confined to short texts quoted apparently *memoriter*, such as occur in the first sixty pages', since not only are the short texts scattered throughout the works but only six quotations out of the twenty-six of what one may call examples of maximum divergence are contained in the first sixty pages of the *Repressor*. There is clear proof, then, that nearly 30 % of Pecock's quotations have their source in the second version of the Lollard Bible.

Secondly, there are some 100 citations in the extant works which are very similar in text to the second Wycliffite version but which cannot be classed as exact quotations because they do deviate from this. In some cases the divergence is so trivial as hardly to merit attention, and here again support must be given to the thesis that Pecock's main source was the Lollard translation of the Bible. Thus when Pecock writes 'This is what' and Wyclif 'This is that',[2] or when Pecock writes 'my silf to him' and Wyclif 'to hym mysilf',[3] or when Pecock writes 'ioie and be ȝe glad' and Wyclif 'but ioye ȝe',[4] we may safely assume that such changes are the faults of the amanuensis rather than of the author. Alternatively, Pecock may have been using a version of the Lollard Bible which itself had deviations from our texts.[5] In other cases it seems fairly safe to think that Pecock is quoting *memoriter* and that in so doing he transposes the words or changes a word here and there according to his own usage. There are, indeed, a number of cases

---

[1] E.g. I Peter iv, 12 (*Repressor*, I, 176–7); John iv, 19 ff. (*id.* I, 196); Acts xvii, 24 ff. (*id.* I, 146); Matthew xix, 16 ff. (*id.* I, 193–4), etc.

[2] *Book of Faith*, 239 (Exodus xiii).

[3] *Repressor*, I, 103 (John xiv, 21); Forshall and Madden, *Wyclif Bible*, IV, 279.

[4] *Book of Faith*, 294 (Luke x, 20); F. and M., *W.B.*, IV, 181.

[5] In their excellent and authoritative edition of the Lollard Bible the Rev. Josiah Forshall and Sir Frederick Madden examined 170 MSS., two of which they printed, one written before 1390 and the second, a copy of which Pecock probably used, before 1420.

where the word change might well be attributed to Pecock's reliance on his memory, for as an Oxford don and as a bishop he would naturally be very well acquainted with what was after all the basis of his study—the Bible. Similarly, his interest in vernacular teaching and his desire to controvert the Lollards would make him equally familiar with the vehicle of Wyclif's teaching—the Lollard versions of the Bible.

Too much importance must not therefore be attached to these cases of minimum divergence from the Wyclif version. Because Pecock wrote 'Y seie to ȝou these thingis, that no man bigile ȝou in heiȝte of spechis',[1] whereas Wyclif wrote 'For this thing Y seie, that no man disseyue ȝou in heiȝthe of wordis',[2] it would therefore be foolish to assert that Pecock's quotations did not in general originate in the Lollard versions of the Bible. Yet there are so many of these trivial deviations from the text that one is tempted to try to think of some other reason, rather than lapse of memory, for the divergences from the accepted source. It is unnecessary to stress the point, but the number and variety of the differences call for attention. 'Zeel of good wille' instead of 'loue of God';[3] 'heerer' instead of 'ech man herynge';[4] 'manie be to thee pesible' instead of 'many pesible men be to thee';[5] 'walke' instead of 'go';[6] 'who may hem explic or opene bi word' instead of 'a man may not declare tho thingis bi word';[7] 'stiking' instead of 'fitchinge';[8] 'ye schulen rere vp titlis' instead of 'ye schulen reise titles'[9] are only a few of the many variations which form cases of minimum divergence. On the whole it is apparent that they may be accounted for by the fact that Pecock is quoting from memory; but certain seemingly trivial features reveal some sort of unity behind a few of the quotations which at first sight may point to

[1] *Repressor* (Col. ii, 4), I, 7.
[2] Forshall and Madden, *Wyclif Bible*, IV, 432.
[3] *Repressor* (Romans x, 2), I, 2; F. and M., *W.B.* IV, 324.
[4] *Repressor* (Rev. xxii, 18), I, 55; F. and M., *W.B.* IV, 681.
[5] *Repressor* (Ecclus. vi, 6), I, 88.
[6] *Repressor* (Psalm cxv), I, 153.
[7] *Folewer to the Donet* (Eccl. i, 8), 5.
[8] *Book of Faith* (John xx, 25), 153; *W.B.* IV, 294.   *Donet*, 124.

an altogether different source—in another version of the Bible. Thus in more than one place the word 'neighbour' replaces that of 'brother',[1] and in other places 'which' replaces 'that'[2] and in others 'sotheli' replaces 'forsoth'. It would be foolish to read anything into these apparently standardised changes were it not for the fact that there are a number of quotations which are nearly or entirely distinct from the Wycliffite version.

Although these 'distinct' quotations only constitute some sixty or less citations out of the total of over four hundred, they have provided the basis for the question—was Pecock using some source to which we have not access or which was different from the Lollard versions or was he himself engaged on a translation of the Bible? The divergences are too wide to be accounted for by lapse of memory alone.[3] Thus where Wyclif writes, 'Thou schalt not make to thee ʒotun goddis', Pecock's version reads, 'ʒe schulen not make blowen goddis, nor goddis molten bi founders craft'.[4] Again, where Pecock has 'be ʒe prudent as addris and symple as colueris', Wyclif has 'therfore be ʒe sliʒ as serpentis, and symple as dowues'.[5]

At first sight these maximum divergences provide a case for the theory of a different or new translation, and it is a case which has seemed tenable to some scholars. The possibility of a different translation cannot be entirely ruled out, and one instance at least[6]

---

[1] E.g. *Donet* (I John iv, 20), 17; *Repressor* (Luke vi, 42), I, 3.

[2] E.g. *Folewer to the Donet* (Gen. i, 31), 169; (Matt. x, 28), 19; *Reule* (Deut. iii, 24), 72; (Rom. ix, 3), 496; (I John v, 9–10), 7.

[3] E.g. *Book of Faith* (Mk. xvi, 20), 243; *Reule* (Matt. viii, 10), 450; *Repressor* (I Cor. xiv, 38), I, 53; (John iii, 19), I, 97; (Psalm xcv, 5), I, 240. Similarly, in other places the word 'avoutrie' replaces the word 'letcherie' (e.g. *Repressor*, I, 63–4; *Donet*, 175).   [4] *Donet* (Exodus xxxiv, 17), 124.

[5] *Folewer* (Matt. x, 16), 167; *W.B.* IV, 24.

[6] This is the sentence mentioned by the reviewer of the *Repressor* in 1875. The word 'undernyme' (II Tim. iv, 2) occurs in Miss Paues's edition of this version (120). The reviewer also seems to have been mistaken in thinking that the word had never previously appeared. It occurs again in the sense of 'rebuke' in Pecock and had been previously used in Wyclif's works (e.g. *Works* (1880), 292). In fact, however, the completed sentence used by Pecock is not the same as that translated by the author of the *Fourteenth Century Version of the Bible*. Pecock's reading of II Tim. iv, 2, is: 'Vndirnyme

points rather strikingly to the portion of the Bible translated into English at the end of the fourteenth century[1] and edited by Miss Paues; but further examination shows that the evidence is inadequate to support this theory. Even if Pecock used this or other similar versions on occasions very little can be said on the balance in favour of imputing the possibility of such a translation to Pecock himself.

All our evidence points to this conclusion. It is clear that, with the exception of the anonymous chronicler, nothing was said in contemporary documents about such a translation. It is practically certain that had such a translation been in existence, it would have found expression in the charges laid against Pecock by his adversaries. Yet such is not the case nor does Foxe, who, it will be remembered, regarded Pecock as a Protestant martyr, mention or even suggest that such a translation was in existence. If it had been in existence, the Protestants would have made very much more of Pecock's fame. The papal bull condemning him says that he was 'worthy of condemnation in respect of certain books or works in English or Latin, and therwith led many simple people astray'. Although the bull goes on to say that the 'said Reginald...had

thou, biseche thou, and blame thou, in al pacience and doctrine', whereas this version reads 'undernyme thou and byseche and blame thou in eferich pacence and intechynge'.

[1] The author was not an extreme Lollard but had Lollard tendencies. The version, which is far from complete, is written in the Kentish and Southern dialects and was probably seldom used. Pecock's use of words is suggestive of acquaintance with it, although in general there seems no real evidence for thinking that he used it. Thus Pecock has 'God aȝenstondith proude men, and he ȝeueth grace to meke men' (*Repressor*, i, 7), whereas the fourteenth-century version reads 'aȝenstondith' but 'humel' instead of 'meke' (24). The Wyclif Bible has 'withstondith' (F. and M., *W.B.* IV, 613). Similarly where the fourteenth-century version has 'And this y seye, that no man bygyle ȝow in hyȝenesse of wordes' (81), Pecock reads 'Ye seie to ȝou these thingis, that no man bigile ȝou in heiȝte of spechis' (*Repressor*, i, 7). The Wyclif version has 'no man disseyue' and 'heiȝthe of wordis'. Cf. also the Acts xxvi, 5, where Pecock and Miss Paues's version have the two words 'certeyn sect'. Wyclif's version has 'oure religioun' (*W.B.* IV, 584). Cf. *Folewer to the Donet*, 106, and the *Fourteenth Century Version*, 202 (Matt. iii, 7) or *Repressor*, i, 68, and the other version (I James v, 21), which show that in general the two editions are very much at variance with each other.

concealed a number of the said books containing manifest heresy composed by him in Latin and also in English and not then published to the intent that they might survive for ever', no evidence was put forward to suggest that a translation of the Bible into English was among them. In addition to this, as Babington and Lewis both admit, Pecock's own vanity makes it extremely unlikely that he would have concealed, even had he only conceived, the plan of a translation by himself.

Yet the chronicler's suggestion remains. If one may hazard a guess one might say that there is a good probability that the idea of this translation arose from one of Pecock's publications which was perhaps most directly concerned with the Bible, the *Just Apprising of Holy Scripture*.[1] Unfortunately this book does not survive, but numerous references which Pecock makes to it in his extant works prove that it was an impressive compilation. It will be remembered how the idea of a new Creed arose. The idea of a new translation of the Bible, an accusation also falsely levelled at John de Trevisa, may have arisen in much the same way.

If this, however, clears up one problem the more important problem still remains. What was the source of the passages of extreme divergence from the Lollard version in his works? It has already been suggested that he may possibly have used another English version of the Bible, but this possibility must be dismissed until further evidence is forthcoming. All the evidence points clearly to the Vulgate, the necessary texts of which Pecock

[1] The aim of this book, of which there was a Latin as well as an English version, seems to have been much the same as that of the *Book of Faith*, to point out that too much significance must not be given to Holy Scripture and to emphasise the basic importance of the 'law of kind'. He tells us in the *Donet* that its aim was to show that divinity was a 'symple and an unsure faculte', and that there 'thou maist se into what effectis such mystyk sensis (i.e. tropological, anagogical, allegorical) or vndirstondingis of holi scripture serven and weren founde' (*id.* 107). Other references (e.g. *Repressor*, I, 20, 29, 40, 70, 127, 128, 130, etc.) show that this was the theme of the *Just Apprising*. There are 45 references to the book in four of his works and he himself tells us that the work itself had been 'wel acceptid and allowid of hiȝe prelatis, and of louȝer clerkis' (*Book of Faith*, 115).

translated as he wrote his work.[1] This would not account entirely for the standardised use of words, but the fact that a certain number of archaisms survive even in passages of extreme divergence does not affect the argument, since Pecock would have had Wyclif's translation, if not consciously, at least subconsciously in his mind all the time. This may well seem to justify Dr Wager's argument that 'in cases of minimum divergence we have in Pecock practically a new translation, based probably upon Wyclif', but it is not so much a justification as a modification, a return to the position held by John Lewis.[2]

Pecock's quotations, then, where they are most divergent from the texts of the Lollard writers, were a haphazard but none the less significant translation of the Vulgate passages which he made when his memory of the Wycliffite version lapsed or when he did not have an English Bible near by. This would account for the fact that the same wording is not always used in identical passages, a fact which would surely never have occurred if Pecock had been working on a new translation. Thus in the passage relating to the Ten Commandments the sentences appear in different places as 'in the seid loues al lawe and prophecies hangen'[3] and 'hangen al the lawe and prophetis'.[4] In other passages a comparison of the Vulgate reading and of Pecock's version reflects the literal exactitude of the translation. Thus where the Vulgate has 'graventur in crapula et ebrietate', the second Wycliffite version reads 'be greuyd with glotony, and drunkennesse, and bisynessis of this lijf', which is far less exact than Pecock's 'be not maad heuy with ouer moche mete and ouer moche drynke'.[5] Similarly, the cruder rendering 'Jesus Crist, the sone of him' instead of 'His Son, Jesus Christ'

---

[1] Pecock rarely quotes the Vulgate in his books, only some fifteen times in the *Donet*, *Repressor*, *Folewer* and the *Book of Faith*, but he makes more use of it in the *Reule*. Here there are 75 citations from the Vulgate as compared with 63 from the English version. This may be due to the fact that the work was intended for the perusal of more learned readers than those of the other books.

[2] 'In his books he translates very large parcels of them into English' (Lewis, *Pecock*, 231).

[3] *Donet*, 17.

[4] *Id.* 164.

[5] *Id.* 138 (Luke xxi, 34); *W.B.* IV, 219.

implies a quick translation from the Latin.[1] On the whole Pecock is unlike his contemporaries in tampering with the sense when the argument requires it, although in one place he apparently interpolated words with this end in view. Thus in the passage Romans iii, 27, the second Wycliffite version has 'by lawe of feith' which is a true translation of the Vulgate 'sed per legem fidei', whereas Pecock's translation reads 'bi lawe of kinde and of feith'.[2] Generally, however, the honesty of Pecock's scholarship is unquestionable. Pecock's quotations from the Bible which are most divergent from the versions of Wyclif and his followers are usually, but not entirely, his own individual translations from, but not a complete translation of, the Latin Vulgate.

Pecock explicitly recognised that his use of English was novel, but, as he urged in the *Folewer*:

Certis, this myche wolde not y haue write here in lay tunge, ne were that y hope this present book schal be translatid into latyn tunge; And parauenture, if y schulde abstene me here now fro writyng herof in lay tunge, y schulde neuer write it, neithir in lay tunge neithir in latyn tunge, and that for greet prece of many othire maters profryng hem silf daili to be writen and to be delyuerid into knowyng; And if y schulde seie in my conscience bifore god: 'this now towchid is oon cause whi y delyuerid bi writyng in lay tunge many maters and treuthis as thei camen to mynde ouer what y entendid bifore forto delyuere in lay tunge, lest if y schulde haue ouer passid hem forto not haue write hem in thilk while, they schulden neuyr haue be write of me; And leefir y hadde forto write suche maters and treuthis in lay tunge, vndir hope that aftirward thei schulen come into latyn tunge, than forto putte hem into perel neuer be of me writen.'[3]

He deprecated the reading of the Bible in the English language without the guidance of an expert theologian or a bishop's

---

[1] *Donet*, 139 (I John iii, 23).

[2] Cf. *Repressor*, II, 420. In some cases texts were tampered with at early dates and retained by later writers. Thus I Peter iii, 15, is quoted inaccurately by Abailard in *Theol. Christ.* III, col. 1217 B.

[3] *Folewer to the Donet*, 29–30.

licence. It can only be studied under the guidance of 'weel leerned clerkis':[1]

> This what y haue now seid of and to Bible men y haue not seid vndir this entent and meenyng, as that y schulde feele to be vnleeful laymen forto reade in the Bible and forto studie and leerne ther yn, with help and counseil of wise and weel leerned clerkis and with licence of her gouernour the bischop; but forto rebuke and adaunte the presumpcioun of tho lay persoones whiche weenen bi her inreding in the Bible forto come into more kunnyng than thei or alle the men in erthe.

But he was fully conscious of the need for books written in English. Why, he asks in the *Reule*, if 'clerkis prechen the maters of these seid bookis to the peple in her comoun langage', should he not write in the same language? Sermons are far more liable to be misunderstood than books.[2] In the same book he tells us of some of the objections which have been urged against his writing in the vernacular. 'Y herde oon man oonys seie that it were not so to be doon', because such matters as Pecock was writing about were fit for scholars only, and could not be properly understood by 'lay men'.[3] On the other hand, such books would encourage the 'lay peple [to] studie ferther in her owne resonyng vpon the leernyng and the knowing of tho seid trouthis'. Finally, it had been argued that such knowledge was itself too 'myche and hiȝe and sutel' for the laity. Pecock replied that an understanding of his

---

[1] *Repressor*, I, 85. He stresses the need for 'substanciali leerned clerkis in logik and in moral philsophie and in dyvynyte, and ripeli exercised ther yn' for the 'trewe vndirstondingis and exposiciouns to textis of Holi Scripture'. A passage in the *Donet* (172) ends: 'fro presumpcioun, and schulen be so clerid in her witt that her reding thanne in the englisch bible schal not hurte hem silf neithir eny othir man.' The passage is incomplete, for there is a gap from the end of chapter xii to the end of chapter xiii. It is very possible that the passage in question related to the reading of the Bible in English.

[2] *Reule*, 21. He distinguishes between Lollard books and the Lollard versions of the Bible, 'tho vnsauery bokis' which are 'loued and multiplied abrood of alle cristen peple' (18), and his own books written for 'weel disposid cristen men of the lay partie'. 'What prechers ben aboute to do bi her preching in the comoun peplis langage, y am aboute to do by my writing in the comoun peplis langage' (19).

[3] *Id.* 87.

arguments is necessary if heretics are to be properly confuted, and that his works do not require more intelligence than the layman uses in secular matters of business of law. He concludes: 'and if suche trouthis mowe be prechid bi voice to lay men withoute eny perel, certis moche rather thei mowe be delyuerid to lay peple in writyng without perel.'[1]

Pecock was not only an innovator but was also one of the first great writers of English prose, a pioneer writing long before even Berners, John Fisher or Sir Thomas More had started their work, before Sir John Fortescue the theorist, Caxton the printer and Malory the story-teller had written their books. It may be true that his prose is cumbrous, at times even obsolete, but it does not deserve the scorn which Dr Greet, for instance, seemingly bestows upon it. It had perhaps little actual influence upon the future development of English prose, less than that of Wyclif or even of Capgrave, but its potentialities were as great, if not greater. Most scholars are well agreed on this point. It may be imprudent to call him the 'greatest prosaist of his time',[2] but his prose, with all its manifest defects, has all the elements of greatness. He was a greater prosaist than Chaucer or Trevisa, whilst his work is of so very different a nature that it does not bear comparison with that of Richard Rolle. At times Hooker's *Ecclesiastical Polity* is not less wearisome than the *Repressor*, and at times Wyclif, with all his vivid phrasing, is insufferably dull. But the dullness in itself should not obscure the merits of any one writer, since the great sermons of one century are more often than not the bane of the next. Yet Pecock has not only managed to evolve a vocabulary that was sufficiently extensive to deal with his subject clearly, emphatically and logically, but he uses phrases quite as fresh and as vivid as those of Wyclif. It is very possible, considering his indebtedness to the Lollard Bible as well as to other Lollard works, that he was influenced by Wyclif in this matter, but he has 'more range and luxuriance of expression...more in-

[1] *Reule*, 99.
[2] Kellner, Introduction to Caxton's *Blanchardyn and Eglantine* (E.E.T.S.), cxi.

tensity of argument'[1] than Wyclif. Finally, and from the point of view of the historian or theologian if not the philologist, this is the most significant fact about his prose: he was the first Englishman to tackle a philosophical treatise in the English language. The magnitude of his task, considered against a background that was full of obstacles, gives him sufficient claim to have an important place in the history of English literature as well as in English history itself.

[1] Hitchcock, Introduction to the *Folewer*, lvii.

CHAPTER XIV

PECOCK THE THEOLOGIAN

WE have been so far dealing with those particular characteristics of Pecock's thought which have made him famous, but we shall be mistaken if we are led to believe that they were not in fact part of a system of moral and doctrinal theology. Pecock was partly a mental opportunist, seeking to use any argument which might controvert his opponents, the Lollards, and to lead the clergy and laity to a better understanding of the Christian faith. His mental opportunism was not, however, a sign of dishonest or unsystematic thinking, but the spearhead of an intelligent and inclusive *Summa Theologica*.

It seems probable that the greater part of the *Summa* did not survive, and even that which does survive, mainly in *The Reule of Chrysten Religioun*, clearly suggests that Pecock would not rank with St Thomas or Alexander of Hales or other eminent theologians whose works have formed a definite and important contribution to the body of medieval theology. Even so, there is much in Pecock's *Summa* which deserves notice, and moreover, from the method of its arrangement and the implications of its arguments, merits close attention.

This chapter is designed to present a brief and all too summary outline of that system of thought which gave rise to Pecock's more startling ideas in order that we may shortly survey Pecock in relation to his significance in fifteenth-century history. As we shall see, in fact, Pecock's system of thought falls into two distinct categories of doctrinal and moral theology, and he would claim that he had laid a new emphasis on several features of the latter.

He commenced his *Summa* (supposing, as the evidence suggests, that the *Summa* was in its essential features a mirror and reflection of the *Reule*) by outlining the reasons for the existence of God. He tells us how 'y fynde that ech tunge, ech lond, ech sect hadde an inclynacioun and o that an actual bisynes forto fynde to hem a god', whilst in respect of the ancient philosophers 'y may fynde that amongis hem the cheef witty pryncis of philosophie were movid in her resoun that thei schulde be oon bigynner and eende of al thyng, best of al other thing',[1] and basing his argument on the fact that 'natural inclinacioun is neuer had in veyn and for nou3t'[2] infers that this gives a reasonable proof of the existence of God.

The fact of our own bodies also presupposes a creator,[3] for just as a series of links in a long chain 'withoute assignable holde aboue may not be assigned neither grauntid to be possible with-oute repugnance', it is equally impossible to think of life without an originator, God the 'maker vnmaad'.

After establishing this fundamental truth, Pecock passes on to the attributes of God, 'what god is in hise worthi dignitees and persoonys of the godhede'. God is infinite, 'inmesurable and infinite',[4] a truth which he picks out with a vivid, happy illustra-tion. London to Rome is a long way, a 'thousand myle', but that distance, even when multiplied to the nth degree, remains finite. God's infinity, which naturally gives rise to praise, wonderment and worship on man's part, provides the clue to His other attri-butes. Pecock writes of these as follows:

A wonderful ricche scile therfore, and ful huge, vnmesurable and vnthen[c]able of dignitee, worthines, preisabilnes and loueabilnes is it forto seie that thou god art a greetnes in beyng infinite, a goodnes infinite, a magiste infinite, fairnes, swetenes and myrthe infinite, my3t, wisdom and love infinite, mercy, merci-ful pitee and desijr infinite, larges, freenes and gentilnes infinite.[5]

He extends his meaning in the detail of the next few pages, pausing here and there to address God rhetorically in tones which betray his devotion and reverence.

[1] *Reule*, 30. [2] *Id.* 31.
[3] 'Certis, lord, thorou3 the si3t and knowing of oure owne body and of othere creturis we mowe bi oure kindeli resoun come to the knowing herof that ther is a maker vnmaad' (*id.* 55).
[4] *Id.* 49. [5] *Id.* 54.

God's nature can only be partly comprehended through a catalogue of His attributes. The nature of the Godhead can only be fully understood through the Trinity of God, Father, Son and Holy Ghost.[1] It is impossible to understand this distinction by reason, 'without reuelacioun maad therupon to vs bi holy scripture'.[2] Pecock's actual references to scripture, to the three-fold cry of the angel from the sixth chapter of Isaiah, and to Psalm xlvii, are more ingenious than intelligent, but he also refers to more relevant quotations from the fourteenth, fifteenth and sixteenth chapters of St John. His views on the relationship between the three persons of the Godhead are wholly orthodox.

It is unnecessary to dwell long on what Pecock has to say on the second person, Jesus Christ, but we may note in passing that, here and there, there is a faint tinge of sweetness about his language which lightens the aridity of his theological style. Jesus is God's greatest gift to man, given of 'thyn vnspekeable largenes and loue'.[3] These lighter devotional touches are rare, but like the illustrations with which Pecock seeks to enlighten his readers they do show the pious and vital temper of the man.

Jesus was God incarnate, 'booth god and man in oon persoon'.[4] His life was a living witness to His divine message, the message foretold by the prophets. 'Thou lividist', says Pecock, 'a moral holy lijf after lawe of kinde, and that in hiȝest and moost parfijt maner fulfillyng the poyntis of lawe of kynde.'[5] This 'peyneful passional lijf' led inevitably to the Cross, and its wonderful consequence, the Resurrection.

The Atonement is then a central factor in his theology, bringing man and God close together. Pecock chiefly emphasises the fact of its opportunity: 'it wrouȝt saluacioun and redempcioun

---

[1] He defines the Trinity in these words: 'In the oon and the same sub-staunce and godhede ben thre persoonys, whiche persoonys ben fadir, sone and holy goost, and of whiche persoonys the fadir bryngith forth, gendrith and bigetith the sone, the fadir and the sone spiren and bryngen forth the holi goost' (*Reule*, 72).
[2] *Id.* 71.   [3] *Id.* 103.   [4] *Id.* 210.   [5] *Id.* 211.

to alle tho that liveden afore thi passioun whiche bileeveden.'[1]
And he shows that it is wrong to say that 'oure lord Jhsus made
not ful satisfaccioun for eny oon hool synne but for summe
porcioun of ech synne'. The onus of making His redemption
fully effective lies with ourselves. Thus:

it wolde seeme that thyn preier with thyn holy lijf and passioun,
crist jhsu, made not remedie, redempcioun, amendis and satisfaccioun for eny synne which was doon aftir the passioun,
fforwhi how may eny synne be forȝouun eer it be doon and
wrouȝt?[2]

He concludes with an illustration to prove this point:

wherfore it is to be vndirstonde that riȝt as if in the kyngis
court y hadde a freend in derist maner loved of the kyng for his
greet vertuose dedis doon to thee king, for whos preier maad to
the kyng, the kyng wold forȝeue to me my trespacis and wolde
avaunce me withoute my deservyng, namelich if y wolde kepe
certeyn smale assignementis which the kyng wolde sette to me for
whos kepyngis y schulde not be so pardoned neither avauncid ne
were the good beryng of my seid freend. It myȝt be seid in this
case that this freend deserued to me my forȝeuenes and that he by
hise good gouernauncis and good beryngis anentis the kyng for
whiche gouernauncis he is ful hiȝly avauncid of the kyng, maade
amendis for my trespacis and that he avauncid me. Neuertheles
ȝitt al this were trewe oonly in an vnproper maner of speche and in
figurative speche bi likenes and not aftir veriest pure trouthe of
spekyng.[3]

The Catholic Church, previewed in the Jewish synagogue,[4] was
founded by Christ through His appointment of the Apostles.
'Thou madist actuely or virtualy alle thyne apostlys prestis,
ȝeving to hem power to make and mynystre thi sacramentis with
othere powers',[5] but the actual establishment of the Church was
wrought through the coming of the third person of the Trinity,

---

[1] We may recall Pecock's comments on the Descent into Hell with some
surprise.
[2] *Reule*, 216.   [3] *Id.* 218.
[4] At any rate so far as its hierarchy was concerned (*Repressor*, II, 436).
[5] *Reule*, 213.

the Holy Ghost with power. Pecock does not tell us very much about God the Holy Ghost. He came at Whitsuntide as the result of Jesus' promise to the disciples 'in more wondirful maner and more effectual maner than thei hadde hym afore'. The Holy Ghost endowed the apostles with the 'kunnyng of alle langagis and kunnyng of oure bileeue to be prechid' and imbued them with the power of love and charity. In the *Donet* Pecock gives his views on the 'seven gifts of the Holy Ghost' in reply to his imaginary questioner who has been puzzled by the passage in the eleventh chapter of Isaiah. He begins by saying that in so far as they were not 'historical or cronical', they might be regarded as but 'vanyte and feynyd curiosite as is said of hem bi manye famose treters of hem'. This is going too far, but it should at the same time be remembered that they do not contain 'alle vertues of goddis lawe'. In fact, these virtues, which are attributed so especially to the Holy Ghost, wisdom, intellect, counsel, knowledge, ghostly strength, pity and dread, are not so very different from other virtues and, in so far as 'thei ben getun bi oure laboure', they cannot be regarded as 'oonly pure ȝiftis of god'. The seven gifts are not, then, in Pecock's view particularly associated with the Holy Ghost, but are almost certainly covered by his own Four Tables.[1]

In another place he mentions the sins against the Holy Ghost. He refers to the traditional threefold division, sins of frailty against the Father, sins of ignorance against the Son, and sins of malice against the Holy Ghost, and asks, if this distinction is true, how it can be harmonised with his view that 'ech vice and synne is doon bi malyuolence or bi malice'.[2] In his answer he shows that sins of frailty and sins of ignorance are in fact closely associated with malice or in his own words:

And for as mych as euer eithir of hem synneth willyngli, therfore euer eithir of hem synneth bi yuel wil, bi malyuolence and bi malice, thouȝ with thilk malice greet freelte, that is to seie, greet difficulte or hardnes ouer comeable, or greet ignoraunce

---

[1] *Donet*, 114–16.   [2] *Folewer*, 158.

ouercomeable, be cause of the deede rennyngli with the wityng and with the willyng.[1]

He also tells us that this threefold distinction is based on the supposition that Power is appropriated to the Father, Wisdom to the Son and Benevolence or Goodness to the Holy Ghost.[2] He is, of course, only following Christian tradition in assuming that the sins against the Holy Ghost are the least excusable, but he refuses to admit that such sins do not merit forgiveness. Such language is in fact 'yperbole' and can only have been intended in a figurative manner. It is, however, necessarily harder to be forgiven this type of sin than other kinds of sin.

The Holy Ghost then affirmed and established the Catholic Church. Pecock's views on the Church were entirely orthodox despite the fact that it was affirmed at his trial that he had questioned the authority of general councils and that he had asserted that it was not necessary to believe in the Catholic Church to merit salvation. There seems no ground for such accusations, at any rate in Pecock's surviving works, but they may be partly accounted for by misreading some of Pecock's implied ideas in the *Book of Faith*.[3] Pecock held an entirely orthodox view of the Catholic Church as the God-given institution through which man merited salvation or came, by the use of his own free will,[4] to damnation. Individualist as he was he had no patience with the anarchistic views of his Lollard opponents on the Church and the hierarchy.

The Church is in fact the means by which man can benefit through Jesus' redemption. Pecock's views on man need only detain us in so far as they contribute to the general argument.

He holds a thoroughly teleological view of man. Man is God's creation, and for this very reason his life is endowed with an objective purpose. 'We ben ordeyned', he says, 'to an eende next

---

[1] *Folewer*, 159.   [2] *Id.* 160.
[3] Vide *Book of Faith*, 176 ff., 283–5.
[4] He deals with the question of willing and 'nilling' at length in the latter part of the *Folewer*.

to oure natural beyng as for oure sovereyn natural good and vttirist natural reste.'[1] Indeed, every creature has been so created that he may achieve 'his hool natural perfeccioun and his rest and grettist natural good', but man is naturally the most important of such creatures. Neither sensual happiness nor material goods have anything to do with such an end, and are in fact indelibly 're-pugnaunt to mannys fynal reste and to his fynal eende'.[2] This end is, as the mystics would say, the *visio Dei*, the sight of the Creator, 'a thing in dignyte and perfecciouns and al goodnes aboue alle creaturis whiche mowe be or thouȝt to be'.[3] Man's purpose in life should then be rightly governed by his desire to attune his personality to this *summum bonum*.[4]

It is for this reason that man has been given body and soul. 'To ech of vs thou hast ȝouun a body with a soule hauyng al the vertu, strengthe and worching of a nourisching lijf which is in herbis and plantis, of a sensible or feelyng lijf as in beestis and foulis, And of a resonable lijf which is fer aboue the lijf of beestis.'[5] These distinctions, which are originally Aristotelian and typically medieval, are, however, interesting because of one or two difficulties which occurred to Pecock while he was writing about them. He was clear about the capacity of vegetable life but far less so about that of the beasts. Was it possible, for instance, to say that beasts could think?[6] 'It wolde seme that grehoundis doon', while 'foxes and apes doon in many of her wiles wirchyng, of whiche wiles y haue herde wondir taalis'.[7] Surely,

---

[1] *Reule*, 40. Cf. man was made to live 'aftir the doom of resoun, or of feith allowable bi resoun, whilis he lyvith in this lijf; that aftir the deeth of this lijf, he be reysid aȝen into bodily lijf, forto lyue in body and soule to gedir euer-lastyng, in ioye and blis, afore the presence of god' (*Donet*, 14).

[2] *Reule*, 41.   [3] *Id*. 42.   [4] *Id*. 107.

[5] *Id*. 101. Cf. *Folewer*, 41–2, where he treats of these distinctions. It is the reasonable or as he calls it here the witty soul which fosters the outward and inward Wits, Moving, the Appetites, Reason and Free Will.

[6] He assumed that the beasts possessed the ten outward and inward bodily Wits (i.e. touch, taste, smell, sight, hearing, common wit, imagination, fantasy, estimation and mind), but neither reason nor free will (*Donet*, 12). Cf. *Folewer*, 43.

[7] *Id*. 35–6.

he argues, common experience makes it likely that beasts can think, although some writers will attribute such intelligence as they show to instinct alone.[1] 'Beestis mowe and kunnen forme proposicions, argue and proue and gete knowyng to hem bi argument of verri silogisme and of induccioun about tho thingis whiche thei mowe bi her outward and inward wittis perceyue', but less perfectly so than man himself. He illustrates his point, for as we have seen evidence to Pecock was the pith of truth, by the case of a dog who refrains from taking scraps off the table for fear of a beating.[2]

He answers a further question of a similar nature, to what extent are beasts immortal, more decisively, for it is the absence of immortality,[3] and of the full power of free will and reason, which differentiates the beast from man.

To revert to our main subject. Man is then differentiated from the beast by the possession of a reasonable soul, by the faculty of reason and free will which that reasonable soul implies, and by the immortality with which God through his soul necessarily endows him. His soul works with his body in this life, but at death the two are parted. 'Oure soule in his hool and ful substaunce is departable from oure body bi deeth maad in the body, withoute eny hurtyng of the soulis substaunce and withoute eny apeirement of his resonyng and his willyng.'[4] He develops this argument at length, showing clearly the mortal nature of the body, and the dependence of reason and free will on the soul and their subsequent immortality.

When death comes,[5] man's soul is joined to an immortal

---

[1] *Folewer*, 37.   [2] *Id.* 37.   [3] *Id.* 17. Cf. *Donet*, 9, 12.   [4] *Reule*, 109–10.
[5] He describes the conflict in the body which results in death: 'Al thing that is bi kynde corruptible and fallable' have come to an end through 'v now to be seid weies'. 'Of whiche weies the first is for the thingis maad of contrarie elementis or of contrarie humoris or of othere thingis hauyng contrarie desiris and contrarie worchingis wherbi ther is contynuel fiȝt bitwixe hem, for which fiȝt there muste be at the laste such feblyng and waasting in it that it muste nedis turne into his noun beyng, as it is of alle bodies in this world mengid and maad of the foure elementis, fier, eir, water and erthe. And as it is of qualitees maad of the firste contrarie qualitees, whiche maner of qualitees

body,[1] for just as the gown is made to be worn and the ball to be played with, so the soul was made by God 'forto be a naturaly and a kyndely soule to a body', i.e. 'forto be in such maner a couenable and joynable thing with a body in sum certeyn wise figurid and complexioned and membrid'.[2] This new and heavenly body which man now receives is not only incorruptible, but 'it neuer schal peyne or greve the soule neither vnobeie to eny thing which the soule wole worche or do by it'.[3] Thus when man comes to receive his final reward at the hands of his Creator, it is the 'hool man maad' of body and soul together who presents himself at the bar of judgement.

The bliss of heaven forms the highest reward for man's conduct of his earthly life. Pecock could hardly find words adequate enough to express his 'moost souereyn and moost desirable and moost fillyng supernatural good',[4] and for the most part contented himself with quoting the Latin of the Vulgate. He does, however, say what other medieval writers had already said on the joys of heaven. The blessed will watch the wicked suffering the pains of hell with noticeable enjoyment.[5] Their other pleasures are hardly less Miltonic. They will have 'myche and cleer kunnyng of hiʒe and priue and wondirful curiose and subtil trouthis and conclusiouns y-had in creaturis',[6] for faith is now merged or submerged in reason in highest heaven. They will also have 'grete sensual delite and sport in oure outward and inward sensitive

ben colouris, for they ben maad of liʒt and derkenes mengid to gidere, and as ben odours and fauouris of taastis and suche othere, for thei ben maad of heete, of colde, drienes and moistenes mengid togidere' (*Reule*, 120–1).
[1] He describes the process: 'a soule oonys fro his body may be joyned aʒen to be a soule to a corruptible body for a while such as was the body to which he was firste joyned, as it bifelle to the soules of tho men which crist and his apostolis and other holy men reisiden fro deeth to lijf, which aftirward dieden aʒen, and so thei dieden twies. And if it schulde like to thee, lord, so myʒtist thou make that a soule schulde an hundrid sithis be departid and an hyndrid sithis be aʒen joyned and at ech of tho tymes to a corruptible body... but at the last ech mannys soule schal be joyned to an vncorruptible and vndeedly perpetual body' (*id.* 128–9).
[2] *Id.* 123. [3] *Id.* 127. [4] *Id.* 129.
[5] *Id.* 148. [6] *Id.* 144.

wittis'.[1] There will be, in addition, considerable mutual admiration and congratulation at escaping the pains of hell, but the degree of rejoicing will not always remain the same lest the saints suffer from too great a monotony. He ends with a catalogue of the heavenly joys.[2]

The pains of the damned are treated in a similar fashion, with that greater realism which life on earth inevitably gives to the picture of hell. There is of course the intermediary state of purgatory to which the would-be-good and the less hardened sinners are consigned.[3] Hell is lurid, for the vicious and the evil are not only deprived of the reward granted to the blessed but are punished by 'peyne of hem to be feelid grevously'. Such pains as they suffer, and one is inevitably reminded of Dante's *Inferno*, they suffer in proportion to the greatness of the sins they have committed. The damned souls are also endowed with a body so that the whole man may suffer the pains of hell—'passyng grete sorewe for the losse of alle tho joies...passyng greet lothynes and gastnes in seyng horrible thingis'.

Whether a man's soul finds its way to heaven, purgatory or hell is determined by the use which he makes of his reason and of his free will, together with the other subsidiary wits, appetites and passions, in this life.[4] It was with this in mind that Pecock constructed that important if formal *corpus* of moral theology to which we must shortly turn. There are, however, certain forces which influence man's actions and which are supernaturally connected with his future life, but which are only partially embraced within the compass of Pecock's Four Tables. They are implicitly rational, but their existence depends more on man's faith or revelation than on the 'doom of reason'.

---

[1] *Reule*, 145.   [2] *Id.* 149.

[3] It is 'tariyng from her supernatural blisful eende'. God will 'caste peyne vpon hem for a while bi a purgatorie in this world or in the world to come' (*id.* 150).

[4] A reasonable soul works through the mediacy of the five outward bodily wits (smelling, seeing, hearing, tasting and touching) and the five inward bodily wits (common wit, imagination, fantasy, estimation and mind) besides reason and free will. *Donet*, 8 ff.; *Folewer*, 20–35.

There is, for instance, the power of grace. Pecock is too orthodox to be sceptical of the force of divine grace, but he is too keen on 'doom of reason' to pay very much attention to it. It is necessary in the sense that when man had sinned Jesus' redemption procured for man 'aftir large maner of speche...so greet grace'.[1] It is a necessary basis[2] for man's good in this life and the next, for no man may 'eny good dede do deservingli for to have for it eny rewarde of blys of heuene' or be protected from 'myschauncis and myscheefis', nor yet obtain God's forgiveness without grace.[3] Grace is of two kinds, grace accepting and grace inspiring:

so that resoun and feith and moral vertuose dedis togidere schulden be oure meenys ledyng vs into oure blisful super-natural ende, thou ʒeuyst to vs othere meenys helping to these now spokun meenys, whiche othere meenys ben thi gracis, of whiche gracis oon kynde of grace is helpyng grace forto make vs stronge to do tho seid vertuose dedis and to aʒenstonde lettyngis and temptaciouns. An other kynde of grace is acceptyng grace bi which thou makist ech of oure moral vertuose werkis to be worth a certeyn blisful mede in heuene.[4]

Grace can be sought, however, through the power of prayer,[5] and it is to this that we now turn.

Pecock has much of interest to say on prayer, but his preference for the active rather than the contemplative life is again apparent.[6] He contrasts those who pray and those who work with the min-strels and servants of an earthly baron, and concludes that the

[1] *Reule*, 205. Cf. *id*. 481.   [2] *Id*. 1.   [3] *Donet*, 46.

[4] *Reule*, 135. His own books are written to show how God 'bi his hiʒest large frenesse ʒeueth to ech man gracis to enforme him in his resoun and to stire him in his wil into thilke moral vertuose werkis whiche god wolde thilk man to do' (*Folewer*, 1–2).

[5] *Reule*, 7.

[6] Cf. *Cal. Pap. Reg.* XI, 76–7: 'The pope has recently learned that lately Reginald bishop of Chichester, solicitous for the welfare of the people committed to him, compiled certain...tractates...in English and Latin, of the Christian religion and a number of others concerning the contemplative life' (June 13th, 1458). He adds that Pecock had been circulating these 'libels' for the past twenty-four years.

lord's greatest debt is to his servants.[1] Yet the *Reule* is interlarded
with sincere and charming prayers,[2] a fact which shows that we
must not overemphasise the seemingly non-spiritual aspects of his
work and character. While he obviously does not deny the efficacy
of prayer—'if we pray and live aright God will hear our prayers on
behalf of sinners, even when the sinner does not deserve the
blessings that he now receives'[3]—he is absolutely certain that
good works are of equal, even of greater importance.[4] Prayer and
worship are the means to action and do not constitute an end in
themselves. This is borne out in the writings of St Hugh, St
Bernard, and of St Jerome, who explicitly urged in his *Epistola
ad Demetriadem*[5] that almsgiving was of greater importance than
worshipping. It is indeed 'synne and vice' to allow prayer to
interfere with such good works towards our neighbour, ourself
and our God. Pecock illustrates his last point by referring to the
duty of penance, but even penance should accompany rather than
interrupt the doing of good works.[6]

With this qualification Pecock commends the practice of
prayer as proper means of 'surest gendring in vs loue toward thee,
desijr, homelynes, trust, hooldnes vpon thee and deuocioun to
wirche and suffre for thee in thi lawe keeping'.[7] He has, however,

[1] The 'mynstrallis pipen and trumpen whanne he risith from bed, whan he
goith to mete and at ech course of seruyce at the table and whan he risith fro
mete and whan he goith to bed and whanne he ridith in his lond into citees or
greet townes. And ʒit thei ben not theryn sette by and apprisid in reward of
othere seruauntis...whiche wirchen his profijt or his desiris and the profijt of
hise cofris and of his tenauntis but as it were litil or nouʒt' (*Reule*, 413).

[2] E.g. *id.* 100, 223–4, 366.

[3] *Id.* 172, 441 (where he says that God will answer the prayers of good men
when they cannot help themselves).

[4] *Id.* 392–5 ('werfore folewith...that but if we haunt preier in thilke bothe
maners in whiche he schal not lette from the vss of eny other moral vertues
worching, ellis we failen as foule aʒenward in the other side bi indiscrecioun'),
id. 408.

[5] *Id.* 384.   [6] *Id.* 394.

[7] 'To aske bi inward speche or outward speche the desirid boonys which
thou thi silf biddist vs to aske vs in the preier callid pater noster' (*id.* 243–4). 'It
availith principaly to gendre, and contynue, and kepe in him whiche preie[th],
the now seid desires toward god forto haue alle necessaries for him whiche
preieth, and for othire, into goddis seruice' (*Donet*, 30–1). He also gave advice
as to set forms of prayer and meditation, *id.* 202–14.

a good deal to say on the practice and method of praying itself. He condemns the practice of making long, formal and unintelligible prayers 'as men vsen in bookis', and he recommends in their place 'schort, smert fiery deuoute preiers' said during or concurrently with good works, whereby the quality of our work is greatly improved.

Comprehension and sincerity are the two most important aspects of prayer with which Pecock deals. Writing feelingly he deprecates prayer 'maad in such langage or vndir so harde or derke clausis that thei mowe not vndirstonde it'. If, however, a man is inevitably so situated that he cannot understand the prayer,[1] he should not allow his mind to wander—'slidernes of her minde'—but should think on some special boon or petition. Finally, prayer must be implicitly sincere: 'in the desijr is al the pith of preier.'[2] The best prayers are the prayers which a man makes of his own accord with his whole heart. 'It were wel doon that thei maden her owen preier thanne at the first whanne thei wolde vse it', so that they 'myȝte esili vndirstonde ech word and ech clause of tho formes'.[3] In some cases men, especially unlearned men, may find it to be easier to pray by fastening on to some prayer or phrase of prayer such as the petitions of the paternoster, but in general all men, especially the more learned, should not abide by set forms.[4]

Grace and prayer are very closely associated with a third means of finding salvation—the sacraments of the Church. Pecock wrote a book on the sacraments, in both English and Latin, which does not survive, but there are plenty of references in his surviving works which show the esteem in which he held them. They are 'outwardli sensible or feleable signes and tokenes dyuers fro spechis, by whiche signes we remembren vs silf or othere persoones with vs in place being, vpon sum persoonys dignite, worthines, benefet or goodnes',[5] signs which 'thou lord god bi

---

[1] There is a further reason for lack of understanding, namely the speed at which some prayers are said (*Reule*, 400).

[2] *Id.* 398.   [3] *Id.* 399.

[4] *Id.* 405.   [5] *Id.* 252.

thin owne persoon inmediatly ordeynedist to be signes of honouring and of worschiping'.[1]

There is baptism, for instance, 'to signifie and bringe into mynde the clensing from oure synne and oure newe goostli bigeting and birthe into thee'.[2] There is the Eucharist which, as we have seen, Pecock as a pious Catholic and as an opponent of Wyclif holds in the greatest esteem. This sacrament, which no one should approach until he has reached the age of discretion,[3] 'notwithstonding it is thin own body and blood', is also ordained as a sign and token to remind us of Christ's holy life and passion.[4] Although it is an article of faith it is eminently reasonable:

it semeth to be hold that the power of presthode ordeynyd bi crist forto make and mynystre the sensible sacramentis...is not a power passing oure power which may be maad and ȝouun bi kynde as bi resoun and free wil, neither the power forto strecche oure deedis of worschipyng into thingis aboue kynde, as into crist as god and man, is a power passing oure power of nature in resoun and wil, neither the power of the hiȝer preesthode forto make the louȝer preesthode into this that the louȝer preesthode make the sacramentis of crist, is a power passing a natural power of oure resoun and of oure wil.[5]

Prayer and the sacraments form a principal part of what Pecock calls in his Four Tables living 'worschipingli', although praying, praising, thanking, worshipping and partaking of the sacraments are actually distinct.[6] Pecock held that worship was also mainly a means to action and that many improvements could be made in the church services. 'The chirche in making the divyne office in latyn intendid and meened that mynistris therof schulde make her attendaunce and her affecciouns answering to the lettir',[7] but we certainly cannot excuse the Church for frequently making her services 'so derke, so looce, so difforme and so vnhanging office

---

[1] Reule, 253.   [2] Id. 247. Cf. Donet, 34.   [3] Reule, 374.

[4] Its purpose: 'that the reycever, in the eukarist receiving, schulde ofte remembre him silf therbi vpon christis holy lijf and passioun, and vpon his benefetis and his lawe, and folewingly schulde take and make a sad purpose to god that he wole be oon to god and to his neiȝbore in charite, and in keping vertues and the lijf whiche crist kepte and tauȝte in erthe' (Donet, 35).

[5] Reule, 313.   [6] Cf. id. 252, 500–7.   [7] Id. 406.

to be rad and seid and into so greet haunte and quantite'. He suggests that a division should be made between the sentences of prayer and praise, which are at the moment so intermingled as to confuse the worshipper, so that there should be a sequence of prayer followed by a sequence of praise, with hymns and verses appropriate to the several themes.[1] The more difficult passages —'not esili to be vndirstonde'—which are of doubtful value, in any case so far as the laity is concerned, could be gathered together and read with an exposition explaining their meaning.

He was also critical of the part which ritual and symbolism played in the church service. 'Liȝtis, encensis, hali watir, gay and riche clothis and garnementis, crossis, ymagis, peyntingis, bellis, organs, myrie songis, stipelis, gay corven roofis with craftiose windowis, dyuersite of deedis to be doon after reule and ordre of the ordinal', together with such practices as wearing one's best clothes on holy days, 'bodili lowȝing vs silf vndir thee, god, lowting, bowing, kneling, falling adoun', are 'wel serven' providing that they are used to remind the worshipper of his obligations. Other rites, which do not recall the objects for which they supposedly stand, and which waste 'greet cost of almes and expensis' that might be put to better use, are worthless. Too great an expenditure on the other proper symbols and tokens should not be allowed.[2] The study of God's word is infinitely more profitable as a means of worshipping and pleasing Him.

Thus what we may call, though the division is by no means a clear one, those means to salvation which are more dependent on revelation than reason have a necessarily less important place in Pecock's scheme of thought than his moral theology based, as he understood it, on the 'doom of reason' and carried out by reason's direction of man's free will.

The 'doom of reason' and the free will which is subordinate to it and which should work under its lead[3] provide the best road to

---

[1] *Reule*, 406. [2] *Id.* 246.
[3] Cf. *Donet*, 12–14, where he discusses the relationship between reason and free will—'the wil is the propre appetite of the resoun and thei abiden to gider in the soule departid from the body'. Cf. *Folewer*, 83–4.

salvation. Pecock continually emphasises man's responsibility for working out his own salvation,[1] a welcome contrast to Wyclif's division of mankind into the saved and the damned, but there is no question of his argument being Pelagian in character.

The relationship between reason and faith, and the critical judgement to which reason gives birth, have been discussed—the best plums have fallen ripe from the tree—but the 'doom of reason' must be mentioned at this place because it is here most apparent as the pivot of Pecock's system. Reason is the basis on which Pecock constructed that stiff and formal system of conduct called the Four Tables of which he was so inordinately proud. Faith also has a part but it is a subordinate one.

The Four Tables formed an all-inclusive, perfectly efficacious guide to Christian living, and, by implication, to salvation.[2] They are incomparably more satisfactory than the Ten Commandments, the Seven Gifts of the Holy Ghost, or any other system of moral theology which has so far been put forth.[3] It now only remains to consider the Four Tables briefly and to examine a few individual aspects of their teaching and thus complete our review of Pecock's thought. In fact the Four Tables formed the greater part and the principal *motif* of *The Reule of Chrysten Religioun*, the *Donet*, the *Folewer* and innumerable other books which no longer exist.

This system which, as he says, is equal to the two commandments of Christ and the teaching of St Paul,[4] consists of four tables, one of 'meenal moral virtues', three of 'eendal moral virtues', covering some thirty-one points in all.[5]

The 'meenal' moral virtues, i.e. those virtues which are the means leading to the 'eendal' virtues, are eight in number: to live learningly, praisingly, dispraisingly, prayingly, thankingly, wor-

---

[1] E.g. *Reule*, 200.

[2] They are a means by which man achieves his supernatural end—'which is forto be blisfulli richid perpetuali in the siȝt of God' (*Folewer*, 77–8). A man should consult the Four Tables before going to Confession (*id.* 117–18).

[3] E.g. *Donet*, 20–1, 136 ff., 161, etc.   [4] *Id.* 24–6.

[5] Some are commandments and some are the counsels of Faith and Reason (*id.* 15; cf. *id.* 191–2). His arguments are somewhat extended in the *Folewer to*

shippingly, disworshippingly and sacramentally. Learning is placed first in the list because Pecock's system was obviously founded upon knowledge or 'kunnyng',[1] and to live learningly is therefore to be interpreted as 'forto wille, chese and be bisie forto knowe, leerne and kunne' all those truths which should be the means whereby faith or reason governs the deeds of our will, or more concretely 'what god is in him silf, whiche ben hise bene-fetis, whiche ben hise punyschingis, whiche is his moral lawe and seruice...whiche ben oure natural wrecchidnessis, whiche ben oure wickidnessis, and whiche ben remedies aȝens hem bothe'.[2] To live praisingly is to praise God by inward or outward speech.[3] Dispraising is the rebuke administered either to oneself or to someone else for faults or sins committed through inward or out-ward speech, so that one may repent of one's sins and amend one's faults in the future. Praying is a pragmatic expression, re-minding the Christian of the obligation of such prayer 'bi inward speche in resoun oonly, or therwith bi outward speche in tunge,

the Donet where he deals more precisely with the natural, moral and 'kunnyngal' virtues (intellect, speculative science, prudence, craft and opinion) and the relations subsisting between them. The moral virtues are 'gendrid in vs' by the 'kunnyngal' virtues. The argument can be best explained by a quotation: 'Certis, sone, natural vertues ben tho vertues whiche disposen, araien and parfiten a creature or power of eny creature bi ȝift of kynde, and not bi getyng in labour or bisines doon and maad therto in resoun or wil of the same crea-ture. And therfore thei ben powers ȝouun kyndeli into a thing folewyngli vpon the natural beyng of the same thing as for her foundement or ground. And thei ben such as we fynden in herbis, spicis, stones, and in alle othire thingis of kynde; as in coral to staunche blood, in the adamaunt to drawe yren, in the malowis to ceese aking...kunnyngal vertues ben tho vertues whiche disposen, araien and parfiten the resoun or the vndirstondyng or the intellect, so that bi hem the hauer of hem, whethir he be man or aungel, is knowyng sum thing, and therfore thei resten and ben placid in the vndirstondyng or in the intellect or resoun....Moral vertues ben tho vertues whiche disposen, araien, inclynen and parfiten the wil forto chese or refuse, and comaunde to be doon or to be left vndoon, what and as resoun or the vndirstondyng avisidli deemeth in sum doom to be doon, or to be left vndoon, or be doable allowabli. And therfore thei resten and ben placid in the wil' (*Folewer*, 46–7).

[1] E.g. *Reule*, 1.   [2] *Donet*, 27.

[3] The benefits arising from this may be thus detailed: although God does not need our prayers yet the 'vse of this office' serves to maintain 'the preisers consideracioun, mynde and affeccioun with god' lest they be con-taminated by worldly and fleshly things (*id.* 29).

or bi othire outwarde sygne'.[1] To live thankingly is to acknowledge God's benefits by inward or outward speech. Worshipping
means a declaration of God's goodness and excellence by 'bowing
or louȝing vs silf ynneforth in the vndirstonding or in the
ymaginacioun',[2] i.e. otherwise than by inward or outward speech.
Disworshipping means the rebuke of our own faults or the faults
of other people by the same means,[3] as for instance occurs when
a man wears sackcloth or puts ashes on his head. Finally, sacramentally means the reception of Christ's sacraments.[4]

The Second Table follows. It is a table of seven 'eendal' moral
virtues, the end being the service of God, 'forto lyve anentis
God'. Ghostlihood, obedience, righteousness or justice, meekness, truth, benignity and largeness make up the table. He defines
ghostlihood or 'goostlynes' as 'forto wille to god al his good,
which is not in a creaturis power forto make him haue, or not haue,
and lacke: as ben his myȝt, his wisdom, his loue, his mageste'.[5]
Obedience means 'Forto seie and kepe hise lawis of kynde',
both commands and counsels.[6] To live to God righteously
he interprets as the performance of our promises to God whether
they were entered into with Him by 'ooth or vowe' or left to the
free will,[7] and resultantly 'to so bere vs anentis alle hise creaturis
and goodis' as He would wish. These deeds in themselves constitute 'truth'. Pecock mentions in relation to meekness that it
includes an obligation on our part to abstain from demanding unnecessary miracles from God.[8] By benignity he means acceptance
of God's 'chastisingis' without grumbling or blasphemy and by
largeness, voluntary gifts to God which He does not demand,
such as vows of chastity or poverty.[9]

The Third Table contains eight 'eendal' moral virtues, the
end being the service of ourselves. The moral virtues are ghostlihood, fleshlihood, worldlihood, cleanness, honesty, patience,[10]

[1] *Donet*, 30.   [2] *Id.* 32.   [3] *Id.* 33.   [4] *Id.* 33 ff.
[5] *Id.* 36.   [6] *Id.* 37.   [7] *Id.* 38–9.   [8] *Id.* 39.
[9] *Id.* 41.
[10] *Id.* 56 ff.: 'Forto holde and kepe (the wil) in a softnes in pees and reste,
withoute disturblaunce and grucching.'

doughtiness and largeness. Ghostlihood here means the willing of oneself towards heavenly goods, 'oure blisful rewardis to be had in heuene and goddis fre gracis thidirward helping here in erthe'.[1] Fleshlihood and worldlihood have much the same meaning, the possession of fleshly and worldly goods, such as wife, children, meat, drink, health, strength and materials in so far as reason countenances it.[2] They are vices when 'vnmesurable' or 'aȝens the doom of resoun'.[3] Cleanness and honesty are concerned with 'resonable vsing of tho same goodis'.[4] Thus cleanness comprises sobriety, the 'taking and vsing of mete and drynk, slepe, housing, clothing, laboure, rest, eir, delectaciouns', fasting, temperance in sexual matters, continence and chastity. Honesty covers both the 'mesurable and resonable vsing of worldly goodis'[5] and honesty of action. Doughtiness, which is connected with all the moral virtues because 'it conteynith an aggregat of manye moral vertues beyng in dyvers tablis',[6] means keeping and following the 'doom of reason' 'in taking and bering and continuyng excellent labouris and excellent peynful dedis for the seruice and lawe of god fynali or eendli'.[7] Finally, there is largeness, or more properly largesse, which is giving to God that which neither He nor the 'doom of reason' demands.

The last and Fourth Table follows the same line as the three previous tables, its end being man's treatment of his neighbour. There are eight 'eendal' moral virtues. The first, 'to live to one's neighbour ghostly', merely means willing to him the heavenly goods previously mentioned in relation to ghostlihood. To live 'attendauntly' 'is the fulfilling of the lawe and boonde of ouerte toward vndirlingis, or of subieccioun toward ouerers',[8] a matter with which we shall deal a little later. The third moral virtue, righteousness towards one's neighbour, has a twofold significance.

---

[1] *Donet*, 42.
[2] He mentions that fleshlihood implies, for example, reasonable attention paid to one's health (*Reule*, 271). His long and not uninteresting discussion on marriage is also related to this virtue (*id.* 275, 341–60).
[3] *Donet*, 43.   [4] *Id.* 45.   [5] *Id.* 50.
[6] *Id.* 59.   [7] *Id.* 57.   [8] *Id.* 61.

It may either mean performing our promises and obligations towards him, or abstaining from spoiling our neighbour's goods, and by implication making amends for a sin of this nature if it has been committed.[1] Meekness as opposed to pride constitutes the fourth moral virtue, whilst to live to our neighbour 'accordingli', i.e. 'forto consent to neiȝboris into the making, keping and vsing of reulis, ordynauncis and lawis to be made, such as resoun wel deemeth to strecche into the comoun availe bodili or goostli',[2] makes up the fifth. Truth, benignity or temperance, largeness, 'willing forto releeue oure neiȝboris lak and nede bi oure habandaunce and plente',[3] complete the table.

These Four Tables, which enabled man to fulfil the purpose for which God has created him, to live morally, virtuously or according to the 'doom of reason', play an important and significant part in Pecock's scheme. The greater part of his books is concerned with an extensive, formal and it must be confessed monotonous and repetitive commentary on some aspect or other of the tables.

It follows from this that if the good life is the life that is lived in accordance with the rules so laid down, the sinful life is its converse. 'As ech moral vertu is a disposicioun or habit or his dede of the fre wil, so ech moral vice muste nedis be a disposicioun or habit or dede of the fre wil oonli.'[4] The moral vices, which are the foundations of sin[5] and the pathways leading to hell, are the opposite of the thirty-one moral virtues detailed in the Four Tables.

There are certain aspects of this general system of moral theology which are interesting because of the light which they throw on Pecock's views on different subjects of topical interest. We have seen, for instance, that he was concerned with the relation-

[1] *Donet*, 62–3.   [2] *Id.* 65.   [3] *Id.* 66.

[4] *Id.* 64. The passions, with which he deals in the *Folewer* (94 ff.), are neither moral virtues nor vices, but they are profitable if they are governed by the will according to our reason.

[5] On this, and relevant topics, see *Donet*, 79–81, 96, 172–5, 177–83; *Folewer*, 81–3, 90–3, 116–17; *Reule*, 361–2.

ship which ought to subsist between superiors and inferiors, between parents and children,[1] between husband and wife,[2] schoolmaster and pupil,[3] craftsman and apprentice,[4] employer and hired labourer,[5] priest and parishioner, king and subject. There is perhaps nothing particularly outstanding about this discussion, which shows that he held the static and hierarchical conception of society[6] common to most medieval writers; but a few points may be of some interest.

The service which the king must pay his subjects and *vice versa* recalls the medieval view of monarchy as a form of trusteeship. The relationship must be determined by the 'lawe of kyndely resoun'.[7] Besides providing for the welfare of the Church and State, the king must see that 'al waastful and vnprofitable parties, statis, degrees, officis, or craftis' are abolished.[8] The laws, which should be as few in number as possible,[9] must be ordained with 'comoun assent of his peple' for the good of the whole community, according to faith and reason, 'which lawe...preestys schulen to him and to his comunalte bi holi scripture treuli and sufficientli ministre'. It is his duty to defend his subjects from all wrongs in respect of persons or of goods and to appoint good and proper ministers.[10] He is furthermore to be content with his 'propre endewing; noon taxe or talage or tribute of hise peple, withoute nede or profite of the comounte, and not without the comounte assent, asking and taking; not taking eny personal service of his peple aȝens her wil, ferthir or more than his lawe resonable, afore made bi consente of his peple, taxith, lymytith and assignith'.[11] Pecock must have written those words, and even more particularly the sentences in which he recommends that kings should provide proper sustenance for scholars and priests,

---

[1] *Reule*, 319–20; *Donet*, 70, 77.
[2] *Reule*, 320–1, 338–9; *Donet*, 71, 77.   [3] *Reule*, 321; *Donet*, 71.
[4] *Reule*, 321–2; *Donet*, 71, 77.   [5] *Reule*, 339; *Donet*, 71, 78.
[6] 'He owith to se and to make be doon how moche and in the maner as to him it longith that alle hise legi men lyue treuly ech in hise party, state, degree and craft which thilk legi is callid to' (*Reule*, 335; cf. *id*. 288, 369).
[7] *Id*. 306.   [8] *Donet*, 75; cf. *Reule*, 334–8.
[9] *Reule*, 335.   [10] *Donet*, 76.   [11] *Id*. 76.

with the experience of a lifetime in his mind. If the prince follows Pecock's instructions he is a 'verri prince', but if he does the contrary then assuredly he 'is a tiran'.[1]

The other point worth mentioning here concerns the relationship which should rightly subsist between the priest and the layman. The prelate is concerned with the preaching and teaching of God's laws, 'conteyned in holi scripture and of moral resoun', with living a good life himself, with administering the sacraments, punishing heretics and rebels, rebuking faults, absolving the repentant and assuring the righteous that they be of the 'soort of savid men'.[2] He will advise the king and help him to make the laws so that his people may serve God better and refrain from 'alle vnskilfulle nouelries, alle wantoun deuociouns'.

The duties of the parish priest, which Pecock details in the *Reule*,[3] are very similar. He is also to be an example of godly living to his flock, whom he will exhort and rebuke according to their deserts. He will additionally 'preie ofte for his peple' and 'be redy to ȝeue counceil and informacioun to pryncis'. He will ask his diocesan to make laws and ordinances wherever necessary, in particular to order the church year. He will not only give alms and hospitality whenever he is able but 'alle these now seid officis he be freely mynistring', preserving for himself only the necessaries of his life and the 'purtynauncis of his cure doyng withoute which his cure may not be parfijtly doon'. It is probable that the sins which Pecock catalogues and which may, he says, confront the parish priest were sins with which Pecock himself as a diocesan was only too frequently faced. They include matrimony, 'ouer ofte and ouer myche drinking of wijnes', 'worldli officis and rekenyngis in court or out of court keping or mynystryng', offices which may involve worldly cares, acceptance of an 'ouer pore and insufficient' endowment, and arrogant bearing.[4] The advice shows clearly that Pecock was wholly aware of the world in which he was living and of his own duty as priest and bishop.

[1] *Reule*, 337.   [2] *Donet*, 72.
[3] *Reule*, 322–7.   [4] *Id.* 325–6.

If his views on usury[1] were typical of his time, his opinions with regard to witchcraft were perhaps less typical, since the fifteenth century was not only the great age of the witch trials, of Joan of Arc, of Gilles de Rais and of the wife of his own patron, Eleanor Duchess of Gloucester, but it also produced Sprenger's *Malleus Maleficarum*, the most ponderous and exact study of the crime which had yet been published. Witchcraft in Pecock's view is but 'foly and yuel', because it 'puttith vertu in wordis and countenauncis and dedis more than bi resoun can therynne be founde'.[2] His views recall the earlier rather than later and contemporary view of witchcraft.

Besides an interesting passage on marriage,[3] Pecock's Four Tables have an implicit reference to monasticism and the monastic life. We might well gather from the way in which he so evidently prefers the active to the contemplative life, although he admits that the contemplative life is the most perfect way of preparing for the perfect active life,[4] that Pecock was no great admirer of the monastic way of life. He admitted the efficacy of the monastic life and even asserted as we have seen in his justification of monasticism in the *Repressor*[5] that bad monks do more good than soldiers engaged in the French war.

Pecock wished that monasteries would return to the customs of the days of their foundation, to the primitive ways of the great saints Benedict and Augustine, for 'certis in this wise as it is now rehercid of singing, reeding or ellis preiyng, it was not in tyme of old fadris in the desertis of egipt and of othere cuntrees'. Formerly monks worked as well as meditated: 'thei were ful bisy in visiting ech other to edifie and to be edified goostly ech of othere, to do deedis of bodili almes to ech othere and to haue exercise of manye foold kyndis of vertu bisidis her exercise of meditacioun, of preising and of preier.'[6] If, he urges, any man believes that reading and singing, continual praying and praising, were the sole ends

---

[1] *Donet*, 68; *Folewer*, 146.   [2] *Donet*, 79, 206.   [3] *Reule*, 340–61.
[4] *Id.* 472–3, 480.   [5] *Repressor*, II, 476 ff.
[6] *Reule*, 416.

for which monasticism was ordained, 'he schulde reuoke thilk conceite and amende it'.[1] In fact the 'greet cost and mych almes', which have been spent on the building of houses for contemplative orders, could have been expended to greater effect on more necessary works.[2] The monastic life should, as the early monastic histories show and as the life of the more recent Cistercian monasteries has revealed,[3] be the life of the world in miniature, lived on a smaller scale to conform more readily to the moral virtues of God's law.[4] He concludes his discussion by recommending religious houses to follow the rules of their original founders, 'forto haue more exercise of ghoostly scole and leernyng among hem than thei han',[5] and to read his own books.

This brief, and all too inadequate, survey completes our study of Pecock's *Summa Theologica*. No one will deny its incompleteness or refute the charge of formalism or of lack of originality. The instruments and tools of the scholastic schools are all apparent from the syllogism downwards. The thought of St Thomas, the references to the writings of the Fathers and of Aristotle—though to a less degree than in other works—are all there. We can, if we will, try to analyse his ideas into their component parts, endeavouring to trace the source of the more original, but it is a relatively fruitless task. Dr W. C. Greet, who attempted a brief analysis in the introduction to his edition of Pecock's *Reule*, arrived at the conclusion that his ideas were an extraordinary combination of opposing schools. There is, indeed, with the exception of the plums which we have already plucked from the tree, nothing very extraordinary about the ideas which we find in Pecock's theology. They are too commonplace, too

---

[1] *Reule*, 417.   [2] *Id.* 416.

[3] 'Whanne thei were as it weren now late foundid forto renewe aȝen the first purite of monasterial lijf or of monkis, thei weren foundid to be bildid in wijlde placis from comoun habitacioun of othere men and that thei schulden haue her erthe tiliyng, her beestis forth bringing, her craftis to hem perteynyng as tailouris craft, coruesers craft and othere craftis sufficient and necessarie bi persoonys bering the habite of monkis in the monasterie' (*id.* 420).

[4] *Id.* 418.   [5] *Id.* 422.

much of the ordinary material of the schoolroom to merit much detailed treatment.

Yet, and this is important, despite its apparent normality his theology has great significance. His material was well worn, but his method of arrangement was novel and full of implications for the age in which he was living. The emphasis on reason, and the critical judgements on all sorts of things to which that emphasis gives rise, all point to the individualism which was inseparable from the Renaissance.

CHAPTER XV

PECOCK'S SIGNIFICANCE

WE have now come to a point where only one question remains unanswered—why was Pecock important? His books were burned and his influence was so eliminated that most men forgot all about him and a mere minority misunderstood him. Yet for all this, Pecock remains an important figure in fifteenth-century history. It would have been interesting and useful to have compared the train of thought revealed in his writings with the ideas of Biel, Luther and other late fifteenth- and sixteenth-century writers. It would have indicated his significance more clearly, but this must wait for a later essay.[1]

Pecock has been repeatedly compared with Richard Hooker who also paid great attention to the law of natural reason in his *Ecclesiastical Polity*. Hooker, identifying reason with man's 'natural faculty of reason', says that 'by reason man attaineth unto the knowledge of things that are and are not sensible'.[2] 'Goodness', he writes a little later, 'is seen with the eye of understanding. And the light of that eye is reason.'[3] Reason is the director of man's will;[4] 'the object of will is that good which Reason doth lead us to seek'.[5] The will, moreover, acts only in accordance with the dictates of reason.[6]

Reason is in fact the voice of God inasmuch as 'God being the author of Nature, her voice is but his instrument'.[7] Reason is the means by which God's commands may be ascertained; 'wherefore the natural measure whereby to judge our doings is the sentence of Reason, determining and setting down what is good to be done.' The laws of nature are identifiable by their perfection, by

[1] Dr E. M. W. Tillyard has stressed the continuance of the medieval tradition in the sixteenth century in his *The Elizabethan World-Picture* (1943).

[2] *Works of Richard Hooker*, ed. John Keble (3rd ed. 1845), I, 219.

[3] *Id.* I, 220.

[4] *Id.* I, 222. 'There is that light of Reason, whereby good may be known from evil, and which discovering the same is rightly termed right.' Cf. 'if reason err, we fall into evil' (I, 225).

[5] *Id.* I, 221.   [6] *Id.* I, 224.   [7] *Id.* I, 227.

their capacity for being investigated by Reason without the aid of revelation, and by their universality.[1] Such laws, however, are limited to 'those duties, which all men by the force of natural wit either do or might understand to be such duties as concern all men'.[2]

The analogy between Hooker and Pecock does not end with the similarity of their views on natural reason. Hooker held that scripture was neither a final nor an all-embracing court of law and conduct. Man was to be guided by 'all the sources of light and truth with which man finds himself encompassed',[3] and more particularly by the law of nature. Moreover, Hooker's view of the Church was not unlike Pecock's[4] as he held that it was an organic body which might be compelled to adapt itself to different situations and needs.

If the comparison between the medieval bishop and the scholarly Kentish rector conveys a positive impression of the significance of Pecock's train of thought, despite the fact that the whole of the Renaissance separates them, a comparison between Pecock and his enemy John Bury is useful from the negative point of view. The comparison shows how Pecock stands out amongst those contemporaries who represented the high level of the ordinary thought of the period.

Little as we know of John Bury's life, his *Gladius Salomonis*,[5] which was a reply to Pecock's *Repressor* written at the request of Archbishop Bourchier, shows that he was no fool. It is a clever, well-argued treatise, full of learning, much of which must have been acquired secondhand. Yet the arguments which he uses are not comparable to Pecock's in importance. Although he admits

---

[1] *Works of Richard Hooker*, ed. John Keble (3rd ed. 1845), I, 233. 'The law of Reason or human Nature is that which men by discourse of natural Reason have rightly found out themselves to be all for ever bound unto in their action.'   [2] *Id.* I, 234.   [3] *D.N.B.* XXVII, 293.

[4] E.g. Pecock hopes to turn the people who 'be so vndisposid that thei louen so vndiscreetly her oold wones and derknessis more than liȝt' to new and better ways (*Donet*, 160).

[5] MS. Bodl. 108. The manuscript is described in the Bodleian *Summary Catalogue* (1922), I, no. 1960. The more important parts of the work are published at the end of Babington's edition of the *Repressor*, II, 570–624.

that human reason may be allowed to interpret or recite the commands and counsels of moral philosophy, Bury is insistent that scripture is the basis on which the moral code must ultimately rest. With this in view, he takes Pecock's arguments and refutes them point by point. Thus Pecock's example of the foundation of a house, which might deceive 'simplices et illiteratos viros', is imperfect, for just as a house is founded in a street and just as a street is part of a city, so moral philosophy is intrinsically part of the law of nature which is itself founded on Holy Scripture:[1]

Sed Scriptura Sancta, quae theologia dicitur, sufficienter per Deum ordinata est ad gubernationes et omnes actus hominum dirigendos in ipsum, nomenque ab eo accepit. Ergo hujusmodi actuum et gubernationum sive regiminum fundatio, quanquam aliunde per naturalem rationem inveniri valeant, ipsius erit Scripturae Sanctae proprium, speciale, et primum ei deputatum officium. Nempe theologia sermo de Deo dicitur.[2]

Thus Bury held that the law of nature is not the fount of faith nor must it be used to ground any article of faith. On the contrary, it is the office of the Catholic Church to put forward the truths which are founded on nature, whilst the truths of divine law are so apparent that no such foundation is required. Further, the law of God may be known and the scriptures may be understood by any man without his being learned in logic or in moral philosophy. The whole of Bury's discussion is well supported by a skilfully wrought mass of references, biblical and classical, but it cannot compare either in form or in substance with Pecock's books.

Friar Bury realised that it was the individualistic character of

---

[1] Taking the city of Damascus as an example he writes: 'Quam insuper vana sit applicatio exempli fundationis domus in loco uno ad fundationem regiminum moralium in ratione tantum, qua nititur probare Sacram Scripturam non valere fundare mores humanos.'

[2] Babington, *Repressor*, II, 577. A little later he writes that scripture existed from the time of creation and that Pecock was wrong in saying that it did not exist before Abraham. Adam learned, for instance, of the indissolubility of marriage from God by divine revelation and not from strength of reason. 'Igitur a primo credente usque ad ultimum credentem una erit lex; lex ecclesiae credentium Scriptura Sancta est; igitur omnium credentium, nedum a lege circumcisionis, sed a lege naturae inchoante, una erit Scriptura Sancta.'

Pecock's ideas which endangered the Church. He pertinently rebuked Pecock 'de jactantia et laude suorum opusculorum, quibus adversarius hic se extollit', and adding that 'nova vero iniquitas pusillorum animos facile contaminat', urged that the very deceitful sweetness of Pecock's views had proved a further incentive to their circulation.

Pecock was certainly not an individualist nor, as we have seen, a rationalist in the modern sense of either of those terms, but the comparison with Hooker and with Bury indicates that it was essentially the way in which he grouped his ideas, the way in which the reason-judgement budded from the medieval syllogism, which determines his place in fifteenth-century history. Politically, it was his partisanship of the Lancastrians. Ecclesiastically, his attack on the Lollards. But both that partisanship and the struggle against the Lollard writings, which partly provided the opportunity for the exercise of his thought, were partly conditioned by the 'doom of reason' and the critical judgements which sprang from it.

In one sense then he was a medieval churchman who represented the medievalism of his times. He was living in days which were still saturated with the emotions and ideas of past centuries. The Pope Pius II still dreamed of a Crusade which would rescue the Holy Land from the Turk. The gild plays and the condemnation of usury together with man's religious devotions all pointed to the intensely medieval cast of men's minds.

Pecock was steeped in the thought and ideas of the past. He was schooled in the medieval scene. He grew up in the controversies of an Oxford which was more interested in nominalist and realist ideas than in the social teaching of the Lollard preachers. He became master of a Collegiate Church in fifteenth-century London, and was equally horrified by Lollards, and conscienceless merchants who spent their time in the buying and selling of material goods. He became a bishop and a royal councillor. He applied himself to the study of logic and the practice of the syllogism with exemplary zeal. Yet even so, there was something of the modernist about him.

In the first place he had come into contact with the Lollards, probably at Oxford and certainly in London, and by reading their works and by conversing with their followers he came to the conclusion that they were challenging the truths of the Church of which he was a minister. He perceived their anarchic individualism in biblical and social matters, and fearing that their teaching might well bring England to the sorry state in which Bohemia now found itself, he determined to controvert and to convert his opponents. It is even possible that he absorbed some of their views to a limited extent. In any case, it is unquestionable that it was this contact with the Lollards which opened the door to his thought, and so to his significance.

Thus the second factor of importance lies in the response to the Lollard challenge. He was not content with merely refuting the Lollard point of view. He may have thought that it was now and again necessary to burn heretics, but he thought that it was infinitely better to convert them. Hence that system of thought and of conduct which we have studied in the preceding chapters.

A new spirit appeared out of the glowing formalism of a medieval system of thought. It is this new spirit which is connected with the 'doom of reason', with the criticism of the Ten Commandments, with the Donation of Constantine and the authority of the Fathers, with the writing in the vernacular, and with his own personal self-confidence. It is idle to pretend that medieval writers had not glorified reason before Pecock and equally idle to assume that the Reformation was the rebirth of reason in theology, when it was, despite Calvin's logical and legal mind, so obviously emotionalistic. It is also idle to deny that other writers were equally critical and far more aware of the new trends in thought which we associate with the Renaissance.

Yet for all that, Pecock's life and thought do represent an unconscious challenge to authority and in this way of course he also mirrors the age in which he was living. Its 'crepuscular character' of which Professor Jacob has spoken is only too apparent, but it was also a period of vital, creative activity. An analysis of the economic trends of the age, the Italian and south

German commercial development and the nascent mercantilism of the *Libelle of English Polycye*, point to this new spirit in the same way as the secularisation of art and of thought. Pecock's 'individualism' reflects the age in which he was living, and so contributes to the interpretation of fifteenth-century history.

He was in brief one of those thinkers, whose greatest representative was Erasmus, who have had their two feet firmly placed on two different soils, the soil of the past and the soil of the future. His life and his thought bridged the gap between the failing scholasticism of the one age and the critical judgements of another. He was of too conservative a character to stand firmly by the decisions which he himself had reached. It was thus part of the tragedy of Pecock's life that his end was as obscure as his beginning. His thought and his achievements were disowned, and, by being disowned and even destroyed, were ever more under-estimated and misunderstood. Raymond of Sebonde,[1] the professor of Toulouse whose naturalism has a far more Renaissance quality and yet whose writings are possibly less important than those of Pecock, had the good fortune to be immortalised in one of Montaigne's essays[2] and to be admired by Grotius. No such reception awaited Pecock. He was dead and buried in an unknown grave. His character and surviving works were used as weapons in the cause of religious controversy. Historians have glanced at him with sober disinterest. The philologist has hunted through his works to find the source and use of words. Yet he was a man who, from nearly every point of view, played a significant and interesting part in fifteenth-century history and whose life and works are not unworthy of being characterised and studied.

[1] His definition of nature and natural law is distinct from that of the English bishop: 'Quamvis autem omnia quae probantur per librum creaturarum, sint scripta in libro sacrae scripturae, et ibi contineantur, et etiam illa quae ibi continentur in libro Bibliae, sint in libro creaturarum, tamen aliter et aliter' (*Theologia Naturalis*, ed. J. E. von Seidel (1852), tit. 212, 314). *Vide* David Matzke, *Die natürliche Theologie von Raymundus von Sebonde, ein Beitrag zur Dogmengeschichte des* 15 *Jahrh.* (1843); D. Reulet, *Un inconnu célèbre, recherches historiques et critiques sur Raymond de Sabunde* (1875); C. C. J. Webb, *Studies in Natural Theology* (1915), 292–313.

[2] *Essays of Montaigne*, trans. John Florio (ed. 1894), 219–310.

APPENDIX I

BIBLICAL REFERENCES IN PECOCK'S WORKS

THE following analysis is based on an examination of the *Repressor*, *The Reule of Chrysten Religioun*, the *Donet*, the *Folewer to the Donet* and the *Book of Faith*.

I. OLD TESTAMENT AND APOCRYPHA

	Quotations	References	Vulgate[1]
Genesis	9	15	.
Exodus	10	11	.
Leviticus	5	4	.
Numbers	2	8	.
Deuteronomy	8	9	1
Joshua	4	7	1
Judges	.	2	.
Ruth	1	.	1
I Samuel	1	1	.
II Samuel	.	2	.
I Kings	1	6	1
II Kings	1	4	.
I Chronicles	.	1	.
II Chronicles	.	4	.
Ezra	.	1	.
Job	5	1	3
Psalms	16	6	5
Proverbs	4	.	.
Ecclesiastes	.	1	.
Isaiah	16	10	6
Jeremiah	4	7	1
Lamentations	1	1	.
Ezekiel	9	5	4
Daniel	3	3	3
Jonah	.	1	.
Micah	1	1	1
Habakkuk	1	.	.
Tobit	.	1	.
Wisdom of Solomon	13	1	3
Ecclesiasticus	4	.	.
Baruch	.	2	.
Susanna	.	1	.
	119	116	30

[1] References to and quotations from the Vulgate are practically confined to the *Reule*. The *Repressor* contains the majority of scripture citations and references.

II. NEW TESTAMENT

	Quotations	References	Vulgate
St Matthew	72	62	18
St Mark	14	26	.
St Luke	35	31	1
St John	37	28	11
Acts	4	27	.
Romans	21	26	7
I Corinthians	20	30	5
II Corinthians	5	8	2
Galatians	5	11	1
Ephesians	4	9	.
Philippians	2	2	1
Colossians	5	4	.
I Thessalonians	1	1	.
II Thessalonians	1	2	.
I Timothy	7	19	.
II Timothy	5	4	.
Titus	3	11	.
Hebrews	11	12	4
James	6	5	.
I Peter	8	10	2
II Peter	3	4	1
I John	10	7	1
Jude	1	.	.
Revelation	6	11	3
	286	350	57

	Quotations	References[1]	Vulgate
Old Testament and Apocrypha	119	116	30
New Testament	286	350	57
	405	466	87

[1] In fairness to the reader, it should be mentioned that the original notes for this analysis were destroyed by enemy action, and an allowance should be made for a small margin of error.

THE WORKS OF REGINALD PECOCK

I. SURVIVING BOOKS:

(a) *The Repressor of Over Much Blaming of the Clergy*. Edited by Churchill Babington, B.D., 2 vols. Rolls Series (1860). The original MS. is preserved in CAMBRIDGE UNIVERSITY LIBRARY. The second volume contains the *Abbreviatio Reginaldi Pecok*, a vindication of the sermon which he preached at St Paul's Cross, written by himself. The MS. is in the Bodleian Library. *The Repressor* is incomplete.

(b) *The Book of Faith*. Edited by J. L. Morison (1909). This edition, based on the MSS. (B. 14.45) in TRINITY COLLEGE LIBRARY, Cambridge, replaces the previous edition by Henry Wharton (1688). *The Book of Faith* is incomplete.

(c) *The Donet*. Edited by Dr E. V. Hitchcock (1921), E.E.T.S. The book was edited from MS. BODL. 916. The title recalls the *Ars Grammatica* of the fourth-century grammarian Aelius Donatus. Hence 'Donet' = grammar. The book contains references to the *Poore Mennis Myrrour* (Brit. Mus. Addl. 37788) which was a slighter edition of the *Donet*, written for the less learned laity.

(d) *The Folewer to the Donet*. Edited by Dr E. V. Hitchcock (1924), E.E.T.S. Based on BRIT. MUS. ROY. MS. 17D. ix.

(e) *The Reule of Chrysten Religioun*. Edited by Dr W. C. Greet (1927), E.E.T.S. Based on PIERPONT MORGAN MS. 519. The MS. is incomplete.

II. NON-SURVIVING WORKS:

(i) *The Afore-Crier or Bifore-Crier*. This little book, probably Bale's *Praeco*, treated of Pecock's reasons for writing in English (*Donet*, 3). If the laity read it, then they will gather information about sundry subjects, the knowledge of God (*Reule*, 3), the knowledge of ourselves (*id.* 4), and other topics. It seems to have been an apology addressed to the laity with regard to the form and method of Pecock's writings—'amonge whiche causis,

namelich amonge tho whiche biholden bothe the seid yuel disposid men of the lay partye and the seid weel disposid men of the
lay partie, summe y schal reherce here for hem which han not redy
atte hand the seid book cleepid the "bifore crier"' (*id.* 19)—and
a slight essay on the model of the *Donet* and other writings.

(*ii*) *Book of Baptism*, mentioned in the *Repressor* (1, 163),
probably dealt with this sacrament and may have been an excerpt
from the *Book of Sacraments*. It was in Latin.

(*iii*) *Book of the Church*, dealt among other matters with
opinional faith (*Folewer*, 78) and was almost certainly the same
as the *Just Apprising of Holy Church* (*id.* 67). It was 'to be maad
in latyn' (*Book of Faith*, 231).

(*iv*) *Book of Counsels*. This book did not deal with the councils
of the Church but with the distinction between counsels and commands (cf. *Donet*, 202). 'More of priuate religiose perfeccioun
and what comparisoun is to be maad bitwix priuate religiouns and
othere statis and degrees of holy chirche schal be tauȝt in the
"book of counseilis"' (*Reule*, 423).

(*v*) *Book of Compendious Logic*. 'Into whos making, if God
wole graunte leue and leyser, y purpose sumtyme aftir myn othere
bisynessis forto assai' (*Repressor*, 1, 9).

(*vi*) *Book of Divine Office*, a service book with a commentary (?).
He tells us that he deals, for instance, with confession of sin
'in fridaies matins' (*Folewer*, 118), 'alle creaturis knowing vn-
knowable, as is knowlechid in "the book of dyuine office", in
seruice of trinite sunday' (*Donet*, 85), 'seruice or office of palme
sundaie weke' (*id.* 89), 'friday seruice, in the bigynnyng of
matyns' (*id.* 97), 'punysschingis for oure synnes...in preiers assigned for thursdaye to alle seintes, and in the preiers assigned
to ech special seynt' (*id.* 93). It also had an exposition of the Pater
Noster (*id.* 204) and contained some special prayers: 'if thou
wolt preie...than thou maist go into al the ii^e party of "the book
of dyuine office", where is rubrisch sett afore in this maner,
"Preiers for euensong", or in this wise, "Preiers for matyns".
And, as I weene, for the now seid iii^e maner of preier, thou nedist
neuer seche eny bettir, swettir, fairer or deuouter than thou schalt
there fynde' (*id.* 205). Probably in English as it is referred to in
Poore Mennis Myrrour. The latter usually contains references to
English books.

(*vii*) *Book of Eucharist*. It is uncertain whether this book was completed or not—'into time leiser schal be to me forto write the book of eucharist'. Cf. *Reule*, 95: 'wel y wote that manye of the lay partye bileeven amys in mater of the eukarist aʒens whom it schal be argued and concludid in the book of eukarist.' Cf. *Repressor*, I, 163, II, 564.

(*viii*) *Book of Faith, Hope and Charity*. Probably a small work relating to the three moral virtues named in the title. 'Whether eny feith in vs be infusid or inhildid and not geten bi labour of our resoun or vndirstonding schal be seid and tauʒte in the "book of feith, hope and charite"' (*Reule*, 435). There is a small fifteenth-century manuscript in the British Museum—MS. Roy. 17 A. xxvi—of which folios 27^b–28^b are entitled 'the thre good uertues that poul clepith feith, hope and charite'. Babington believed that this work, and probably some others dealing with the Ten Commandments, the Seven Deadly Sins, the Deeds of Mercy Bodily and Ghostly, the Visitation of Sick Men, were probably written by Pecock. The similarity of the style and sentiment, and the fact that the descent into hell is omitted from the interrogatories put to the sick man made Babington incline to this view (lxxviii). Dr Hitchcock thought that there were no certain grounds for attributing this work to Pecock (*Donet*, 217 n.).

(*ix*) *Book of Lay Men's Books*. Probably a slight work which concerns the writing of books—and Pecock's in particular—in the English language (*Folewer*, 7).

(*x*) *Book of Legends*. 'Namelich sithen in legendis ben founde manie ful vntrewe fablis, as in a book therof to be mad schal appeere' (*Repressor*, II, 354). Therefore probably only promised.

(*xi*) *Book of Learning*. This dealt with the question of wisdom founded on 'philosofre and scripture' (*Folewer*, 55, 60) and wise clerks. In it 'is witnessed bi holy scripture in greet lengthe the first poynt of the first table' (of Pecock's Four Tables) (*Donet*, 177). It was written in English (*Book of Faith*, 255).

(*xii*) *Book of Lessons*. This deals—or was going to deal—with dispensation from monastic vows among other matters. 'More and in better wise y hope schal be sett in *The book of lessouns* to be rad perauenture in the chaier of scolis' (*Repressor*, II, 518).

(*xiii*) *Book of Matrimony*. 'Sir, seie to me where in Holi Scripture is ʒouen the hundrid parti of the teching upon matrimonie
which y teche in a book mad upon *Matrimonie*' (*Repressor*, 1, 15).
The contents of the book are thus obvious. He speaks of marriage in *The Reule of Chrysten Religioun* (274 ff.) and says 'that
ech fleischly deede doon bitwix man and womman out of the
seid couenaunt of matrimonye is vnleeful and synne aftir doom of
natural resoun but if sum special circumstaunce excuse it, schal
be perauenture schewid aftir in this same iii tretice or perauenture
in the "book of matrimonye"' (*Reule*, 276).

(*xiv*) *Book of Nature and Creatures in General*. Seems to have
dealt with morals. Probably an excerpt from a larger work
(*Donet*, 181).

(*xv*) *Book of Orders and Pastoral Care*. Concerns the duties of
the hierarchy, of princes, etc. 'More of this what longith to
pryncis schal be sett in the "book of ordris and of pastoral cure"'
(*Reule*, 338). Cf. *Reule*, 365.

(*xvi*) *Book of Penance*. Talks of doctrine of deadly and venial sin
(*Donet*, 193) and of the office of the minister (*Repressor*, 11, 427).
'How euer it be her of that we mowe or no satisfie sufficiently and
verrily and euenly to god for synnys beyng grettir than tho of
whom spekith the next bifore goyng trouthe...schal be maade in
the "book of penaunce"' (*Reule*, 151). Cf. *id.* 154.

(*xvii*) *Book of Priesthood or of Priests' Power*. It deals with the
duties and office of the Priest (*Donet*, 38; *Reule*, 214, 444). There
is also some work on the sacraments (*Reule*, 309). 'Also thou
[God] ʒauyst to hem power forto make othere preestis in lijk
power and to multiplie hem after that the multitude of cristen
peple to haue preestis schulde haue nede, as groundis herof ben
writun in the "book of preesthode or of preestis power"' (*Reule*,
213–14). 'Also alle the gouernaunces of prelatis or ouerers which
thei maken and vsen anentis her vndirlingis and netherers bi
strengthe of her prelacie or ouerte, and that whether thei ben
princis or preestis, and so folewingly alle lawis maad bi men forto
reule hem the better in the othir pointis of the lawe of kinde or of
god forto the bettir serue god, ben conteyned' in the *Spreading of
the Four Tables*, the *Book of Priesthood* and the *Book of Orders* (*Reule*,
365). Cf. *Repressor*, 11, 427, 451. It dealt with 'what the chirche of
God is' (*Book of Faith*, 168). It was written in English (*id.* 225).

(*xviii*)   *Book of Questions*. This book was largely concerned with moral questions (*Donet*, 181; *Reule*, 192–3), among them lying (*Folewer*, 137). It also apparently dealt with the powers of the soul when the soul was freed from the body by death and the powers of angels (*Folewer*, 99–100).

(*xix*)   *Book of Sacraments*. This was undoubtedly a notable compilation from the number of references made to it (e.g. *Repressor*, I, 163, II, 564; *Reule*, 7, 248, 252, 266, 282, 504). It contained work relating to 'ech suche sacrament' (*Donet*, 117). 'How many grete sacramentis ther ben ordeyned bi crist in the chirch and which thei ben schal be tauȝt pleynly ynouȝ in the "bokis of sacramentis" in latyn' (*Reule*, 309). Cf. *Reule*, 365. Pecock mentions another book in the *Repressor*, the *Book of Faith and Sacrament* to be written in Latin (*id.* I, 38, 42, 80, 92, 99, 101). This may either be identified with the *Book of Sacraments* or was an abridgement of the *Book of Faith* and *Book of Sacraments* in combination. The *Book of Baptism* and the *Book of Eucharist* would be offshoots.

(*xx*)   *Book of Sentences*. This largely deals with moral virtues and such questions as were contained in the *Book of Questions* (*Folewer*, 82, 100, 166, 179; *Reule*, 232, 297).

(*xxi*)   *Book of Usury*. As the name implies it was concerned with the attitude of the Church towards usury. The law against unjust usury was a law of reason rather than an ordinance of the Church or State (*Folewer*, 146). In the *Donet* he writes: it 'schal be tauȝt', but the book was probably completed later.

(*xxii*)   *Book of Worshipping*. This probably overlapped somewhat with the *Book of Divine Office* and the *Book of Sacraments*. It was concerned with image worship (*Donet*, 126), and worshipping generally. 'The vse and haunt which may resonably and therfor vertuosely be doon of signes in the chirche—as ben ringing of bellis, pleiying at organs, singing bi noote, peyntid ymagis, crossis, preciose vestimentis, baners, halowid watir and halowid candels, halowid palmys, laumpis, torchis, tapirs and such other, and al the vse and haunt of sacramentis as of baptym, of eukarist and of other' (*Reule*, 364). Cf. *Repressor*, I, 119, 156, 166, 253, 254 (pilgrimages), 267, 273.

(*xxiii*)   *Concio ad Clerum*. A sermon which Pecock made on the text 'Montes Israel, ramos vestros germinetis et fructum viridem afferatis'[1] to the 'clergie in London...and which sermon y wolde

---

[1] Ezekiel xxxvi, 8.

summe kunnyng man wolde turne into the comoun peplis langage' (*Reule*, 500; cf. *Folewer*, 81, 104–5, 108).

(*xxiv*) *Declaratory* (*Declaratorium* of Bale). Probably the Prologue to the *Donet* (6). The 'litil book to be a declarative' may be separate but it was quite possibly the second part of the *Donet* which was written 'for a defensorye and an excusatorye and sumwhat a declaratorye of the other first seid party' (*Donet*, 176). Dr Hitchcock inclines to the view that it was probably a separate work (215 n.).

(*xxv*) *Enchiridion or Manual*. Written 'for vnlettrid men in latyn' (*Reule*, 403). Among other things, it contained material dealing with the office of prayer (*Donet*, 204–5).

(*xxvi*) *Greater Book or Rule of the Christian Religion*. The relationship of this and the *Less Book* to the *Reule* is uncertain but it was probably along very much the same lines as the *Reule*. It may have been more extended but it may on the other hand be less in size than the *Reule* but greater in size than the *Less Book*. References in the *Donet* are numerous (e.g. 36, 42, 47, 56, 61, 100, 172, 184, 192, 196).

(*xxvii*) *Improving of Men's Insufficient Forms*. 'Tretice therfore speciali to be made, whos name schal be this, "the inproving of mennys insufficient foormes"' (*Donet*, 81).

(*xxviii*) *Just Apprising of Doctors*. It contains a number of quotations from the different doctors of the Church (*Folewer*, 66). It also discusses how great their authority is (*id.* 72), comments on the folly of certain doctors who call themselves 'leernyd men' but 'as children thei muste al thilk while be vndir credence of othire, and so be oonli vnsure trowers and not prouyng knowers' (*id.* 68). In the *Reule* he points out that the greatest doctors can err in their search for truth 'wherof lengir proof is maad in the book clepid the "just apprising of holi scripture" and in the "just apprising of doctouris"' (*id.* 466). Cf. *Book of Faith*, 146.

(*xxix*) *Just Apprising of Holy Scripture*. From the numerous references undoubtedly an important work dealing with the whole question of faith and reason, the authority and bases of Holy Scripture. *Vide* n. 1, p. 199. He reaches the same conclusions as we have them in the *Repressor* and his other extant works but the *Just Apprising* may have been rather more extensive.

(xxx) *Less Book (Rule) of the Christian Religion.* Vide (xxvi).
Donet, 21, 23, 42, 60, 113, 184.

(xxxi) *The Proof of the Christian Faith.* A 'trewe preciose
book' (*Donet*, 101) containing full and decisive arguments on behalf
of the Christian faith, useful for converting all doubters or un-
believers (*Reule*, 133, 427, 429). Cf. *Repressor*, I, 99. It is different
from the *Book of Faith* and although it was noted in the *Poore
Mennis Myrrour* (fol. 63 a) it seems to have been written in Latin
(*Book of Faith*, 133).

(xxxii) *The Provoker or Caller Forth of the Christian Religion.*
Contains teaching on the moral virtues (*Folewer*, 166, 188, 214,
225). It was a 'lasse compendious' version of the 'Witnessing of
the Four Tables' (*Donet*, 177), but it treated the Christian articles
of belief in 'ful compendious maner'. 'Of this same mater
[Pecock's reply to Lollard dependence on Holy Scripture] it is
quikli and smertli spoken in a litil book therto and therfore maad,
which y clepe *The Prouoker of Cristen peple*' (*Repressor*, I, 47–8).
References in the *Reule* (10, 241, 287).

(xxxiii) *The Spreading or Filling of the Four Tables.* From the
very large number of references—17 in the *Reule*, 4 in the *Folewer*,
11 in the *Donet*, and 9 in the *Repressor*—fairly obviously an important work. Probably an expansion of the Tables which
Pecock believed would replace the Ten Commandments as a
system of moral teaching and which he treats in the *Donet*, *Folewer*
and *Reule*. It is also different from the *Witnessing of the Four
Tables*.

(xxxiv) *Twelve Advantages of Tribulation.* This 'preciose litil
book' (*Donet*, 56) treats of wilful mortification (*Donet*, 98, 100) and
patience in suffering adversity. 'And also sumtyme forto leerne
vs in vertu of pacience, that we haue therby to come the riccher
reward and crowne in heuene, and sumtyme for other good causis
wherof mencioun is maad in the trety of the "xii auauntagis of
tribulacioun" in the comoun peplis langage' (*Reule*, 139, cf. 164).
Dr Hitchcock refers to a little anonymous printed book, bearing
the device of Wynkyn de Worde called the *Twelve Profytes of
Tribulacioun* (*Donet*, 219 n.). Three of the 'profytes' are similar to
the 'auauntagis' which Pecock mentions.

(*xxxv*) *The Witnessing of the Four Tables*. Different from the *Spreading*. Contains an account of the relation of scripture to the Four Tables—of which 'y haue bigunne make a special book by himsilf' (*Donet*, 84). It was a 'ful longe...and ouer costiose to pore men' (*id*. 177).

(*xxxvi*) *Epistle to William Goddard the Franciscan*. A reply to one of his opponents who was provincial minister of the Friars Minor in England. There is some confusion because 'there were two friars of the same name, and it is not always clear which of them is referred to' (A. G. Little in *E.H.R.* vi, 749–50). In all probability Pecock's opponent was William Goddard the elder, but the question is obscure. Dr Little added that this MS. might still be 'in the library of Bramshill House, Hants.'

(*xxxvii*) Other works, some of which Bale mentions, may or may not be by Pecock and may or may not have been written, e.g. (i) *De providentia Dei*; (ii) *De libertate Evangelii*; (iii) *De saecularium potestate*; (iv) *Contra mendicitatem impiam*; (v) *De usa palinodia*, probably the letter to the Pope which he wrote after his abjuration.

Other works mentioned by Bale may be identified as follows— or rather have been rightly identified by Babington—*Defensor*, the defence of his sermon at St Paul's Cross contained within the *Abbreviatio*, the *Sequax* to be identified with the *Folewer to the Donet*, and the *Symbolum* which relates to Pecock's views on the Creed. *Contra donationem Constantini*, *De aequalitate ministrorum*, *De legibus et doctrinis hominum* relate to parts of the *Repressor*. *De communione sub utraque specie* was either part of the *Book of Eucharist* or *Book of Sacraments* or both.

The difficulty of establishing the date or even the completion of Pecock's works is impeded by his method of working on a number of books at the same time and including cross references (vide *Reule*, 22).

APPENDIX III

GLOSSARY

The Glossary is only intended as a guide to the less obvious words, and does not give the variations of Pecock's spelling.

Abriggyng, abridging
Accordingli, suitably, agreeably
Adamaunt, adamant
Aferd, afraid
Affeccioun, affection
Aȝens, against
Aȝenstondith, withstand
Aking, aching
Algatis, altogether
Allegorik, allegorical
Amys, amiss
Anentis, in respect of, with regard to
Anoon, straightway
Apaied, contented
Apechyd, impeached
Apeirement, impairment, injury
Apprisid, appreciated, valued
Araie, arrange in position, dress
Ascrive, ascribe
Aspie, espy, observe
Assaie, try
Assignementis, commands
Assoilyng, refuting
Assumpt, assumption
Attendaunce, ministration
Avises, considers, advises
Auctorite, authority
Aungel, angel
Auters, altars
Avisidli, advisedly, attentively
Avisyng, consideration
Avoutrie, adultery
Awaiter, one who lies in wait for

Baar, bare, naked
Babilony, Babylon
Bacbiter, secret calumniator
Bateil, battle
Beeme, Bohemia
Beere, bore
Ben, been
Beryngis, bearings
Bigenyng, beginning
Bigile, cheat out of
Bigunnen, began
Bitwixe, between
Biwamblen, vomit
Blindingis, blindings
Blowen, cast (of metal), puffed up
Boisteȝ, rough, coarse
Boistosenes, roughness, coarseness
Bokis, books
Boonys, boons
Bras, brass
Brennyng, burning
Brent, burnt

Cantilbiri, Canterbury

Carect, character, letter
Certis, certainly
Chanoun, canon
Chargis, duties, responsibilities, burdens
Chese, choose
Cisme, schism
Clausul, little clause
Clennes, purity
Clepe, clepid, call, called
Cloutis, patches
Cofris, coffers
Colueris, doves
Comberose, cumbrous
Comounte, community
Complexioun, temperament (combination of body fluid and humours)
Compowne, combine
Comprehensiveli, comprehensively
Comunalte, commonwealth
Comuning, having fellowship
Conceit, conception, idea
Coniuncciouns, conjunctions
Connable, knowledgeable
Correpcions, rebukes
Corrupcioun, perversion of speech
Cors, body, corpse, amount, substance
Coruesers, shoemakers
Corven, carved
Costiose, expensive
Couenable, convenient
Coueryng, covering
Couthe, could
Covyns, cunning, deceit
Craftiose, artistic, skilful
Cristen, christian
Cristenhode, christianity
Cronical, in the nature of a chronicle
Crownes, tonsures
Cumpenyng, intercourse
Cuntree, country
Curiose, perversely minute in enquiry
Curteis, courteous
Customabli, customarily

Deel, grief
De(e)me, judge
Defaut, fault
Defensory, defence
Delid, dealt
Demene, manage
Demeritorie, unworthy of merit
Denouncing, proclaiming
Derke, dark
Derthe, famine
Dette, debt
Deuise, devise
Deynte, deinte, fondness, honour, esteem
Dew, due

Digne, worthy
Discherid, disheartened, distressed
Discorden, disagree
Dispreise, blame, censure
Disworschip, dishonour
Donet, grammar
Doom, judgement
Dossers, baskets
Douȝtines, energy
Doutis, doubts
Dowues, doves
Dradde, feared
Dresse, direct, arrange
Dukis, leaders

Eendal, final, ultimate
Eftsoones, again
Eir, air
Encensis, incense
Encerche, search
Encresing, increasing
Endewe, endow
Endewing, endowing
Ensaumpling, giving an example
Entent, intent
Entermeting, having dealings with, mixing
Errouris, errors, mistakes
Erysys, heresies
Evir, ever
Excusatorye, apology
Exortacioun, exhortation
Explaying, explaining
Expowned, expounded

Fader, father
Fauoure, favour
Feelshipp, fellowship
Fer, far
Fersly, fiercely
Feyn, glad
Feynyd, feigned, pretended
Ffeendly, fiendishly
Fier, fire
Fitchinge, fixing
Folewer, sequel
Forȝouun, forgiven
Formfaderes, ancestors
Foundamentali, fundamentally
Freelnes, frailty
Freelte, frailty
Freenes(se), generosity
Freris, friars
Fro, from

Gaderers, gatherers
Gadir, gather
Garnementis, garments
Gastful, dreadful
Gastnes, terror
Gendrith, beget
Gileful, deceitful
Gilti, guilty
Glotonye, gluttony
Godis, gods
Goodis, goods
Goostli, spiritually
Gouernaunce, practice
Graved, engraved
Grauntiden, grant
Greet, great

Grew, Greek
Grounde, ground
Grucching, grousing

Ȝeue, give
Ȝere, year
Ȝhe, yea
Ȝifte, gift
Ȝitt, yet
Ȝotun, molten
Ȝouun, given
Ȝowre, your

Habandaunt, abundant
Halewid, hallowed
Hali, holy
Halyday, Holy day
Han, have
Happe, happen, befall
Hastynes, haste
Haunt, custom, practise, familiarity
Heiȝte, height
Hem, them
Here, hear
Homelynes, intimacy
Hond, hand
Hool, hoole, whole
Hosil, sacrament

Iȝe, eye
Immediacioun, immediacy
Immouable, immovable
Induccioun, induction
Inhildid, poured in
Inmesurable, immeasurable
Inparfitnes, imperfection
Intelleccioun, intellect, reason
Interesse, concernment
Iyen, eyes

Jheus, Jesus
Joon, John
Joynt, joint
Journeie, journey

Kete, bold
Kindeli, by nature
Knoulech, acknowledge
Kunnen, can
Kunnyng, knowledge
Kunnyngal, having to do with knowledge
Kunnyngist, most knowing
Kuting, cutting
Kynde, nature, natural reason

Ladde, led
Laife, laity
Large(ne)s, generosity
Lasse, less
Lauȝe, laugh
Laumpis, lamps
Leccherie, lechery
Leechouris, fornicators
Ledyng, leading
Leefir, rather
Leeful, lawful
Leefulli, lawfully
Leene, lend
Leener, lender
Legi, vassal, subject

Leie, lay
Lesingis, lies
Lette, hindrance
Lettyngis, hindrances
Lewidnes, ignorance
Leyser, leisure
Liflode, livelihood
Ligge, lie
Liuiden, lyueden, live
Lodowic, Louis
Lond, land
Longith, belong
Looce, loose, inattentive
Lothynes, loathing
Loueabilnes, lovableness
Louȝing, abasing
Louȝer, lower
Lousid, released
Lowting, bowing to, worshipping
Lyenage, lineage
Lymes, limbs
Lymytith, limit
Lyuynge, living

Malencolie, melancholy
Malouis, mallows
Malȝuolence, malevolence, malice
Manassing, menacing
Maure, Maurice
Mede, reward
Medid, rewarded
Meened, intended
Meenys, means
Membrid, mentioned, remembered
Mencioun, mention
Mengid, mixed
Merytorie, meritorious, worthy of merit
Mete, meat
Miscallen, miscall
Mo, more
Modiris, mothers
Morther, murder
Movid, moved
Mowe, to be able
Myche, much
Myddis, middle, midst
Mynistrid, ministered
Mynstrallis, minstrels
Myrie, merry
Myrthe, mirth
Myschauncis, mischances
Myscheefis, mischiefs

Namelich, especially
Ne, nor, not
Netherers, inferiors
Nilyng, not willing, unwilling
Noe, Noah
Noon, noun, none, no one
Nouelries, novelties, novel things
Nyrcromancie, necromancy

Obeischaunce, reverence
Officyng, the performing of divine office
Ordynaries, ordinaries (of the Church)
Ouerer, superior
Ouerte, superiority
Outre, utter
Oynement, ointment

Pacchis, patches

Panyeris, baskets
Parchemyn, parchment
Parfiten, perfect
Parfitest, most perfect
Parteyners, partners
Parti, part
Passiden, pass
Passional, pertaining to the Passion
Paynemys, pagans
Peas, peace
Peinturis, painters
Peple, pepull, people
Perfeccioun, perfection
Pesible, peaceful
Peyneful, painful
Pilers, pillars
Pilioun, a doctor's hat
Plees, pleas, lawsuits
Plegge, pledge
Plesaunce, pleasure
Plijte, plight
Porelier, poorer
Potestatis, potentates, powers
Poul, Paul
Prece, press (of people), advance eagerly
Preisable, worthy to be praised
Preynge, praying
Prisonyng, imprisonment
Priue, private, secret
Probabilnes, probability
Processe, passage of a book, argument
Profis, proofs
Profrid, preferred
Propirtees, properties
Purtenauncis, appurtenances
Puttiden, put

Questmongers, informers
Quyk, alive
Quykli, quickly, lively

Rad, read
Rateler, a rattling spouter (of Biblical texts)
Receyueden, receive
Rekenyngis, reckonings
Religiose, monks
Remanent, remaining
Remembrauncing, reminding
Rememoratijf, reminding
Rennyngli, rapidly
Rennyth, runs
Repugnaunce, inconsistency
Resonyng, reasoning
Reuelat, revealed
Reulis, rules
Reuth, pity
Reyne, rainy
Reysid, raised
Rewe, row, order
Rewme, realm
Rialte, royalty
Ricche, rich
Richid, enriched
Rische, rush
Rode, cross, rood
Rombe, remote
Rubrisch, rubric
Ruydnes, rudeness

Sad. grave, serious

Saff, save, except
Saluacion, salvation
Satanas, Satan
Sauerith, savours, perceives
Schapun, shape
Schendith, puts to shame
Scherpli, sharply
Schulden, should
Se, see
Seable, capable of being seen
See, sea
Seuyng, seeing
Sewt, suit
Seyng, saying
Seyntis, saints
Sikirli, certainly
Sire, Syriac
Sithin, since
Sithis, times
Skile, scile, reason, cause
Slauȝtir, slaughter
Slidernes, slipperiness
Smatche, taste
Soche, such
Sonondaye, Sunday
Soolnes, solitude
Soore, sore
Sophym, sophism
Sotheli, truly
Sotyll, subtle
Sowles, souls
Sowneth, sounds
Sownyng, signification
Specis, spicis, species, kinds
Spiren, breathe, inspire
Squaymose, repugnant
Stabili, establishing
Statis, estates
Stipelis, steeples
Stiking, sticking
Stok, stick
Strecche, stretch
Strengir, stronger
Substancial, solid, learned
Supportacion, support
Sureli, certainly
Sutel, subtle
Sweten, sweat
Swettir, sweeter
Symount, Simon

Talage, tax
Tariaunce, delay
Tariyng, tardily
Thanne, then
Thidir, thither
Thilk, that
Tho, those
Thome, tomb
Thritti, thirty
Tilier, tiller
Tiran, tyrant
Togyder, together
Tonne, town
Toure, tower
Towchid, touched
Tre, tree
Tropologik, tropological

Trowen, believe
Trumpen, sound with a trump
Tunge, tongue
Tweyne, two

Vce, use
Velim, vellum
Vnaȝendressabli, obstinately
Vnaȝenseiabli, uncontrovertibly
Vnavisednesse, heedlessness
Vncessable, unceasing
Vncurtesie, discourtesy
Vnderlingis, inferiors
Vndirnyme, blame, rebuke
Vndiscreccioun, want of discretion or discrimination
Vneth, hardly
Vnformal, wanting due form or method: unmethodical
Vnhangingli, unconnectedly
Vnied, vnyed, united
Vnmoueable, immovable
Vnobeie, disobey
Vnouercomeable, invincible
Vnperfitli, imperfectly
Vnpiteful, ungodly
Vnquyk, slow
Vnredili, inconsiderately
Vnriȝt, wrong, not right
Vnsauery, insipid
Vnscapabili, inevitably
Vnskilfulle, unreasonable
Vnthen(c)able, unthinkable
Vpon, upon
Vttirist, speak

Waisch, wash
Wantoun, unrestrained
Ware, wary
Wasingam, Walsingham
Weerned, forbade, refused, warned against
Welwilling, consent
Wel y-nouȝ, well enough
Wenen, think
Wepeable, deplorable
Were, wear
Weren, were
Wijnes, wines
Wijte, punishment
Wite, know
Withinforth, inwardly
Withoutforth, outwardly
Witt, knowledge or one of common wits
Wolde, would
Wones, customs
Wonyd, accustomed
Worcher, worker
Wote, knew

Ymaginatif, imaginative
Ymaginacioun, imagination
Ynke, ink
Ynner, inner
Ynouȝ, enough
Yperbole, hyperbole
Ypocrites, hypocrites
Yren, iron
Yuel, evil

BIBLIOGRAPHY

This bibliography is not intended as a complete summary of all the sources used for this essay, but it contains details of the chief books to which reference has been made in the notes. In general detailed references to the works of medieval and patristic theologians have been excluded, except where they have a direct bearing upon the text of the essay, e.g. in the case of John Wyclif.

Abailard. *Sic et Non*. Ed. Henke et Lindenkohl. 1851.

An Apology for Lollard Doctrines. Ed. Todd, J. H. Camden Soc. London, 1842.

An English Chronicle from 1377 to 1461. Ed. Davies, J. S. Camden Soc. London, 1856.

Aquinas, St Thomas. *Summa Theologica*. Trans. London, 2nd edn. 1927 ff.

Aristotle. *Nicomachean Ethics*. Trans. Welldon.

Bale, John. *Index Britanniae Scriptorum*. Ed. Poole, R. L. and Bateson, M. Oxford, 1902.

Baronius. *Annales Ecclesiastici*. Ed. Theiner. Vol. XXVIII.

Barraclough, G. *Papal Provisions*. Oxford, 1935.

Bekynton, Thomas. *Correspondence*. Ed. Williams, G. 2 vols. (Rolls Ser.) London, 1872.

Betts, R. R. 'John Hus' in *History*, vol. XXIV, n.s. 94.

— 'English and Czech Influences on Hus' in *TRHS*. 4th ser. vol. XXI, 1936.

Bibliographica Britannica. 1766.

Blackie, E. M. 'Reginald Pecock' in *EHR*. July 1911.

Bradwardine, Thomas. *De Causa Dei*. Ed. Savile. 1618.

Brewer, Thomas. *Memoir of John Carpenter*. London, 1856.

Calendar of Charter Rolls. Henry VI. Vol. VI. (Cal. S.P.) London, 1927.

Calendar of Close Rolls. Henry VI. Vol. III. (Cal. S.P.) London, 1927 ff.

Calendar of Fine Rolls. Henry VI. Vols. XVIII, XIX. (Cal. S.P.) London, 1931 ff.

Calendar of Papal Letters. Henry VI. Vols. X, XI. (Cal. S.P.)

Calendar of Patent Rolls. Henry VI. Vols. IV, V, VI, VII. (Cal. S.P.) London, 1906–11.

Calendar of State Papers (Venetian). Vol. I. London, 1864.

Cambridge Antiquarian Society Communications. Vols. I, XXXIII.

Cambridge Medieval History. Vols. VII, VIII.

Capes, W. W. *The English Church in the fourteenth and fifteenth centuries*. London, 1900.

Capgrave, John. *Liber de Illustribus Henricis*. Ed. Hingeston, F. C. 2 vols. (Rolls Ser.) London, 1858.

Chronica Monasterii S. Albani Registrum Abbatiae Johannis Whetehamstede. Ed. Riley, H. T. (Rolls Ser.) Vol. I. London, 1872.

Chronicle of the Grey Friars of London. Ed. Nichols, J. G. Camden Soc. London, 1852.

Chronicon Adae de Usk. Ed. Thompson, Sir E. M. London, 1904.

Churchill, I. J. *Canterbury Administration*. 2 vols. London, 1933.

Collier, Jeremy. *Ecclesiastical History*. Vol. II. Ed. Barham. 1840.

Dante. *Divina Commedia.*

Deanesly, M. *The Lollard Bible.* Cambridge, 1920.

Dictionary of National Biography. Ed. Stephen, L. and Lee, S. London, 1885–1900.

D'Oyly, G. *Life of William Sancroft.* London, 1821.

Douglas, D. C. *English Scholars.* London, 1939.

Douie, D. L. *The Nature and Effect of the Theory of the Fraticelli.* Manchester, 1932.

Dublin Review. Vol. xxiv, n.s. (1875).

Dudden, F. Homes. *St Ambrose.* Vol. ii. Oxford, 1935.

Dugdale, W. *Monasticon Anglicanum.* Ed. Caley, J., etc. 6 vols. in 8. London, 1846. (Reprint.)

Duns Scotus. *Opus Oxoniense.*

— *Reportata Parisiensia.*

Dymok, Roger. *Liber contra XII Errores et Hereses Lollardorum.* Ed. Cronin, H. S. Wyclif Soc., n.d.

Esame del Calendario Protestante detto Foxiano. Ed. Morelli, F. G. Vol. ii. Ed. 1753.

Fabyan, R. *The New Chronicles of England and France.* Ed. Ellis, H. London, 1811.

Fasciculi Zizaniorum. Ed. Shirley, W. W. (Rolls Ser.) London, 1858.

Forshall, J. and Madden, Sir F. *The Holy Bible in the earliest English versions made by J. Wycliffe and his followers.* 4 vols. Oxford, 1850.

Foxe, John. *Acts and Monuments.* Vol. i. Ed. 1684.

Fueter, Eduard. *Religion und Kirche in England im fünfzehnten Jahrhundert.* Tubingen and Leipzig. 1904.

Fuller, T. *Worthies of Wales.* Ed. Nuttall, P. Austin. 1840.

Gairdner, J. *Lollardy and the Reformation in England.* Vol. i. London, 1908.

Gascoigne, Thomas. *Loci e Libro Veritatum.* Ed. Rogers, J. Thorold. Oxford, 1881.

Gee, H. and Hardy, W. J. *Documents illustrative of English Church History.* London, 1896.

Gilson, E. *La philosophie au moyen âge.* 2 vols. Paris, 1922.

— *Reason and Revelation in the Middle Ages.* 1939.

Gospel of Nicodemus. Ed. W. H. Hulme.

Gower, J. *Works.* Ed. Macaulay, G. C. 4 vols. London, 1899–1902.

Green, V. H. H. 'Bishop Pecock and the English Bible' in *CQR.* vol. cxxix.

— 'Donation of Constantine' in *CQR.* vol. cxxxv.

Greenwood, A. D. *Cambridge History of English Literature.* Vol. ii. 1908.

Hall, Edward. *Chronicle of Lancaster and York.* Ed. Ellis, H. London, 1809.

Hannick, F. A. *Reginald Pecock.* Washington, 1922.

Hartridge, R. A. R. *History of Vicarages in the Middle Ages.* Cambridge, 1930.

Hastings, J. and Selbie, J. A. *Encyclopaedia of Religion and Ethics.* 13 vols. Edinburgh and New York, 1908–26.

Harris, C. R. S. *Duns Scotus.* 2 vols. Oxford, 1927.

Historical Manuscripts. 12th Report. Appendix. Part VIII. 1891.

Hoccleve, T. *Minor Poems.* Ed. Furnivall, F. J. and Gollancz, I. 2 vols. EETS. London, 1892, 1925.

Holinshed. *Chronicle*. 1808.

Hook, W. F. *Lives of the Archbishops of Canterbury*. Vol. v. London, 1867.

Hooker, Richard *Works*. Ed. Keble, John. 3rd edn. 1845.

James, M. R. *Apocryphal New Testament*. Oxford, 1924.

Lechler, G. V. *John Wycliffe and his English precursors*. Trans. P. Lorimer. London, 1884.

Leland, J. *Commentarii de Scriptoribus Britannicis*. Ed. Hall, A. Oxford, 1709.

— *Collectanea De Rebus Britannicis*. Ed. Hearne, T. London, 1770.

Le Neve, J. *Fasti Ecclesiae Anglicanae*. Ed. Hardy, T. D. 3 vols. Oxford, 1854.

Lewis, John. *Reginald Pecock*. Oxford, 1820.

Libelle of English Polycye (1436). Ed. Warner, Sir G. Oxford, 1926.

Little, A. G. *Studies in English Franciscan History*. Manchester, 1917.

Loserth, J. *Hus und Wiclif*. 2nd rev. edn. Munich, 1925.

Mandonnet, P. *Siger de Brabant et l'averroïsme latin au xiii siècle*. 1911.

Manitius, M. *Geschichte der lateinischen Literatur des Mittelalters*. Munich, 1911 ff.

Manning, B. L. *The People's Faith in the time of Wyclif*. Cambridge, 1919.

Matzke, D. *Die natürliche Theologie von Raymundus von Sebonde*. 1843.

Migne, I. P. *Patrologiae cursus completus. Series Latina*. Paris, 1844–64.

Monnier, Jean. *La Descente aux Enfers*. Paris, 1905.

Myrc, John. *Instruction for Parish Priests*. Ed. Peacock, E. EETS. 1868. Rev. edn. London, 1902.

Myroure of Our Ladye. Ed Blunt, J. H. EETS. London, 1873.

Netter, Thomas. *Doctrinale Antiquitatum Fidei Ecclesiae Catholicae*. Ed. Blanciotti, F. B. 3 vols. Venice, 1757–9.

Newcourt. *Repertorium Ecclesiasticum Parochiale Londonense*. 1708–10.

Nicholas of Cusa. *De Concordantia Catholica*. Basle, 1565.

Oman, Sir C. *History of England*, 1377–1485.

Owst, G. R. *Literature and Pulpit in Medieval England*. Cambridge, 1933.

— *Preaching in Medieval England*, 1350–1450. Cambridge, 1926.

Palmer, H. P. *The Bad Abbot of Evesham and other Medieval Studies*. Oxford, 1929.

Paston Letters, 1422–1509. Ed. Gairdner, J. (Library edn.) 6 vols. London, 1904.

Paues, A. *A Fourteenth Century version of the Bible*. Cambridge. 1902, 1904.

Pecock, R. *Book of Faith*. Ed. Morison, J. L. Glasgow, 1909.

— *Book of Faith*. Ed. Wharton, H. 1688.

— *Donet*. Ed. Hitchcock, E. V. EETS. London, 1921.

— *Folewer to the Donet*. Ed. Hitchcock, E. V. EETS. London, 1924.

— *The Reule of Chrysten Religioun*. Ed. Greet, W. C. EETS. London, 1927.

— *The Repressor of Overmuch Blaming of the Clergy*. Ed. Babington, C. 2 vols. (Rolls Ser.) 1860.

Petrus Alphonsus. *Dialogi in quibus impiae Judaeorum opiniones confutuntur*. Cologne, 1536.

Petrus Comestor. *Historia Scholastica*.

Pierce the Ploughman's Crede. Ed. Skeat, W. W. EETS. 1867.

Poole, R. L. *Wycliffe and movements for reform*. London, 1911.

Poole, R. L. *Illustrations of the History of Medieval Thought and Learning.* 2nd edn. London, 1920.

Proceedings and Ordinances of the Privy Council of England. Ed. Nicolas, N. H. Record Commission. Vol. VI. 1837.

Pronger, W. A. 'Thomas Gascoigne' in *EHR.* LIV.

Ramsay, Sir J. H. *Lancaster and York.* Vol. II. Oxford, 1892.

Rannie, D. W. *History of Oriel College.* London, 1900.

Rashdall, Hastings. *Universities of Europe in the Middle Ages.* Ed. Powicke, F. M. and Emden, A. B. 3 vols. Rev. edn. Oxford, 1936.

Raymond of Sebonde. *Theologia Naturalis.* Ed. Seidel, J. von. 1852.

Registrum Sacrum Anglicanum. Ed. Stubbs, William. 1897.

Religious Pieces. Ed. Perry, G. G. EETS. 1867.

Remonstrance against Romish Corruptions in the Church. Ed. Forshall, J. H. London, 1851.

Reulet, D. *Un inconnu célèbre, recherches historiques et critiques sur Raymond de Sabunde.* 1875.

Richards, G. C. and Shadwell, C. L. *The Provosts and Fellows of Oriel College.* Oxford, 1922.

Schirmer, W. *Der Englische Frühhumanismus.* Leipsic, 1931.

Schmidt, F. *Studies in the Language of Pecock.* Upsala, 1900.

Seeberg, R. *Die Theologie des Duns Scot.* Leipzig, 1900.

Short, Thomas. *A Sketch of the History of the Church of England to 1688.* London, 1840.

Sikes, J. G. *Peter Abailard.* Cambridge, 1932.

Smalley, B. *The Study of the Bible in the Middle Ages.* Oxford, 1941.

Smith, H. Maynard. *Pre-Reformation England.* London, 1938.

Snappe's Formulary. Ed. Salter, H. E. Oxford, 1924. (OHS.)

Stephens, W. R. W. *Memorials of the See of Chichester.*

Stone, Darwell. *History of the Doctrine of the Holy Eucharist.* Vol. I. London, 1909.

Stow, J. *Annals.* 1602.

— *A Survey of London.* Ed. Thoms, W. T. London, 1842.

— *Memoranda.* Ed. Gairdner, J. Camden Soc.

Ten Brink. *History of English Literature.* Ed. Robinson, W. Clarke. New York, 1893.

The Lay-Folks' Mass Book. Ed. Simmons, T. F. EETS. 1879.

Thomson, S. H. 'The philosophical basis of Wyclif's Theology' in *Journal of Religion,* XI (1931).

Three Fifteenth Century Chronicles. Ed. Gairdner, J. Camden Soc. London, 1880.

Trevelyan, G. M. *England in the Age of Wyclif.* London, 1899.

Ueberweg, F. *Grundriss der Geschichte der Philosophie.* 12th edn. Ed. Frischeisen-Kohler and Praechter, K. Berlin, 1926-8.

Valla, Lorenzo. *Opera.* Basle, 1540.

— *The treatise of Lorenzo Valla on the Donation of Constantine.* Trans. Coleman, C. B. New Haven, 1922.

— *Laurentii Vallae de falso credita et ementita Constantini Donatione Declamatio.* Ed. Schwahn, W. Leipzig, 1928.

Vickers, K. H. *England in the later Middle Ages*. London, 1913.
— *Humphrey, Duke of Gloucester*. London, 1907.
Wager, C. 'The Language of Pecock' in *Modern Language Notes* (1894).
Walsingham, Thomas. *Historia Anglicana*. Ed. Riley, H. T. 2 vols. (Rolls Ser.) London, 1863–4.
Waterland, Daniel. *Works*. Ed. Van Mildert. Vol. x. Oxford, 1823.
Webb, C. C. J. *Studies in Natural Theology*. Oxford, 1915.
Wilkins, D. *Concilia Magnae Britanniae*. Vol. III. London, 1737.
Willis, Browne. *Survey of St Asaph*. Ed. Edwards, E. London, 1801.
Wood, Anthony à. *Historia et Antiquitates Universitatis Oxoniensis*. Oxford, 1674.
Workman, H. B. *John Wyclif*. 2 vols. Oxford, 1926.
Wulf, Maurice de. *History of Medieval Philosophy*. Trans. Messenger, E. C. 2 vols. London, 1935.
Wyclif, John. *De Compositione Hominis*. Ed. Beer, R. 1884.
— *De Dominio Divino libri tres*. Ed. Poole, R. L. 1890.
— *De Ente librorum duorum excerpta*. Ed. Dziewicki, M. H. 1909.
— *De Eucharistia Tractatus Major*. Ed. Loserth, J. 1892.
— *Dialogus sive Speculum Ecclesie Militantis*. Ed. Pollard, A. W. 1886.
— *Opera Minora*. Ed. Loserth, J. 1913.
— *Opus Evangelicum*. Ed. Loserth, J. 2 vols. 1895–6.
— *Miscellanea Philosophica*. Ed. Dziewicki, M. H. 2 vols. 1902, 1905.
— *Polemical Works*. Ed. Buddensieg, R. 2 vols. 1883.
— *Select English Works*. Ed. Arnold, T. 3 vols. 1869–71.
— *Select English Writings*. Ed. Winn, H. E. Oxford, 1929.
— *Summa de Ente. Libri primi tractatus primus et secundus*. Ed. Thomson, S. H. Oxford, 1930.
— Summa Theologiae:
　　I and II. *Tractatus de Mandatis Divinis. Accedit Tractatus de Statu Innocencie*. Ed. Loserth, J. and Matthew, F. D. 1922.
　　III–V. *Tractatus de Civili Dominio. Liber primus*. Ed. Poole, R. L. 1885. *Liber secundus*. Ed. Loserth, J. 1900. *Liber tertius*. Ed. Loserth, J. 2 vols. 1903–4.
　　VI. *De Veritate Sacrae Scripturae*. Ed. Buddensieg, R. 3 vols. 1905–7.
　　VII. *Tractatus de Ecclesia*. Ed. Loserth, J. 1886.
　　VIII. *Tractatus de Officio Regis*. Ed. Pollard, A. W. and Sayle, C. 1887.
　　IX. *Tractatus de Potestate Pape*. Ed. Loserth, J. 1907.
　　X. *Tractatus de Simonia*. Ed. Herzberg-Fränkel and Dziewicki, M. H. 1898.
　　XI. *Tractatus de Apostasia*. Ed. Dziewicki, M. H. 1889.
　　XII. *Tractatus de Blasphemia*. Ed. Dziewicki, M. H. 1893
— *Tractatus de Logica*. Ed. Dziewicki, M. H. 3 vols. 1893–9.
— *Tractatus de Benedicta Incarnatione*. Ed. Harris, E. 1886.
— *The English Works of John Wyclif hitherto unprinted*. Ed. Matthew, F. D. EETS. London, 1880. (Not all genuine works of Wyclif.)
　　(N.B. *The Cambridge Bibliography of English Literature*. Vol. I. Cambridge, 1940, contains a bibliography (307–11) compiled by Mr B. L. Manning.)
Wyld, H. C. *History of Modern Colloquial English*. London, 1936.
Young, K. *The Drama of the Medieval Church*. Vol. I. Oxford, 1933.

INDEX

The index is intended as a rough guide rather than as a full analysis of contents. It deals with persons, some places and selected topics.

CAMBRIDGE : PRINTED BY
W. LEWIS, M.A.
AT THE UNIVERSITY PRESS